Aristotle

Aristotle

Democracy and Political Science

DELBA WINTHROP

Foreword by

Harvey C. Mansfield

The University of Chicago Press

Chicago and London

The University of Chicago Press, Chicago 60637
The University of Chicago Press, Ltd., London
© 2019 by The University of Chicago
Published 2019
Printed in the United States of America

28 27 26 25 24 23 22 21 20 19   1 2 3 4 5

ISBN-13: 978-0-226-55354-2 (cloth)
ISBN-13: 978-0-226-55368-9 (e-book)
DOI: https://doi.org/10.7208/chicago/9780226553689.001.0001

Library of Congress Cataloging-in-Publication Data

Names: Winthrop, Delba, author.
Title: Aristotle, democracy and political science / Delba Winthrop ; foreword
   by Harvey C. Mansfield.
Description: Chicago ; London : The University of Chicago Press, 2018. |
   Includes bibliographical references and index.
Identifiers: LCCN 2018031114 | ISBN 9780226553542 (cloth : alk. paper) |
   ISBN 9780226553689 (ebook)
Subjects: LCSH: Aristotle—Political and social views. | Democracy. | Political
   science.
Classification: LCC JC75.D36 W56 2018 | DDC 320.01/1—dc23
LC record available at https://lccn.loc.gov/2018031114

⊖ This paper meets the requirements of ANSI/NISO Z39.48-1992
(Permanence of Paper).

CONTENTS

FOREWORD

"Nothing is so obscure that it is not meant to be found. . . ."

—Delba Winthrop, on Aristotle's text

This study of Aristotle is the doctoral dissertation of my late wife, Delba Winthrop (1945–2006), submitted to the Harvard Government Department in 1974 but not to a publisher during her lifetime. Published now with every word of hers unchanged, it is an interpretation of Book III of Aristotle's *Politics*. Without getting ahead of the reader's judgment, one can say with some confidence that no other study of Aristotle is quite like it.[1]

Aristotle's interpreters may be divided into the philosophical and the philological, though not distinctly, because each makes unacknowledged use of the other. The philosophical ones were the dominant voices of philosophy in the medieval era, and they were disparaged if not refuted in the early modern era, as shown in the sarcastic formulation of "Aristotelity" by Thomas Hobbes, and by the huddled shame they reveal in the presence of their master in the underworld of Glubbdubdrib in Jonathan Swift's *Gulliver's Travels* (3:8). Dr. Winthrop, however, had to deal with the authority of Aristotle's philological interpreters, particularly the half dozen she names as editors of rival texts of the *Politics*, for whom knowledge of Greek takes precedence over Aristotle's lost philosophical eminence. In judging the work of these eminent scholars, she took refuge and modest satisfaction in a rediscovery of Aristotle's eminence. She had no authority of her own, and she was not one to broadcast her own originality.

Yet in the "Note on the Translation" (appendix 1), a personal statement from which the reader might want to begin, she made her situation quite plain—though it still requires an inference on the reader's part. Remarking

on her translation rather than her interpretation, she says that she was forced
to make her own translation because previous translators were not literal
enough. They did not reproduce Aristotle's ambiguities, but rather narrowed
them, foreclosing possibilities that Aristotle had left open. With a more literal translation a more imaginative interpretation becomes possible, indeed
necessary; for "nothing is so obscure that it is not meant to be found." Ambiguities must be explained—not set aside, overlooked, or ignored. "Most authorities are not on my side," she admits, or rather asserts. Her "argument"
has to be "judged on its merits." The literal translation serves her argument,
her interpretation; and the error of "previous translators" supports an error
of interpretation. Nonliteral translations are the consequence of a lack of
"serious reflection" not compensated for by superior knowledge of Greek.
Dr. Winthrop means to restore the superiority of Aristotle's philosophical
interpreters over the philological ones. Most authorities are against her, and
she does not cite any on her behalf except for Thomas Taylor, a now obscure
figure of the early nineteenth century whom she discovers and appoints as
a predecessor.[2] Her interpretation is rather terse and demanding; it serves
as both an education and a test of the reader's interpretive capacity. As one
reads through it, one becomes aware of the maturity and quiet insistence, as
well as the boldness, of the tester.

Dr. Winthrop's argument, as stated very briefly in this "Note," is that Aristotle's *Politics* is "intentionally written in an ambiguous manner" because,
though philosophers do not tell untruths, not all their truths or speculations "can be baldly announced." This is as if she were announcing that
she is a member of the school of Leo Strauss (1899–1973), an historian
of philosophy well known for his rediscovery of the fact that philosophers
once wrote in an intentionally ambiguous manner of this sort and for this
reason.[3] But Dr. Winthrop does not acknowledge this authority for her
proceeding. Instead, she says that her "procedure in translating" is not a
"presupposition," as if of a school of thought, but "a conclusion painfully
arrived at." She was indeed a "Straussian," but not one who took Strauss's
premise for granted. Or one could say that when accepting the Straussian
premise, the hard work of applying it is equivalent to the task of proving
it. To specify—and connect—the many ambiguities in Aristotle's text is to
justify, and not merely presume upon, the premise that Aristotle put them
there intentionally.

What are the distinctive features of Dr. Winthrop's understanding of Aristotle's *Politics*? She presents them in contrast to the many modern scholars,
not philologists, who have attacked Aristotle, and also to the not so many
who lately have defended him. First, there is the fundamental ambiguity

underlying the many other ambiguities in Aristotle's text: this is that he speaks at the same time and in the same words of politics and philosophy. Thus "democracy" refers both to a political regime and to an understanding of nature, a demos or democracy of matter, one that understands the whole of things as body and all things as bodily quantities. Some have seen metaphysical implications in his political remarks but have not gone so far as to imagine and develop an entire metaphysical argument from all of his words.[4] In Dr. Winthrop's examination, democracy is shown first as the simple numerical equality of material bodies and then qualified and corrected to comprise an equality of worth or virtue. This reforming occurs in politics, obviously, and at the same time but more hidden in metaphysics. To identify and elaborate what is hidden gives her account a much greater emphasis on Aristotle's ontology and a fuller consistency of detail, going beyond isolated suggestions, than in other accounts. The political reform requires that political thinkers move to metaphysics on the one hand and, on the other, that metaphysical thinkers not depart from politics. Political thinkers must examine and go beyond the "inclusiveness" of today's political discourse to consider the content of what, as well as whom, it is necessary to include.

The whole of a political community must be made a genuine whole. A genuine whole as one would define it turns out to be an articulated whole of differing parts, no longer a "democracy" of matter. Here is support for the politically ambitious who are unsatisfied with mere numerical equality that will also be news to the natural philosophers powerful in Aristotle's time and ours. The two reforms, political and philosophical, are mixed with each other as well as parallel to each other. To explain this distinction, Dr. Winthrop discerns a difference in Aristotle's text between "the common benefit (or good)" and "the benefit in common." The common benefit is a sum of benefits to each as equal members of an "all"—a raw democratic or demotic addition of the necessities of bodily survival, as in today's welfare benefits taken individually. The benefit in common is the whole with parts that make diverse and unequal contributions to it—for example, the whole welfare state as an experiment in common living, with earners, old folks, congressmen, and bureaucrats serving partial roles in it.

Second, Aristotle's argument addresses both philosopher and citizen, teaching each party the virtues of the other. He begins with the natural philosopher and turns him into the political philosopher, or political scientist. The philosopher is not to turn his back on politics or merely criticize politics, or even rise above politics, but to learn from politics. Nor is he to learn that nature is an "organic" whole, in the way that some interpreters

exaggerate Aristotle's purposive (teleological) viewpoint to mean that everything grows spontaneously. To be sure, the polis is natural, as "man is by
nature a political animal," but it is not a natural organism like a tree. The
polis has to be founded and fashioned with conventions or opinions that
could be other than what they are; hence there are several regimes, not just
one. Nature is not a homogeneous but a heterogeneous whole. Politics is not
an instance of the universal purposiveness or teleology of nature, but rather
the reverse: politics is the model by which nature's teleology is demonstrated
and from which it is derived. One must explain not *to* but *from* politics.

Third, the central topic of both politics and philosophy is the discovery
of the whole that is their end, separately and together. The common good
or common benefit in each of them is the bringing together of parts. The
political nature of man stated in Book I of Aristotle's Politics is explained
by reference to the faculty of speech peculiar to man, by which men perceive and express good and bad, just and unjust. These are terms implying
that they belong to a community, a whole of some sort. But how, and of
what sort? Dr. Winthrop considers and answers that question. She brings
up the relevance of Greek mathematics to such terms as "numerical equality" and "multitude" in democracy, and to "one" as a unity and not a number in monarchy. Her reliance on Jacob Klein's indispensable work *Greek
Mathematical Thought and the Origin of Algebra* (trans. 1968) is apparent
throughout (p. 85n15). Applying Klein's analysis to politics (as Klein did
not), she finds it appropriate to the heterogeneous whole proposed by Aristotle in contrast to the democratic whole, an "all" of equal numbers presupposed by modern mathematics. Aristotle's mathematics is alive to the nature
of things counted, and has room for the terms of speech that humans insis-
tently use. In her discussion of the only mention of "political philosophy"
in Aristotle's *Politics* (125–27) she makes a nice distinction between ethical
mathematics and mathematical ethics. Ethical mathematics teaches philosophers to count men with a view to ethical differences, and mathematical
ethics teaches political men, who may be all too aware of such differences,
that justice is a kind of equality.

Fourth, what the philosopher learns from politics is the truth of human
freedom, shown most obviously in political debate and most surely in moral
virtue. Debate presupposes choice, and choice presupposes freedom; moral
virtue is voluntary, and as such it declares and guarantees the freedom that
humans can achieve against the enslavement with which their bodies appear
to threaten them. Aristotle is a philosopher of freedom—freedom in virtue,
not virtue versus freedom. Freedom requires an education in moral virtue; it
is not handed to us by nature, as modern philosophers assert.

A fifth feature is the importance of assertiveness—to be found in philosophy as well as in politics. Dr. Winthrop's book could be understood as a treatise on the Greek verb *phemi*, meaning to assert, and implying an accompanying demand to be honored or in a situation of risk, as opposed to saying something when little or nothing is at stake. Assertion is a large topic in the philosophy of language today, and it is discussed in Aristotle's *De interpretatione*, but I have been unable to find any study of Aristotle's *Politics* that makes a point of the quality of assertiveness that Dr. Winthrop finds to be crucial in it.

Sixth, while we ponder the fine distinction between asserting and saying, one can add to the list the careful study of each word of Aristotle's text, not only in a phrase but in all of Book III (on the choice of which more later). For example, a poet is literally a "maker," but with Dr. Winthrop's guidance one is led to notice that "making" is quite different from "making manifest." Aristotle's frequent resort to the poets in the *Politics* transforms their work from making to making manifest. This takeover makes manifest that Aristotle too is a poet, an award or accusation that Dr. Winthrop pins on him. Another example of her meticulous care: on an occasion when Aristotle says "some" say a certain thing, she takes two pages to identify who or which "some" they are (pp. 26–27).

These distinctive features do not leave her book so original as to be isolated from scholarly conversation, however, for she takes on a question that political theorists in particular have posed today. Does Aristotle favor democracy, and if so, how and why? Dr. Winthrop puts the focus on democracy in her book's title, and she adds the supplemental matter of how political science in its practical aspect can improve democracy. For in her view Aristotle's political science is a practical science, but it needs the nourishment and support of a theoretical science of nature to sustain its assumption that politics for all its necessities is fundamentally a matter of a choice, and a choice well made. Her intent is similar to that of the political theorists who now study Aristotle, hoping to profit from him and often presuming to instruct him. But she finds much that would help them.

Legend has it that there was once a professor who believed two things: that Aristotle was the greatest philosopher who ever lived, and that democracy is the best form of government ever discovered. Hence Aristotle was a democrat, he concluded. Dr. Winthrop shares the conclusion but provides a better argument for it. She does her best to rescue Aristotle from democratic disesteem and at the same time to make democracy more reasonable and more defensible than its complacent supporters in today's politics and political science can show. One theorist who did not study Aristotle but still desired to use political science to improve democracy, Robert A. Dahl, was the subject of Dr. Winthrop's senior thesis at Cornell University in 1967. It too was titled "Democracy and Political Science." In the dissertation (now this book) she wrote not long after, she uncovered a better modern guide to democracy in Alexis de Tocqueville's *Democracy in America*. This she cited in order to explain Aristotle and all but declare Tocqueville to be Aristotle's modern representative. Later in life (2000) she published a translation of that work, as coauthor with this writer.

Dr. Winthrop's introduction to her book reveals a concise style suited to an argument that moves one step at a time to surprising conclusions. Just the first paragraph sums up the whole of it. Dr. Winthrop begins from today's uncritical estimation and espousal of democracy, to which there is no respectable alternative or competitive choice. Even its most vocal partisans will fall silent before the polite request, to say nothing of a demand, for a defense of it. Aristotle too, begins from democracy and from the words of its partisans. He begins from political dispute, since the word "partisans" implies contrary partisans. Why do the democrats speak first? And why are qualifications to democracy, rather than democracy itself, in dispute?

It turns out that for Aristotle the beginning of political dispute is the same as today's. We moderns are not as parochial as one might think from the dominance of "democratic theory" in our academic discussions. There is good reason, prima facie justice, in the democratic claim that ruling should be shared equally. Prima facie justice is very different from Thomas Hobbes's rather contrived and artificial "state of nature" in which all are equal, but the result is the same—an initial advantage for democracy. The advantage is in our thinking, but note in this first paragraph the development of the "we" who think. Dr. Winthrop takes us from "democratic citizens," to whom democracy is obvious, to "good citizens," who want to be sure it is truly just, and then to "political scientists," who are concerned for human beings. These are three separate communities of a hierarchy, already suggesting the character of Aristotle's argument on different levels. But in Aristotle, the words addressed to the three communities are the same, and the levels are not spelled out. That is a task for Aristotle's readers to whom she gives guidance. Aristotle has the faculty of speaking directly to all and indirectly to some here and some others there; and a good fraction of Dr. Winthrop's perceptive imagination is devoted to sorting out what goes to whom.

One must first appreciate the natural appeal of democracy, which explains and to some extent justifies the complacent and parochial satisfaction with it today. Quoting from Aristotle in Book VI of the *Politics*, Dr. Winthrop shows that men want democracy because they want freedom, the raw freedom of living as one wishes. To be free is to not be a slave, hence to affirm oneself as a human being. In this affirmation men are equal, which means equal numerically rather than proportionately equal by worth or capacity. As such, men living as they please do not want to be ruled, which means each rules on his own as a king or tyrant. This condition of anarchy forces men to accept the apparently lesser freedom of democracy, which is that of ruling and being ruled in turn. As said above, this democracy is a democracy of bodies, all equal as being body, and it is consistent with an understanding of nature as being composed of bodies and a human nature that is an unexceptional part of the rest of nature. Such a democracy of all nature can be found in the natural philosophy of pre-Socratic philosophers known in Aristotle's time, and also in the political philosophy of Thomas Hobbes and his successors, known in ours. Thus Aristotle is relevant to our time because he shares our central concern for democracy and is aware of the natural science and democratic political philosophy that are advanced to support it. Aristotle is not remote from us, but on the contrary begins his political thinking in Book III of the *Politics* from the democratic premise of modern thinking about both nature and politics.

Aristotle's democrat, like that of Hobbes, makes a claim to justice. Since all are equal, all must be included in a whole as equal parts of the whole. But does a whole of equal parts truly make a whole? It seems that the freedom to live as one wishes includes more than can be counted in the equality of bodies, and that the very desire for freedom distinguishes humans from the slavishness of the rest of nature. Is a political order, in Aristotle's term a "city," a whole that can politically accommodate desires that go beyond those necessary to sustain a slave? Can visible nature be understood—that is, understood as a whole, as a multitude of things? Are those things equal parts or pieces of matter, or different sorts of parts in a whole? The question of the political whole raises the question of the natural whole, and Aristotle attempts to solve the problem of the whole in both politics and philosophy. This attempt takes place in Book III of the *Politics*.

Dr. Winthrop has given reason for a book on democracy, on politics, and on philosophy—but why study Book III by itself? To show why, she provides a very quick summary of Books I and II. Book I also deals with the city as a whole, but from the standpoint of the household or "one's own" (*oikeia*), and it concludes that politics is distinct from economics and that another beginning is needed. In Book II one finds a study of what is common in politics as opposed to what is one's own, and a study of opinions about the best regime. The best regime runs aground on the shoal of the human body, the matter of one's own, so that Book II is as partial as Book I, though in reverse. The reason in the best regime is without soul because it is abstracted from body. Book III combines these two aspects, one's own and the common, focusing on the whole from the standpoint of the whole, and making the new beginning called for at the end of Book I. Book III, one might say, begins from the part of the city that coexists with the city, the citizen, which is a part created by the city, whereas Book I deals with the genetic parts of the city, those that precede its creation, the household and the village, its genetic parts. Book II deals with the community as opposed to its parts, and with the best regime, whether in the form imagined by philosophers and law-givers or as glimpsed in actual regimes such as Sparta, Crete, and Carthage. Book III then brings one's own together with the common to make a whole distinct from its origins, and a community that does not neglect or abstract from one's own. It discovers a whole made by human choice and freedom rather than one determined by the economic necessities of acquisition and slavery discussed in Book I—and a whole within the limits of nature rather than one merely wished for as in Book II. The beginning of Book III replaces the failed beginnings of Books I and II that consider what is before politics, hence beneath politics (Book I), and what is beyond politics (Book II) because it tries to rise above, rather than meet, the necessities set forth in Book I. According to Dr. Winthrop, Aristotle seems to have come upon a political situation in his lifetime, not prior to or innocent of philosophy but already influenced by philosophy—one that needs to be cleansed of error unfortunately introduced by philosophy, both by pre-Socratic natural philosophers and by Socrates and Plato. Both politics and philosophy need the new replacement beginning of Book III.

If Book III is placed where it needs to be, what about Books IV to VIII, the rest of the *Politics*? Dr. Winthrop asserts that the rest of the *Politics* must be seen in the light of the more fundamental discussion in Book III of the city as a whole and in its parts. These later chapters deal with different sorts of men and the educations they require, culminating in the consideration of the best regime as Aristotle has it in Books VII and VIII. Democracy is, of course, brought up after Book III, but it can and must first be understood in its fundamentals in Book III alone. Having read Dr. Winthrop's book, readers might want to seek confirmation of her statement about the rest of the *Politics* on their own. The success of her interpretation, however, depends on whether she shows that Book III stands on its own or that it needs to be corrected by later statements of Aristotle's in the rest of his book. She gives the example herself of Aristotle's openly "immoderate attack on immoderate democracy" in Book IV (p. 179n89) in contrast to the qualified approval of democracy in Book III that stands unaffected by it.

After this summary of Dr. Winthrop's introduction, it is time to leave the reader to examine the more subtle and exact exposition of her argument.* A number of eye-opening remarks of hers, best discovered in context, await one's attention. One consequence of her introduction may be noted here: two of the staple conventions or debates of modern scholarship—that Aristotle's *Politics*, given its inconsistencies and imperfections, consists of lecture notes, and that the traditional ordering of its books does not make sense and needs to be reshuffled—fall by the wayside, unnecessary and properly forgotten, as examples of the conscientious underestimation by modern scholarship of Aristotle's greatness. To restore a vivid sense of his greatness, more awe-inspiring as it becomes more intelligible, is a benefit not incidental to Delba Winthrop's intent and to the long-delayed publication of this book. She wrote a number of articles on Aristotle, on Tocqueville, and on Alexandr Solzhenitsyn, but this is her first book.[5] For a scholar of reputation, this publication might be an act of sentimentality or of biographical interest; in this case it does more to establish than to honor a reputation. For Delba's book, which she completed at the age of twenty-eight, is—if you will allow me this intimacy and this declaration—a work of stunning originality and maturity.

Harvey C. Mansfield
Cambridge, Massachusetts
October 17, 2017

---

* To understand Dr. Winthrop's (and Aristotle's) argument, the reader should take advantage of the many endnotes she supplies, especially in chapter 3, directing attention *supra*, to previous discussions in her text left incomplete. Her argument follows Aristotle's, and to make sense of either—which means to unify them as a *whole*—later statements must be compared to, and reconciled with, earlier ones.

Were someone to ask today, "Why democracy?" the mouths of its most vocal partisans might well drop in surprised silence. That democracy is the best, not to mention the only legitimate, form of government is undoubtedly the most vigorously asserted and least examined political opinion of our day. Every qualification of democracy is perceived as a deviation from the right order, and it is attempts to justify these suspect qualifications, rather than democracy itself, that are likely to cause disputes. Is this reaction peculiar to our contemporaries? Or is there some prima facie justice in the claim that all citizens must share equally in the responsibilities and benefits of ruling? That this claim is surely just is obvious to us as democratic citizens. That the claim is truly just is a concern to us as good citizens, and that it is truly beneficial is a concern to us as human beings. Why it is or is not so is a question for us as political scientists.

Actually, the democratic partisan, after recovering from his initial shock, might well produce what seems to be a reasonable and even respectable argument for democracy. No doubt his reasoning would be similar to what Aristotle speaks of as the democratic hypothesis:

> The hypothesis of the democratic regime is freedom. They are in the habit of saying this, as if only in this regime did they partake of freedom, for they assert that this is an element of every democracy. One freedom is to be ruled and to rule in turn. And the demotic justice is to have equality according to number, but not worth, and, this being the just, the multitude is necessarily sovereign, and whatever seems to the majority is the end and the just. For they assert that each of the citizens must have the equal. Thus, in democracies it happens that those at a loss are more sovereign than those with resources. For they are more, and the opinion of the majority is sovereign. Therefore, this is one sign

of freedom, which all the demotic set down as the boundary of the regime. But one is to live as someone wishes. They assert that this is the work of freedom, if, indeed, the life of being a slave is not as one might wish. Therefore, this is the second boundary of democracy. From this has been unleashed (the wish) not to be ruled, most of all by no one, but if not this, in turn. In this way it contributes to freedom according to equality (VI, 1317a40–1317b17).

According to Aristotle, the democrat wishes to live the life of a free man, and he believes that political freedom is the condition of living as one wishes, that is, with the liberty befitting a man. Aristotle's democrat recognizes that the end he seeks is in some way dependent upon a particular political order. Doing as one wishes requires that one not be ruled by anything or any man. But the freedom of each man to do as he wishes—for example, to appropriate his neighbor's patrimony or to become a tyrant in order to rape any man's wife—may conflict with the freedom of every other man to do the same. Therefore, one agrees to rule and be ruled, so far as is necessary, equally with other men who similarly do not wish to be ruled. Only for this reason does political equality seem necessary and desirable. Rule over others is sought in order to safeguard or increase the liberty or license that would otherwise be endangered. The democrat finds politics neither unavoidable nor something serious in itself.

That democracy may, in fact, ensure liberty only for most—that it is, in effect, a tyranny of the common or poor men—is a problem that the democrat chooses to ignore. But the good citizen cannot overlook the possible injustice of democracy. And the political scientist must be open to the possibility that some other regime might meet the democratic demand of freedom for each better than the democracy of strict numerical equality.

The democrat also presents us with a more serious consideration. As Aristotle portrays him, he implies that politics in general and any political order that one would choose to defend in particular must be evaluated in the light of the end it purports to serve. Political freedom and sharing equally in rule are for the sake of whatever might be said to constitute the freedom of a man. This the democratic citizen believes to be living as one wishes. Thus, prior to an opinion about the best regime is an opinion about what leads a man to be concerned with politics at all, an opinion about what is good, or beneficial to a man. If the democrat submits to being ruled and ruling, then the democratic hypothesis reveals an opinion that no political order can accommodate the desires of all to live as they wish, or unruled. Must we, with the democrat, acknowledge that man's freedom necessarily conflicts with or transcends the political? Or is it rather the case that the democrat has misunderstood the meaning of being a free man and that for which freedom is deemed good? Not only must we raise the question of whether democracy is the regime that most allows each to live as a free man, but we must consider whether the democrat's understanding of freedom is really what is meant by living as someone would wish. If ruling and being ruled is the necessary form of political order, perhaps there is some other understanding of being a free man and of how a man would wish to live that is wholly consistent with ruling and being ruled.

Whatever our final reflections on this question, we must begin where democrats naturally begin. The democratic claim is that the rule of all, and only the rule of each and all, makes the city a whole. Political claims are claims about justice, and justice, in its most fundamental sense, is the common benefit. The common benefit is known only by knowing the extent of the "community" to be benefited as well as what is beneficial. What the whole is must be known in order to make an argument about the nature and order of what can then be said to be its proper parts; and from a consideration of these parts, inferences about what benefit is common to them can be made. A whole is complete in itself; there can be no just reservations against any regime that lives up to its claim to make the city a whole, properly so called. Presumably in arguing that only a democratic city is a city, properly so called, the democrat means that the democratic whole makes manifest, as much as is necessary and possible within the political horizon, all that is in each man. The democrat's opinion about what a whole city is depends upon his opinion about what a whole man is. The latter opinion is perhaps not independent of an opinion about what a whole is and, therefore, what man's relation to the whole of which he forms a part is. This opinion, of course, is not merely political.

When do we say that a thing composed of many parts is "a whole" rather than "a multitude of things"—for example, a city of men, or visible nature? Each of the many citizens or natural beings seems itself to be some thing, a one and a whole. How then do we speak of all these many as uniting to form a whole? And what of wholes composed of dissimilar parts? A man, for example, is generally admitted to have not only a body, as do other beings, but also some capacity for articulating his passions and anger, if not for reasoning; he has what is often called a soul. How do body and soul form a whole man? Do all wholes consist of both these kinds of parts?

Even if the democratic partisan is not fully aware of all the questions raised by his claim, we must admit the possibility that the democrat's opinion is in fact a dim reflection of the insight of someone who has thought more seriously about the principles of the democratic hypothesis. We must also entertain the possibility that the democratic partisan has either not fully comprehended the implications of his hypothesis or has distorted it to serve his own interests.

Both of these possibilities are suggested by Aristotle. He specifically connects the demotic opinion that justice is being ruled and ruling in turn to an understanding of equality as numerical equality. Each citizen is an equal one among many citizens, as each man and each thing are ones among many countable things in nature, and nature is the countable units that a mathematician examines. The demotic opinion, however, is also connected to the recognition that man is a being with a capacity to choose to live as he wishes, which means that he is not simply a one among the many other countable ones in nature. The first principle reflects an argument from natural science, not political science. The second principle is given in the form of a quote from Euripides—a poet, not a political philosopher.[1] Euripides, however, is often considered a philosophic poet, and here and in the *Ethics* Aristotle indicates that Euripides does attempt to connect his assertions about political and human things to a "higher and more physical understanding."[2] Nonetheless, Euripides is portrayed in the *Politics* and *Ethics* as being far from concerned with or adept at politics, and as still further from being a loyal democrat.[3] The teaching about the natural or divine things that he may hold to be true supports regimes in addition to democracy, especially tyranny. Thus, the democrat seems to have chosen his friends imprudently.

The difficulty with political democracy and the demotic principle of justice is that man seems to differ qualitatively from the beings he counts. Therefore, his finding in nature a whole of equally countable things might tell him nothing about how a whole consisting of qualitatively different parts, human and nonhuman, might be ordered. It would seem that only by abstracting from man's peculiar quality, his freedom or political capacity, can democracy be shown to be just according to nature. Yet the very act of demanding to choose one's own way of life reveals the absurdity of the abstraction. Moreover, to abstract from a consideration of what natural wholes are is an example of the arbitrary use of man's freedom, and it suggests the possibility of tyranny. The democratic argument, it seems, would offer the political man no defense against tyranny, the freedom of one. At the least we may conclude that a defense of democracy requires an explanation of what a man's place in nature is. Democracy needs philosophy.

Our immediate point is that in order to understand democracy fully we, beginning as democrats, must conclude as philosophers do, examining not only the claims democracy makes, but the grounds on which the claims are held to be just or true. In raising these questions we move far from a consideration of democracy proper, but they must be raised in order to answer the primary question with which we are concerned: Does democracy make the city a whole, and if so, what kind of a whole is it? Can a democratic or any other city be understood as a whole that makes possible the exercise of man's freedom and permits his living as he would wish? Can the regime be defended against its critics because it can be demonstrated to be the very order necessary for the exercise of man's freedom and humanity?

Democracy as a fitting subject for study suggests itself to us naturally. We live in a democracy, and democracy or the anticipation of democracy, liberal or socialist, is such a universal phenomenon that at present it hardly seems necessary to justify its examination. Its examination through the use of Aristotle, however, does seem to require justification. We dismiss challenges to our enterprise on the ground that we cannot learn anything meaningful from Aristotle because he wrote long ago and in circumstances different from our own. This is a challenge to the utility of the history of political philosophy altogether. The relevant doubt would be not that we are unable to understand Aristotle, but that he was unable to conceive of the possible circumstances that would necessitate a rethinking of his judgment on democracy and its alternatives.

What immediately comes to our minds is the seemingly comprehensive defense of the principle of modern representative democracy in the work of Thomas Hobbes. Although Hobbes favored monarchy in practice, we term his teaching democratic insofar as he makes the legitimacy of all regimes rest on the natural rights of free and equal men and the universal consent embodied or represented in the sovereign. Whatever our opinions about the relative merits of aristocracy and democracy might be, Hobbes' argument strikes us as theoretically superior to Aristotle's because it incorporates the principles of modern natural science, which we accept as true. Hobbes' argument further strikes us as practically superior: democratic justice based upon the self-serving rights of man, universal enlightenment, and modern technology seems a more realistic way to ensure order than does aristocratic benevolence based upon moral virtue. Nevertheless, one might challenge the theoretical superiority of Hobbes's teaching if it cannot explain in the same terms of modern natural science the teacher himself, and one might challenge its practical superiority if it has not proved to be beneficial without qualification. Our contention is that Aristotle does in fact conceive of the conditions that would make democracy seem the most defensible political order, and that he rejects a solution similar to that of Hobbes on grounds that Hobbes would have acknowledged as not unreasonable. We therefore examine Aristotle's account of democracy on the hypothesis that it is the comprehensive judgment upon democracy.

Aristotle's comprehensive judgment upon democracy, we contend, is found in Book III of the *Politics*. That Book III appears to be concerned with democracy is of course not sufficient; it treats oligarchy, aristocracy and kingship no less. Nor are Books IV through VI any less obviously concerned with democracy. However problematic its self-understanding might be, democracy is, according to Aristotle, the natural form of politics. By natural we mean both according to the understanding of nature that preceded political philosophy, and according to the political perspective of most men prior to political philosophy. Aristotle's discussions of democracy are therefore often discussions of politics simply. Book III of the *Politics* is Aristotle's fundamental discussion of politics and of the city. From the beginning of Book I the reader might infer that it, too, dealt with the city as a whole,[4] yet the most obvious theme is economics and its locus, the household, not the politics of the agora. Furthermore, the thesis of the book is that economics and politics are distinct,[5] and the conclusion of the discussion is that another beginning must be made if one wishes to understand politics.[6] Book II is explicitly an examination of what others have said about the best regime.[7] We neglect it not so much because it purports to be a criticism of others, for certainly one could learn about Aristotle from considering what he chooses to criticize and why he does so. Rather, we neglect it because it, no more than Book I, treats politics from a perspective that would allow us to speak about politics proper. The best regime with which Aristotle is concerned in Book II seems to exceed the possibilities of even the best actual city.[8] The explicit theme of Book III, however, is what each of the regimes is, seen in the light of what the city is; or the theme is the city and its parts and how those parts are ordered to each other and to the whole. Politics is thematic, and the relation of politics to the private, the economic, and the universal, the political community, is clarified. From Book III we can understand much of what we would need to know about Books I and II.

In turn, the rest of the *Politics* can best be understood in the light of Book III. The remainder is, simply stated, the education of men of differing interests and capacities in the manner befitting each individually and all together. That there need be several educations, that they can and should assume the form they do, and that the political educations presented are the comprehensive human educations are grasped as implications of Book III once that teaching is understood. In particular, why democracy is treated as it is throughout the *Politics* can then be made clear without a detailed analysis and comparison of each passage in which it is mentioned. Hence, the subject of this volume will be Book III.

In Book III all men are given the outline of a teaching about the just, the good, and the beneficial, and some men are gradually led to understand what just and beneficial regimes are and why they are necessarily so. At the same time as citizens and political scientists are instructed, there is an inquiry for the benefit of philosophical men about what the whole and being as such might be. Eventually we shall consider why this inquiry occurs within the *Politics*. Does philosophy concern itself with politics merely for the sake of defending political men or in order to defend philosophy from political men, or does the philosopher learn about wholes and being only from taking the political seriously?

Whatever else it is, Book III of the *Politics* is manifestly political. It virtually begins with a political dispute. The language suggests that someone demands that he not be held responsible for what appears to his interlocutor to have been an act of his city. He attempts to absolve himself of responsibility by asserting that the act was not one of the city, the whole, but of the oligarch or tyrant, a part. The city is for him a city only when it is a democratic whole, though he cannot offer a coherent argument in defense of his claim. This assertion we take to be that of a democrat, an assertion which is the basis of a dispute between political men and of an inquiry by theoretical men. Book III begins with the clumsy assertiveness of a democrat and his opponent who, in disputing about politics, reveal to a theoretical man the nature of what is political and of a whole. Book III virtually ends with an explanation by a theoretical man of what the democrat intended to say, and with a qualified defense of democracy before political men.

For the above reasons we will turn to an examination of Book III. We examine it in detail, with pedantic insistence on distinctions among words and between what is said and what is not said or said ambiguously. Eventually we shall defend this procedure by an account of the reasons Aristotle himself presents in Book III for the necessity that political treatises be written in the manner in which he writes. His insistence upon this necessity and the cause to which he attributes it cannot but be a part of Aristotle's explanation of the nature of political and all things and, in particular, of demotic and democratic things.

ONE

1. Beginnings (1274b32–41)

Book III concludes with the suggestions that the form of the book has been
several arguments,[1] and that the content has been the education of a serious
man and of a statesman and king.[2] These and other indications lead us to
propose that the organization of the book is as follows. First, the education
and habits that make a man serious and that make a statesman or king are
said to be almost the same. If they are almost but not simply the same, then
they differ, and Book III consists of two educations. The first is that of a
political man who, taking himself and his manliness seriously as men are
wont to do, learns what manliness is and what about himself is worth taking
seriously. He learns about philosophy. The second is that of a philosopher,
a would-be knower of the whole of nature, who learns that what most men
take seriously but he finds ridiculous—politics—is far more important than
he had thought, for the city in speech is the only whole man knows. Both educations culminate in a teaching about the human soul and about what one
might surmise about politics and all things in the light of that knowledge.

Since the starting points of the educations differ, the steps in them necessarily differ. Therefore, we are not surprised to note that the divisions of the
arguments in Book III are twofold. Five times, arguments conclude with the
comment that things have been distinguished,[3] and twice the phrase "one
must distinguish" prepares for the resolution of a difficulty or a clarification
making possible the conclusion of an argument.[4] Six times, what appear to
be identifiable sections are commenced with the mention of something that
needs to be inspected or examined.[5] The themes of the first three examinations bear a clear resemblance to three reasons, given at the beginning of the
book, for examining the city in order to learn about the regime. First, there
is a dispute about what can be said to constitute the deed of the city. Can a

part ever do the work of the whole? Second, we all see that statesmen and legislators are busy in the city. Third, the regime is some ordering of those who make their homes in the city. The first three examinations are (1) what it is necessary to call a citizen and what a citizen is, which is connected to the dispute about whether a deed was or was not done by the city; (2) whether the virtue of the good man and a serious citizen is or is not the same; and (3) whether there is one regime or several, what they are, how many, and what the differences are. The last three examinations are (4) the regimes, how many they are in number, and what they are; (5) a crossing over and examination of kingship; and (6) an examination, brought on by the argument and made out of necessity, of the king who does all things according to his own intention. These latter examinations seem to repeat, in reverse order and from a new perspective, the first three themes: the ordering of what composes the city, the business of the ruler, and the part that is responsible for the doings of the whole. As we shall soon learn, it is the democrat and the natural philosopher who are unable to make the kind of distinctions they should, and consequently their education is repeated in understanding what distinctions are made. This is the education in politics. It is the oligarch, the discriminating political man but also the potential student of the philosopher, who proceeds by examinations and learns what constitute fitting subjects for examinations. Because we flatter ourselves in thinking that we are both discriminating citizens of a democracy and potentially wise human beings, we shall follow the order of the examinations.

Before we commence the first examination, it will be useful to notice some distinctions implicit in Aristotle's speeches from the very beginning. What is "asserted" in politics may differ from what "is," as well as from what is "set down" as a philosopher's tentative position, from what is "spoken" as in a private conversation between reasonable men, and from what is "mentioned" or "caused to be said" in the sense of answering a question only if raised by the reader himself.

For example, let us consider Aristotle's reasons for studying the city, given at the beginning of Book III. There is a dispute about responsibility for a political deed, and assertions are made. We might remind ourselves of what a dispute is not—that is, the quiet, rational inquiry and discourse that characterizes dialectic. What we see of a statesman's or legislator's activities does not comprise all of his doings if some of a man's doings, notably speeches, are heard but never seen. That the regime is an ordering of those who make their homes in the city does not mean that this is the only ordering of things that is of consequence. This order may be caused by those who rule in the city, and one can ask where they learned the principles according to which they order. We mention these possible inferences about what is *not* said from what *is* said, because these possibilities will readily occur to men who think as philosophers do. The education of philosophers is presented in this way, and it passes unnoticed by those who do not take speeches seriously. But we shall find that these inferred topics—the order outside of the city, the ruler's unseen activities, and a dialectical inquiry into causes—comprise the last three examinations. If this analysis is correct, our suspicion that we profit from keeping these three topics in mind throughout is confirmed.

The beginning of Book III, then, presents two different beginnings at the same time. Book I begins with what is seen, and it treats all things—the household, economics, and nature—from the perspective of concern for oneself and one's family and what is necessary and useful to what is most one's own. Book II begins with what we choose to contemplate, and it treats the whole of things—the regime, speeches about the life according to wish or prayer, and man's cities—from the perspective of the concern for what is most sharable, reasonable speech, and what it finds noble or beautiful. In neither book is there a possible politics. But in Book III both perspectives are brought together, although not initially combined. The asserted, the sensible, the private, and the necessary are juxtaposed with the spoken and silently articulated, the logically distinguished, the sharable, and the choice-worthy. These perspectives are the two different *archai*, "beginning points" or "first and governing principles," by means of which one organizes all that is sensible and knowable into a whole, and through which one comes to understand what a whole is. Book III is political in a way that Books I and II are not. Is the city, then, not a whole like either of these two apparent wholes, one's own and reasonable speech? Is neither of these the first principle of politics? What the city is is "almost" the first inquiry of Book III. The first inquiry, which is perhaps not first in time but first in importance, is the inquiry about the first principle, the *archē*. Only after the mention of philosophizing about political things, when the two perspectives are combined, is the city said to be a whole.[6] And only at the conclusion of the discussion of kingship does an *archē*, although of very great age, perhaps come into being.[7] Thus, to learn why and how the whole is made through the combination of the two *archai* and why and how the first principle is intelligible through politics is the education of the philosophic reader of Book III of the *Politics*.

Our education begins with the observation of political men disputing, citizens acting and asserting themselves, though asserting themselves by speaking, giving opinions. Thus begins Book III; it ends with political men speaking and dialoguing. From the beginning, Aristotle corrects the perspectives of Books I and II, the economic and the best regime, and he gives us our first hint about the nature of the city and politics proper. The citizen voices an opinion about political deeds, and his judgments reflect his thoughts, only gradually articulated, about the just, the noble, and the beneficial. Citizens' speeches constitute political deeds. The form in which they become manifest reveals an element not essential to the economic and philosophic: assertion, the desire to be free and the demand to be honored. Is it this element of assertiveness that makes the political the realm in which the whole man is manifest? The citizen first appears as a man who asserts an opinion he must then defend with argument as well as force. The philosopher first appears as a man who raises doubts, and has an opinion he must defend with force as well as argument. In political disputes asserted and spoken, the private and the common, the beneficial and the noble, the necessary and the choiceworthy are brought together, and a whole is made.

The citizen is the subject of the first examination, one would suppose, because he is a part like the whole. From knowing "citizen," one should know "city." But this assumption is questionable from the beginning, for the first thing we observe is that a citizen of a particular city disputes with another man about what the city is. From knowing an oligarch, one knows only oligarchy, not "city" nor even all of an oligarchic city if the poor within it are democrats. Perhaps it is more reasonable to suppose that Aristotle first examines the citizen, not the city, precisely because the citizen's assertion brings to light the difficulty in a part's claiming to bespeak the whole. The philosopher, too, is a part of nature who must speak for the whole. We learn in Book III that no particular city is a whole. But in our reflection on the inadequacy of each and our consideration of what would be necessary to make it a whole, we make a political community in which men have the possibility of becoming whole men and of understanding what a whole is.

2. Citizens (1274b41–1276b15)

A citizen in a democracy is not always a citizen in an oligarchy, we are told, and therefore democrats and oligarchs dispute about what a citizen is. To this dispute we are witnesses. A definition of a citizen is proposed, and a correction is offered and apparently accepted. The definition first proposed seems to be the democrat's, but it is said to be one of the citizen simply, and it does seem to be applicable to all cities.

The speaker begins by excluding those who are not full citizens, rather than by specifying the qualities entitling one to be a citizen. We would expect someone engaging in a dispute to make an argument justifying his exclusions, but the citizen gives no reasons. What he asserts is that a citizen is not a citizen merely by living and laboring in the city; the work of a citizen differs from what is necessary to sustain his physical being. Nor is one a citizen in having legal rights and duties toward other citizens that might be enforced in the courts; the citizen's work differs from what is necessary to ensure legality. Nor would one be a citizen if he were too young or too old; the work of a citizen does bear some similarity to the work of one in the prime of manhood. The principles of exclusion and inclusion are said to be the same as those employed in disenfranchising and exiling citizens—that is, in unmaking them—but the claim is that at least some citizens are not made. Presumably a citizen must then be born a citizen. This explains why resident aliens and slaves are not citizens, but not why children and old men are incomplete citizens. Children and old men must be excluded because the citizen is one who is fully a man. But being fully a man is manifested in doing the work of a citizen, in ruling, or in partaking in jury and assembly membership. We then wonder why able metics and slaves are excluded, especially if all citizen-born are presumed to be able men and are included equally. What does being able to rule and being a man have to do with being born in a particular city? A citizen is a citizen in being a citizen, but this statement cannot consistently explain both the origin and the quality enabling one to be a citizen. The citizen has not thought much about what the causes of being a citizen are.

Regardless of applicability to other cities, the form as well as the content of the definition meets our expectation of what a democratic definition might be. As in a democracy, and particularly in the Athenian democracy, a citizen is one who partakes without restriction of time in jury and assembly membership. The man offering this definition, presumably having always lived in a democracy, speaks of offices limited or unlimited in time because he is unfamiliar with offices filled by election instead of lot or rotation. He substitutes membership in the assembly for the magistracies because the assembly is sovereign in a democracy. In expressing his views, the citizen of a democracy begins from his own city, which is all he knows. For him a democratic citizen is the same as a citizen simply; of other possibilities he is unaware and cares nothing. He knows that some men are excluded from Athenian citizenship, yet he cannot specify a consistent principle of exclusion or inclusion. He does not argue or speak well. In fact, he expresses disinterest in quibbling about names and definitions and rests content with only a more or less fitting definition. Why Aristotle seems to agree to set this down as the definition of a citizen is another matter.

Others, however, do seem to be interested in precision and in making fine distinctions. Someone objects that the definition does not give due weight to the obvious, for we see that regimes do differ. In some regimes, not all men have a part in rule. The immediate insistence on differences by the man offering the objection contrasts with the democrat's desire to find a definition roughly fitting most cases, and his mention of regimes, not cities, contrasts with the democrat's disregard of them. It is he who identifies the first definition of a citizen as peculiar to democracy. This speaker takes as his point of reference what he sees, not what he knows by custom; but he nevertheless prefaces his correction of the first definition with the elaboration of an abstract principle. Perhaps both politics and perception require arguments that were absent in the first speech. The principle he elaborates, that things differing in form are more different than similar, will be considered later, for its connection to the objection made to the definition of a citizen is not obvious. Nor indeed is there a clear basis for the distinctions this man does make, though he insists upon them. He seems to identify the unerring with the prior, the erring and deviant with the latter, as if he had some inexplicable attachment to the old. He readily calls to mind regimes in which there is no demos, or in which the many need not be given a part in rule. The bulk of his supposed argument consists of giving examples that contradict the democratic definition, and the examples he offers are of more or less aristocratic or oligarchic cities in which only a part rules or judges. His knowledge of these regimes is somewhat deficient, however; he does not know that the other office in Sparta is called kingship, and he does not recognize that the Carthaginian procedure differs slightly from the Spartan.[8] Nevertheless, on the basis of what he can distinguish, he suggests that the democratic definition be revised. The particular office in which a citizen partakes must be delimited, for not in every regime are all given the right to deliberate and try cases; but only one who does have this right or possibility is a citizen. Thus all freeborn men are not full citizens in all regimes. He also improves the democratic definition in suggesting, ambiguously, that the origin of doing the work of a citizen is in a right or a capacity, and that the quality of a citizen is doing the work with skill. Furthermore, he adds an end: Citizenship is for the sake of the self-sufficiency of the city. He thus clarifies the first definition without giving any more reasons.

If the first definition was set down by an Athenian democrat, this correction does seem to be made by an Athenian oligarch of sorts. He is a man of greater awareness and confidence, who is used to making authoritative statements. He speaks of necessities and self-sufficiency as might a businessman. He begins by distinguishing himself from other citizens, thus revealing a distaste for the demos, and by mentioning by name only regimes in which a part rules the whole. Although his knowledge of these foreign regimes is imprecise, he wishes to have it known that it is not always necessary to allow the many to rule. Citizens are only those who have the power or ability to rule. What kind of oligarch this speaker is may be shown in the relative emphasis he puts on power and ability, as well as in his ambiguous reference to earlier or prior regimes.

The democrat implied that there might be a connection between being a citizen and being fully a man. Neither disputant denies that all cities share to a certain extent this understanding; each understands politics to comprehend everything human. The oligarch, nonetheless, by suggesting that citizenship is a right given or taken by someone, or a power, implies that citizen birth is at best a necessary but not sufficient condition. He further specifies that the citizen must have some skill, and that citizenship has some end. But what kind of power ensures skilled deliberation and judgment? He no more than the democrat adequately explains the connection between the origin of a citizen and the quality of a citizen. We hear no democratic challenge to the oligarchic correction. Yet if the oligarch can convince or silence a democrat, he might well be defenseless before a man who has asked him about the efficient cause of citizenship, and who can tell a good argument from a bad one.

Whatever disagreement there might be between democrats and oligarchs, in what follows Aristotle causes us to realize that there is more agreed upon than not. A citizen is one who was born a citizen or is now a citizen, and who is more or less able to take his part in the affairs of the city. In practice, one who is descended from citizen stock on both sides is a citizen, and no question is raised. That deliberating and judging be done well does not seem to be as essential to the citizen as is the concern for unimpeachable ancestry. Presumably one could argue, if pressed, that the citizen's ability is somehow heritable, and that one knows that the first citizen was himself singularly skilled at deliberating and judging.

Now the citizens are pressed to argue precisely this point, for Gorgias's bon mot does impeach their ancestors. Gorgias urges that Larissaean citizens have been "made" by Larissaean magistrates (called *demiourgoi*) in the same way that other "Larissaeans" (a Larissa was a kettle) are made by other *demiourgoi* (the word for craftsmen). The opinion Aristotle reports is that the title of citizen is inherited chiefly from one's father and, we suggest, that the matter or quality of a citizen comes from one's mother just as the female is material for the male to form.[9] It would seem that both form and matter make a citizen. The difficulty in this understanding is that the first citizen could not have inherited his title. If his ancestors had the same matter, what does his title add? Why, in other words, does the citizen insist that

title to rule is conferred by citizen birth as well as ability? Aristotle's definition of a citizen was politic because it ambiguously reproduced the city's
characteristic unconcern with excellence and its attachment to the ancestral.
Gorgias, to his own profit, mockingly exposes the citizen's difficulty. Gorgias, a foreigner, claims to teach an art of rule to citizens of many cities. His
pun means that all cities are conventional, or made, and that the ruler is the
maker, a man who has learned an art of rule. If all citizens are made like
artifacts, then not the antiquity but the intended use of the artifact and the
skill of the maker in fulfilling his intention are what we must want to know
in determining citizenship. The best city for Gorgias would be one that had
been shaped into something useful by an artisan. Gorgias, however, either
out of delicacy or carelessness, neglects to specify the user. He does succeed
in calling into question the claim that a democracy or any ancestral order
might have on a citizen's allegiance.

If democrats and oligarchs are closer to one another than to foreign rhetoricians, it is unclear where Aristotle himself stands. He seemed to be satis-
fied with the ambiguous correction of the democrat's definition by someone
we tentatively identified as an oligarch. The definition gave citizenship to
those who had the right or the ability. Because of the ambiguity, Aristotle
may be far closer to Gorgias in the concern for excellence than he is to the
citizen's unconcern for it. Skill in deliberating and judging may well be an
art like kettle-making, and the previous specification of sufficiency as the
end is not unlike a concern for utility. What Aristotle apparently opposes
most is Gorgias's outspoken mockery: He contrasts Gorgias's assertion with
the previously "orated" definition, and thus contrasts Gorgias's rhetoric with
another kind of public political speech.

If Gorgias mocks, the "Little Lion" perhaps seeks to know as well.[10] What
claim should the ancestral have on the citizen, and why is the question of
efficient causes not an important one? These may also be Aristotle's own
questions, but they are not the citizen's. Gorgias, the skilled speaker and the
man who "raises a doubt," reveals to us the city's incompleteness, both in
its unconcern with the human qualities exhibited by Gorgias and in its inability to defend itself. Moreover, for good or ill, it is only Gorgias's assertion
that causes a philosopher to make his first assertion. Making speeches and
raising doubts are not of the essence of the city, yet it would seem that any
city, democracy or oligarchy, that finds it politic to exclude foreign rhetoricians and what they represent is not a whole in which the whole of man is
manifest. The city can neither defend itself from rhetoricians nor defend its
exclusion of them to us.

Regardless of whether strangers are present, the illegitimacy of the first citizen and the conventional character of the city would be apparent to all citizens whenever a revolution occurred. A revolution is in effect a new founding, and the Athenian order about which the democrat and oligarch now dispute had for its founder a man who made Athenians out of non-Athenians. None of the original citizens could have been descendants of two citizens. Under the tyranny, their fathers were not citizens, and to the extent that their mothers were respectable, their virtue would inhere in non-citizens now. The citizen is not senseless in avoiding the question of origins. In any case, how well the city provides for sufficiency could be said to be more important than the ignobility of the beginnings. But if the citizen can ignore the first part of Gorgias's challenge, he must take seriously the joke about artisans. The citizen who speaks so poorly on his own behalf and has claimed no craft would then have little to hope for in continuing the argument with Gorgias.

Rather, we suggest, it is Aristotle himself who continues, as if disputing with men like Gorgias. The possibility that there is an art of ruling has not been denied, but Aristotle, in tacitly stressing his attachment to Athens, indicates that the best attained by any actual Athenian ruler is more likely to be rule in accordance with the best Athenian custom than rule with some transcultural art. The speaker clearly identifies himself by his examples as an Athenian, but he does not identify himself with any particular regime. He speaks of two Athenian regimes, the old tyranny and the new democracy, neither of which he praises or blames. He is then attached to Athens in a way that the democrat and oligarch are not, although he is attached to it as Gorgias is not. He is both theoretical man and citizen. But he is not therefore less harsh on the Athenians than on Gorgias. He tells them not that they need an art of rule which he might teach them, but that they need justice. Athenians, being "made" citizens, are not true citizens, and are at best just citizens. The proper concern of these citizens is justice, which is apparently not an art. This is not to say, however, that artful rule would not be more beneficial than just rule, or that the two might never coincide. Nor is it to say that justice is ever achieved by the Athenians. It is to say that Aristotle announces his intention of protecting a kind of good citizenship that is at least possible for Athenians, assuming that it is impossible for Gorgias to educate them all in the art of rule.

Aristotle makes clear his intention in the following way. He reminds us of the opinion of some that the unjust has the same capacity as the false, hence the just as the true, and he further says that we see citizens ruling unjustly, hence not truly. According to this opinion, the just is the true, being in completion, and a kind of being not seen, or at least not seen in actual cities.

We are reminded of Socrates' opinion in the *Republic*.[11] The city we see has no true or just citizens. Aristotle even informs us that his own public speeches in this city may be false. He says that we shall assert that these rulers who rule not justly, hence not truly, still do rule, although unjustly. The assertion contrasts with what is; indeed, what is has dropped from sight. A citizen was said to be one who has the possibility of sharing in office, requiring skill in deliberating and judging; but we are now reminded only that a citizen is one who shares in some defined office. Aristotle even goes so far as to say that he has already asserted this when he has made no assertions thus far. The just and true and skillful rule lies in the realm of the unseen and unasserted. Aristotle in no way expresses disagreement with some who say that the unjust has the same capacity as the false, yet he allows the city its own kind of being and, therewith, its own kind of justice. Is he all too aware of the extent of the capacity or power of the false and the unjust? Aristotle saves the city from foreign rhetoricians who ply their trades, and from men who inquire about the true and the false, but not from those who demand justice. Aristotle's first political act is an attempt to save the dignity of the city in order that one can be indignant with it when it is not dignified.

Aristotle may have some additional purpose in making justice the focus of the citizens' dispute. The reason for the ambiguity in the definition of a citizen is now clearer. A citizen is one who has the right or possibility of deliberating and judging with skill. Legality, or right, is closer to the forceful; and possibility, or capacity to do well, is closer to the true. Aristotle says that the dispute about the citizens made into lawful Athenian citizens after the expulsion of the tyrants is a dispute not about what a citizen is, but about whether one is justly a citizen. The dispute to which we have been witness is then not a dispute about the "what is" of a citizen, but a consideration of those "who must be called citizens." This, we recall, was also said to be one subject of the first examination.[12] But if the Athenian citizens have not been disputing about the "what is" of the citizen, to whose dispute about the "what is" have we been witness? The dispute about justice, the citizens' dispute, is said to be bound to the previously "mentioned" dispute. This might be taken as a reference to the first announced dispute, the one about whether a deed was done by the city or by the oligarch or tyrant.[13] Aristotle, however, now calls this not a dispute but an inquiry or difficulty, which takes place after a democracy has come into being. We have interpreted Aristotle's text thus far to represent a public dispute in democratic Athens, but perhaps our interpretation has been incomplete. We thus find it necessary to reexamine the arguments that have been made.

In the first definition, the citizen is one who partakes in the *archē* which is beyond definition. The man offering this definition begins a political dispute with a statement of what one might say is the true beginning as cause and substance of all things. In this first principle man partakes by judging. Later this definition is said to be most fitting to a citizen in a democracy, whatever is meant by democracy, though its proponent does not offer it as such. Rather, the definition is that of a citizen simply, and to repeat, Aristotle looks at the citizen because he is the part of the whole that should reveal the whole. Why in politics or in speaking about political things the first cause and substance of all things becomes manifest will be seen to be the theme of Book III of the *Politics*.

Because the first principle is undefined, the speaker begins by saying what the citizen is not. The citizen simply is not a citizen by chancing to be a citizen; therefore he is a citizen either always or by some regular or explicable cause. While Aristotle speaks of other offices as being limited in time and as not having the possibility to be wholly the same twice, this office, spoken of in the singular, is unlimited.[14] He finds it ridiculous to deny its title of rule with respect to the most sovereign things. *Archē*, we stress, means not only office or ruler, but beginning and first and governing principle. This *archē* is some first cause that is responsible for the being of all or of the most sovereign things by having begun or by ruling them. These things the "democrat" takes seriously. The citizen partakes of this rule not by making his home someplace, as does a slave or a metic. The being of the citizen is neither his physical being nor his work in the household. (What these points mean will be explained as we proceed.) The true citizen is never too young or too old; his being is always being in completion. Politics, however, is not something he habitually takes seriously; he presently partakes of the city in which he dwells and in its legal justice only incompletely, standing accused before it and in need of a champion to justify him before the city and to defend him in its law courts. The citizen reminds us not so much of Socrates, who, when suspected of inquiring into the heavens and under the earth, was compelled to defend philosophy, but rather of what Socrates inquired after: the first or governing principle by which the being of all things and of their being a whole is known.

Reference is also made to a citizen who partakes by judging, however, and the judge does suggest a man, albeit a wise one. If a man does not rule the whole, his full citizenship is exercised in judging the whole. But there is perhaps something common to judge and ruler. Man's judging is ruling if he thereby duplicates what the ruler, or first cause, has done. To speak of partaking in the first principle by judging suggests, therefore, that the first principle is something intelligent and/or intelligible. Yet this is not specified; the first principle is undefined, and what is common to judge and ruler is nameless. In saying that what is common has no name, one might mean that this substance has no particularity and is therefore beyond naming and explanation by formula. Throughout the *Politics*, Aristotle frequently reminds the reader that what is intelligible to intelligence transcends what speech can express.[15] Or else, the namelessness of the community might call into question its very existence. The mind that judges has nothing in common with what has brought all things into being if all things are body in flux, neither caused nor governed by intelligence. That all things came into being by a first cause similar to intellect is surely open to doubt. But it is to this first cause, sought by the natural philosopher regardless of the political consequences of his pursuit, that the definition of the citizen simply, the democratic citizen, makes reference.

That the search for the first cause is conducted without regard for political consequences might be significant for the following reasons. As we asserted in the introduction, there may well be some connection between what political opinions men hold and what their loftier thoughts are, be they naive or sophisticated. If this is also Aristotle's understanding, we are then prompted to consider why the search for the first principle or substance simply is tacitly identified with democracy and what this suggests to us about Aristotle's use of democracy throughout the *Politics*. If one partakes of citizenship in being a judge who thereby shares in some community with what rules, then only in grasping this primary substance is one a citizen. Needless to say, the number of noncitizens among men, not to mention all other beings, would be large. Insofar as no man knew the most sovereign things or the one thing responsible for all things being a whole, there would be no citizens in this democracy. But this only a wise man would know; it is what the philosopher still seeks to know. Thus there would at best be incomplete citizens, metics and slaves—that is, philosophers ever at work acquiring wisdom. Or, more likely, if there is no community between judge and first cause, either because no wise man is present or because the first cause is unintelligible, then all men and all perceptible beings can reasonably be said to partake of another substance which is body. This democracy is the ruleless rule of each and every body: a chaos, not a whole that is ordered according to laws. Should the democrat wish to imitate this unruled disorder in his city, he cannot consistently do so. His first difficulty is that the Athenian democracy is established and maintained as Athenian and as a democracy by some sort of custom or law. According to the philosopher's argument, however, men could not reasonably be distinguished by custom or by law, or at all from other beings with bodies, even though these beings do not often attempt to sit as judges on Athenian courts. The democratic citizen could not account for his inclusion of freeborn Athenians and his exclusion of beasts, much less metics and slaves; his law would seem to have no basis in reason. The democracies found in the philosopher's argument have either far too few or far too many citizens to comprise a human city. The definition does not take into account both the unique way in which man, the only being that judges, partakes of some first principle, albeit imperfectly, and the way in which beings with bodies can be said to partake in some first principle. Neither the city like a democracy of the equally wise nor the one like a democracy of equally unruled bodies can be a city in which men as we know them live. Given this conclusion, the Athenian democrat is necessarily forced to argue in defense of his order that the Athenian laws and customs of some unknown origin now make all Athenians, but only Athenians, equally fit to judge. This, of course, is precisely not using one's judgment about the most sovereign thing, which is the wisdom of the law.

The philosopher who seeks to make a whole in this way, grasping for being itself but speaking nothing about it, is like the democrat who could not say anything more than that a citizen is one who does what a citizen does. Being is. The philosopher's difficulty seems to lie in his inability or unwillingness to articulate the manner of being of that indefinite first principle. In saying only that a citizen participates in being, he does not tell men what they need to know about being. If the philosopher is not confused, he is far from politic.

We can now better understand the objection offered by the man who seemed to be an oligarch of sorts. He does not deny that all things somehow partake of the first principle, but he does insist that, nonetheless, all things are subordinate to *eidē*, forms or species. His argument begins with the obvious and reasonable criticism to which the first definition of a citizen is subject. A man using his senses, not to mention a sensible man, perceives, for example, that a man looks and acts, and therefore perhaps *is*, different from a beast. The visible differences in things are indications of real differences. A citizen is understood by understanding his "regime," his visible form, if, as it is argued, things that differ in form have little or nothing in common. An alternative reading of the argument would be that all the things that have regimes have little or nothing of what is common in them, or that most beings do not share in a community as judges. If the whole is composed of parts subordinate to different forms, and difference in form is more important than the identity of the substance in which some or most of the parts partake, then to say that man partakes of some first principle does not require that a beast therefore similarly partake. Perhaps the differences in form are even indications of differences in substance. There need not be as many citizens as the democrat found.

In fact, the oligarch proceeds to explain that in the regimes we see, one judges only partly by the first principle, or one judges some things by one principle and others by another. Without the presence of a certain kind of demos, or lacking certain beliefs, one does not grasp the first principle but seems to find several. The oligarch refers to the situation in which a democracy of wise men is not to be found and in which a democratic city has not been established by custom and law. (The word for law and customary law is *nomos*; "to believe," *nomizō*, is from the same root.) The situation in Carthage is correctly said to be the same as in Sparta because in neither place are judgments made according to one first principle. Moreover, these best existing yet less than perfect political regimes, Sparta and Carthage, correspond to man, actual and less than perfect. Men know only the parts or some of the parts of being, but they must make do by combining partial wisdom and opinion in forming judgments. Hence the democrat's other difficulty, that of too few citizens, might be overcome by the need to combine partial opinions to form worthy but imperfect judgments.

In characterizing the first definition of a citizen as democratic, the oligarch says that in some regimes, the nondemocratic ones, partaking is possible but not necessary. In a democracy, the parts are fully what they are supposed to be as well as what the whole itself is supposed to be. In the other regimes of which the oligarch speaks, this completion is only a possibility, not a necessity. The oligarch assumes, as his examples indicate, that man's regime is not necessarily a democracy. Man's perfection does not fall within the necessary workings of nature. But it is perhaps also unnecessary in the sense that judging the just or believing in certain things might be a sufficient, if imperfect, substitute for wisdom. A limited or defined ruling principle—for example, that by which men but not other beings are ruled—might be the principle according to which man deliberates and judges and is a citizen. And among men perhaps some, but not all, judge according to this principle.

If the democrat, looking toward being simply, neglects to distinguish from others' being the peculiarity and problematic character of man's being, the oligarch neglects to say how the various parts or regimes, which may partake of different first principles, partake of one and how they might be ordered. He does not speak of what rules the whole. He seems to speak most clearly about man. Man is a citizen in having the possibility of sharing in the first principle of deliberating and judging with skill. Because he has, as other beings we see do not have, the capacity for intellect, he judges; but his having only a capacity, a potential, means that he can do it well or poorly. And because he may partake of two first principles, body and intellect, he does not know which is the ruling principle; so he must deliberate and choose, not rule. And because his wisdom is incomplete, he needs the help of others: The city is composed of some multitude aiming at self-sufficiency. The democratic definition must be corrected in accordance with the realization that beings differ in their qualities, and that in the case of the being called man, being itself or self-sufficiency may be actualized in no particular instance, but in the completion toward which philosophy aims.[16] The end is actualized in greater or lesser degrees in various men. Human cities obviously differ, as do the ways in which they are ruled. To ignore similar distinctions among men, as well as between men and other beings, seems unreasonable. According to the oligarchic understanding, a man in whom there is not wisdom, but a substance enabling him to deliberate and judge with skill, is a citizen. The oligarchic correction substitutes forms for first substance, and potency for actuality; yet in doing so, it tells us more about man and the political, if not about the cause of all being and being as such.

The philosopher's attempt to define the citizen simply alienates him and the first cause, if it is intelligible substance, from the city in which he dwells. While he lives as a stranger to political men, they, totally immersed in their own order, identify their particular order with all things simply. Both the pursuit of the highest and the inability to recognize the particular as not being all that is contravene common sense and human necessities, though the democratic philosopher and citizen are not therefore incorrect. What we have been calling the oligarchic correction is closer to both reasonable nonphilosophic common sense and political science. It begins either with distinctions based upon sense perception, or with a teaching about forms. In each dispute, human common sense and political science take the same side against democracy and natural philosophy. Any further dispute or inquiry based upon common ground would have to take place between an oligarch of some sort, the man who emphasizes the distinctions in what he sees, and a more politic and political philosopher who teaches about forms and about man. From their interchange might emerge the city's justice and an articulate explanation of what makes a whole a whole.

The reasonable correction has the potential dangers of either identifying, as does the oligarch, the visible with being simply, or of forgetting, as does the political scientist, that the human whole, a partial whole or a regime, is not necessarily identical with the whole or the city. Nevertheless, Aristotle tentatively accepts the oligarchic correction. The citizen is man, potentially not actually wise, and the city is a multitude of these men, not all things or the cause of all being. The philosophic dispute is connected to the citizen's dispute about which things of those we see do rule justly. In order that the corrected definition, the one seemingly more useful to politics, be ultimately acceptable, Aristotle will have to make the teaching about justice true. He will have to provide for the first danger of identifying the visible with all that is, so that if one forgets about anything other than what one sees, one will not therefore understand a whole incorrectly. The citizen whom one sees ruling justly must make manifest what is. At the end of Book III, Aristotle speaks of some or many men who *see*, judging with their eyes and ears; that is, in the light of what has been explained, Aristotle will have to provide for the second danger of forgetting that the human whole is not necessarily identical with the whole by considering whether or not the nature of all things is in fact the same as human things, or as that of the citizen who rules justly. At the end of Book III he raises the question of whether the best political order corresponds to a natural order. That is, he returns to a search for the citizen simply, but in a way that the search is shown to be necessary for the sake of justice and just in not seeming to challenge cities that do achieve a semblance of political justice.

The philosophers' dispute about what the citizen is, not the citizens' dispute, is the dispute about whether the cause of a deed was the city, the whole, or a part that rules it: the oligarch or tyrant. The first definition spoke of the first or ruling principle, the matter or substance in which as many parts as are in the whole partake and by which they are made a whole. The cause of the city's deed might well be a tyrant. The second definition spoke of the partial wholes of which the whole is made. The cause of the city's deed might be said to be an oligarchy, a small part. If number is not the criterion for responsibility for deeds of the whole, then what is?

Gorgias suggests that intention and skill in execution are the criteria. Gorgias raises the question of the efficient cause. But he forgets that neither citizens nor natural beings seem to have been made in the way that man makes artifacts, for a well-made artifact does reveal the intention of an artisan. Can one similarly discern the intention of the whole by seeing who has been made a citizen? To explain the intention of man's productions, moreover, is less problematic than to argue that both the whole city and the whole of nature were made with some intention. Unless Gorgias means to attribute to nature and to the political an intelligent first cause, then he antagonizes the city without being wholly serious. If he is serious, his irony hides little. Speaking about the first cause will lead the citizen to attribute his city's founding to a divine or semidivine being, but it will lead the philosopher to admit that the wise man contemplating is the efficient cause of there being a whole. In speaking of these questions initially as Gorgias would, rather than last as Aristotle does, one destroys the possible basis of agreement between philosophers and political men who can be educated only dually. The question of whether the legislator had an intention and what it was can only make sense to philosophers who have understood the importance of politics and to political men who have learned the full range of their choices. For a political philosopher to assert, as Gorgias in effect does, that man makes his own whole, that there is no first cause outside of man's arts, arises from a very different opinion about what political education is.[17]

Aristotle does not deny the importance of Gorgias' difficulty, and it is he who mentions that the more serious difficulty is to account for changes in regimes, visible forms, which are perhaps also changes in being. This inquiry, as a public inquiry, must be closed off, however.[18] The strength of greater lions is to be sealed up, as Cleisthenes is said to have done when, after the expulsion of the tyrants, he enrolled foreign and slavish metics. To whom Aristotle refers in speaking of tyrants and foreign and slavish metics becomes clearer to the reader as we proceed, but we suggest now that the former are philosophers who rule according to nature and the latter are philosophers at work philosophizing, who, in being foreign, are alienated from politics and who, in being slavish, are studiers of nature and not of men. Indeed, Gorgias, the "Little Lion," takes seriously only man and his arts, and Cleisthenes, "Strength Locked Up," succeeding the tyrants, makes philosophers take the political seriously. Attention is forcefully turned to the citizen's concern, justice, and to what the citizen takes seriously. The dispute about the "what is" of the citizen and the inquiry about the efficient cause are replaced by a consideration of justice. The approach to these questions through an inquiry into justice may, however, be a necessity and not the philosopher's choice.

Yet Aristotle mentions an inquiry beginning when a democracy comes into being. The origin of the new Athenian democracy was reputedly Cleisthenes' making free citizens of the basest sorts of men, slaves and metics. Perhaps the other democracy of the philosopher had an equally mean beginning—in politics. The citizens' dispute reasonably takes place in a democracy where one finds disgruntled unequals sharing equally with the base. But the dispute becomes an inquiry. Not the dispute about justice, but an inquiry by some men, emerging from it, is the beginning that culminates in a philosophic judgment upon the first things. The reader witnesses this ascent throughout Book III of the man of the few. Aristotle's announced silence about philosophy, his locking up of his strength, is to enable him to teach all men about justice, and to teach some about political science or prudence and some about philosophy. That he can teach these things simultaneously is shown in our ability to make sense of the arguments thus far in several ways. Democratic and oligarchic citizens are made to distinguish between lawful and just citizens. Justice is what the citizen must take seriously. Ruling justly may require some skill that men have unequally, but we do not yet know how it is acquired, whether inherited from one's ancestors, taught by Gorgias, or in neither or both ways. Philosophers are forced to make a new beginning in their search for the ruling citizen of nature, the first thing. It is now necessary to speak to political men about political things, thus to appear to take politics seriously, but we do not yet know whether philosophers wish to take seriously nature or man—and, if man, his arts or his politics. What is taught to whom and how it is taught is to be determined by the requirements of justice. But by justice does Aristotle mean the philosopher's repaying a debt because he too has learned something from the political? Or does he mean benefiting the city incidentally by teaching it to be just to philosophers?

3. To Be or Not to Be (1276a6–1276b15)

Whether citizens whom we *see* ruling rule justly is bound to the "mentioned" dispute; that is, the one that is less obvious. This dispute, we have learned, is the philosophers' dispute about the "what is," or the being, of citizens, or parts of the whole. The "democrat" argued that being was to be found in the cause of all things and in what makes judgments. The "oligarch" stressed that being of various kinds was found in the various things that had been brought into being. One kind of being, human being, was only being in potency, but was being nonetheless. The philosophers' dispute, therefore, raises the question of whether it is true to speak of at least two different kinds of being: one visible, another unseen and the same as intellect. Because the dispute is bound to the question of justice, the answer, Aristotle announces, either is determined by the requirements of justice or itself determines the meaning of justice, or both. In other words, if being is the bodily being in which most men can well be said to partake roughly equally, insofar as the true and the just are meant to be the same, then the rule of all men, which duplicates the natural equality of bodies, is just. If being is the intelligible or intelligent being in which men can well be said to partake very unequally, then the rule of the wiser or wisest is just. If the former, the deeds of the city are justly done by the democracy; if the latter, they are justly done by an oligarch or a tyrant. If being is of both kinds, as does seem to be the case, then there are two justs; and in what proportion they are to be combined and who therefore is to rule are most problematic.

The importance of who is justly or legitimately responsible for the deeds of the city becomes apparent when some men attempt to argue that they are not going to keep their legal obligations to the city if those obligations were contracted for them by an illegitimate ruler. For example, a democrat might well argue that the laws made by a former ruling oligarch or tyrant do not bind him. But is not the primary meaning of justice also keeping one's contracts, or obeying laws?[19] If so, by what considerations of justice could a citizen claim to break a law? He would have to say that deeds lawfully done are not necessarily justly done because the lawful ruler was not a just or legitimate ruler by some standard of justice. Perhaps he did not rule for the benefit of the whole city. The citizen's difficulty leads to the inquiry: "When did the city do something and when did not the city do it?" Yet Aristotle concludes the discussion with a statement about when the city can be said to be the same or another city. The question of when one can justly dissolve a contract with the city is expressly not answered, for it belongs to "another argument." Hence the argument that follows from the inquiry is a consideration of what constitutes being, but not yet according to which kind of being justice is.

The inquiry into whether a deed was done by the city or "not the city" replaces the dispute about whether a deed was done by the city or by the oligarch or tyrant. By omitting "the oligarch or tyrant" as the antithesis of the city, Aristotle indicates that the inquiry is no longer undertaken by a democratic citizen who identifies the city with the democracy; the mere fact that all rule does not distinguish democracy from regimes in which only a part rules. By substituting "not the city," Aristotle further indicates that what rules the city is not external to the whole of it, even if the whole does not mean all. What is "not the city" may have no being at all.[20] Yet Aristotle does speak of cities being the same or "other"; there are, it seems, two cities: one that is distinct from "not the city" and one that is distinct from other cities. These two cities represent two kinds of being. How one speaks of the two kinds of being as one philosopher to another, and what one asserts about them as a philosopher to political men, are questions of truth and justice.

The inquiry begins with an allegation put forth by "some": They choose not to keep their contracts because the contracts were undertaken not by the city, but by the tyrant. These some, who no longer oppose oligarchy to the city, are presumably oligarchs of sorts who are now more concerned with justice than with obedience to any law or regime merely because it is lawful. These some specify the conditions under which they might keep their contracts by distinguishing regimes that are for the sake of the benefit in common from regimes that *are* by being strong. Democracies, Aristotle now asserts, can be distinguished in the same way as can other regimes, and their deeds are the deeds of the city in the same way as are those of other regimes. There is a democracy that *is* the city by virtue of the many's being strong enough to rule the few, and this is the democracy to which an oligarch might object. There is also a democracy that *is* the city by virtue of its having as its end the benefit in common, and to this democracy no citizen of good intention could object.

The distinction that "some" make, by which these "some men" might be more clearly identified, depends on "the benefit in common." The reader will first find it useful to distinguish "the benefit in common" (*to koinē sympheron*) from "the common benefit" (*to koinon sympheron*) and, second, to keep in mind that the word used by Aristotle for "benefit" (*sympheron*) also means "the bringing together." A benefit in common means either a benefit attained by common efforts (*koinē* used adverbially) or a benefit to what is common (if "what" is a feminine singular noun, as is, for example, *archē*, the first principle or ruler). The common benefit, however, is a benefit to the community; *koinon*, in fact, also means the public and the common as opposed to the rare. Then the first, "the benefit in common," is a benefit attained by all, but not necessarily one by which each shares in the same benefit. The second, "the common benefit," is a benefit that is restricted to what can be distributed to all as a community. The reference at this point in the argument to regimes that are for the benefit in common, or for the bringing together into the common thing, is, we suggest, a reference to regimes that make a whole and a one by the common though perhaps dissimilar efforts of dissimilar parts, rather than to regimes that make a whole by benefiting the public or by bringing themselves into a community. It is the kind of benefit or bringing together that an uncommon man or a philosopher who seeks to know how the parts of the whole are one is likely to have in mind. It is not the kind that a democrat or a man thinking of all the parts of the whole would have in mind. The regimes that *are* by being strong are parts that make laws for their own benefit while claiming to rule for the whole or regimes that have physical strength, but the regimes that are for the benefit in common are not necessarily strong and, therefore, perhaps never make laws for any actual city or have physical being. The some who speak of regimes in this way are men who talk as if the kind of political rule that would be beneficial required no strength, and as if the kind of being that can be common by being the first principle had nothing to do with bodies, which are ruled by strength. The same are men of perhaps unreasonably high political standards and impolitic philosophers.

Restating the inquiry as he does permits Aristotle to remind the philosopher that being with strength is being nonetheless. Politics and the democracy of the city must be taken seriously by him at least to the extent that they are strong, whether or not they are for his benefit. But the political man with whom Aristotle speaks had seemed to think that regimes *are* essentially by being strong, by having the force of law. Justice at first seems to be nothing so much as keeping one's contracts, and legality seems to be obedience to cities that do not appear to serve the benefit in common; this is the usual political situation. A change of regime, however, means that the power of law no longer obtains, and the political man is presented with an opportunity to pass judgment on the law and to choose whether or not to continue to obey it. The necessity of choosing requires some standard for choice, and the standard that is first proposed is the benefit in common. From this perspective, a man and a citizen could reasonably and justly distinguish between regimes that are merely strong and regimes that might be strong *and* beneficial. Whether from the point of view of achieving the end of an actual city, and the manner of being required by that end, one would wish for an opportunity to dissolve the connection between the strong and the beneficial is a question that Aristotle does not now address. That connection is the just by law. It would seem, however, that this connection is always dissolved in the philosopher's city of intelligibles, and that it can be approximated at any time in the private speeches and inquiries about the just by critical citizens and philosophers.

The argument that there are regimes that are for the benefit in common but are not strong, and that by reference to them one justifies breaking contracts and doing other things, is said to be akin to, or "of the household of," another difficulty. Throughout the *Politics*, the term "household," whose secondary meaning is "akin to" or "belonging to," seems to mean man's soul. The city to which these regimes pertain is perhaps understood by reference to man's soul, and the city of the strong regimes understood by reference to man's body. In human being both kinds of being are found, even if specifically human being is the intellect. One can therefore consider whether to say that the city is the same, not the same, or other, for one can compare the soul both to the body and to another soul. The difficulty with regard to soul and body is not simply the same as the difficulty with regard to intelligible wholes and actual cities, however, because while a body *is* in having physical being a city is by virtue of its laws and customs; it has no physical being of its own. The laws, the city's formalities or forms, are its being, and this is a kind of being that is neither simply intelligible nor bodily. Hence, the comparison of city to human being is as imprecise as is the comparison of law to intellect.

The search begins literally superficially, because it begins with a search of the place and the men—that is, of physical location. The superficial search is nonetheless a real search, for Aristotle speaks of men making their homes in places that are "other" to one another. Each place, therefore, *is* because what is "other" *is*; Aristotle does not deny that body is being. But he also speaks of a search that is now tamer because human beings have been "unharnessed" from place and make their homes in a city "spoken about." Aristotle consistently compares the city and the spiritedness of political men to a horse and its horsiness.[21] The search is tamer here because it takes place not amid the clamor of the *agora* but in a city created in speech. The search is tamer also because the men spoken of do not exhibit the characteristics of horsy bodies, for they can be separated not only from this or that place but from place or body altogether. In other words, Aristotle attempts to speak of a kind of being that is what disembodied reason might be like: a soul devoid of human passions. Such a soul would also be devoid of what might be necessary to explain the effect of the soul's being found in particular bodies. This soul is, of course, not human soul as we know it; and in being separate from body, it is not human being as we observe it.

The city composed of human beings whose being is disembodied can presumably be a whole and a one, and therefore have a regime that is for the benefit in common. The city composed of rational souls in bodies, of human beings who have settled or "made their homes down," is "believed" to be a one. This city is only *believed* to be a one; it either is not or cannot be known to be a one simply. The city of men who speak—in contrast to the city spoken about, whose whole being is speech—cannot be a one because the beings who speak have distinct bodies. Physical continuity cannot make one whole of the parts, as the Peloponnesus could not be made one by a wall surrounding it.[22] The name "Peloponnesus" means "Dark-Toil," and it refers, we suggest, to the philosopher's toil, which is never made publicly respectable in actual cities.[23] Shared place cannot be the cause of unity; a community of philosophers would not be a one. Nor, however, is one nation—for example, Babylon—a city more like a nation than a city, a one. If we correctly understand the Peloponnesus to be several nations and Babylon one, then Babylon may be one philosopher. Babylon, it seems, should not be spoken of as a one, because someone will surely assert that three days after its capture a part of the city did not *sense* the capture.[24] The philosopher's being itself presumably combines several kinds of being, one kind of which either does not sense or perceives in a different way. Not only is it the case that many bodies cannot be not be made one body, but a soul and a body cannot be spoken of as one. A consideration of whether philosophic souls can somehow be brought together—"whether one or more nation is beneficial (brought together)"—is postponed, because the relationship of soul to body must first be defined.

Furthermore, whatever one might conclude about the possible unity of souls, each distinguishable unit of matter, each body, seems to be. Yet the city has no matter different from the many bodies composing it. The city with bodies in it can therefore only be believed to be a one. If the city can *be* and the city's justice can *be* only because of its laws and customary beliefs, then one must protect the forms that give it being. Therefore, what must be asserted or said in public about being and the cause of sameness and other-ness is made more problematic, because one may not be able to assert as much as one could say, even if what to say should be clear. Or, for the same reason, perhaps one must assert more than one could reasonably say with confidence about the kinds of being and their unity.

If one must speak of matter as being in the case of natural beings, and of intellect as being in the case of human beings because it is true to speak this way, then the political consequences of one's assertions, as distinct from speeches, must be considered. Aristotle poses two alternatives with respect to assertions about natural wholes: Either one asserts that the city remains the same if its race or genus of settlers is the same, "exactly as we are in the habit of saying that a river or stream remains the same even as its matter is corrupted and born," or one asserts that the human beings are the same but the city is other. Of course, not all of us are "in the habit" of speaking about rivers in this way. Heraclitus said that one can never step into the same river twice because the river is its particles of matter, and these, always being corrupted and born, are not the same particles but different ones. To say that a river remains the same is to ignore the problem that being seems to consist only of instances of being, and that each particle of water is a one and a being. Maintaining the identity and continuity of the river, as com-mon sense might lead a man to perceive a flow of water within unchanging boundaries, requires the argument that particular things have being only insofar as they partake in a genus. The cause of a particle of water's being is the class of wet, colorless, odorless, tasteless matter called "water." The class *is* more than any of its members, and the class remains the same. That all particles of water are meant to be members of a genus is, of course, due to man's classifying them as a genus—that is, his positing of abstract ideas. Thus, the common sense that says that one can step in the same river twice requires the support of a theoretical argument, insofar as it is opposed by Heraclitus's theoretical argument.

If one asserts that being is in the genus, the difficulty with respect to political beings is whether to assert that the being pertains to the settlers-down or to the human beings composing the city. Genus, as applied to cities, means the race—the stock from which Athenians or Persians come, for example. But man may partake of two genera, matter and intellect, corresponding to the settlers and the human beings. To assert that humans *are* only in being parts of the city, city being understood as genus of settlers, is to subordinate individual men to their ancestral laws and customs. But individual men, who manifest rational soul or human being, may differ in more important respects from each other than do particles of water, which have body only. Yet to assert that humans are the same but the city other, that the genus pertains to human being and is the same regardless of the matter, is to deny that the body and the political and cultural have any connection to man's humanity. It is to assert that human beings do not have to "settle down." The second assertion, in denying a reason for the city, virtually washes the city away. If in the first case man's unique substance is engulfed in the tide, in the second his dependence, for good or ill, is lost sight of. The city in which human beings settle down needs to combine both ancestral law and reason, body and soul—each as a being and all as a whole. Hence the difficulty in making either or both assertions.

The comparison of man's city to a natural being like a river does not seem helpful. Whether being is understood as body or as intellect, neither kind of being allows us to explain how the city is a whole of parts that are men. And neither allows us to explain why the questions raised by political men are significant—that is, which parts of the Athenians, democrats or oligarchs, should rule. The city needs to be understood neither as a whole by virtue of a genus in which its parts partake nor as only its parts and not, therefore, as the cause of their being a whole. Rather, the city needs to be understood as a whole whose parts have no being as what they are without their being parts, and as a whole that is as it is because its parts are what they are. For example, one would not speak of oneself as an Athenian or an Athenian democrat unless there were some community identifiable as Athens, a whole distinct from oneself or one's family and from all of humanity. But neither could one speak of Athens or an Athenian democracy unless there were human beings who consciously constituted themselves as Athenians or Athenian democrats. The difference between thinking of oneself as an Athenian and as an Athenian democrat would seem to be that one does not choose to be Athenian; but one might perhaps choose to be an oligarch rather than a democrat. In either case, the city is its citizens, but a man's being a citizen is not anything that arises naturally from either his physical being or his intellect. The city is not a natural compound, but an artificial one like a chorus.

Aristotle therefore offers what "we assert": If the city is some community, it is a community of citizens in a regime, and becoming other in form and different in regime, it necessarily seems to be not the same, exactly as we assert that a chorus is "other" when comic and when tragic. The uses of regime thus far (Book III, 1275a39–40, 1274b38) have led us to understand it first as the visible manifestation of the form (*eidos*) of a group of things and second, as the ordering of intelligibles ("those who make their homes") into a whole. These two meanings now seem to be combined. The regime becomes an ordering of visible things. The assertion that a chorus is other when it is comic or tragic means that each chorus has being, but its being is determined chiefly by its form; not by the genus, which is chorus. Comic and tragic choruses differ not only in what would be their *eidē* because they serve different ends—that is, comic or tragic—but also visibly in form. Although the parts dance and sing in each chorus, the arrangement of chorus members in lines and files in comic and tragic choruses differed according to Greek conventions. The audience could tell whether the play was a comedy or a tragedy without even bothering to listen to it; the visible order was a sufficient indication. This assertion about choruses represents Aristotle's explicit modification of the Platonic teaching: the forms are in matter, and presumably one knows a form when one sees it.[25] Citizens have bodies, but they are understood as citizens not by virtue of having body, but by being parts of a whole that has distinct form. Not only the kind of being, the *eidos*, but the order of the parts, the regime, makes the whole what it is. A tragic chorus *is* a tragic chorus, not just a kind of chorus, and democratic Athens is not just one form Athens can assume; the democratic order *is* as much as Athens *is*. One needs to know how Athenians have constituted their political order, as well as that they are Athenians, in order to determine whether Athens is or is not the same city. For Athens to be a different city its *eidos* must be other— Persia instead of Athens—and its regime must differ—monarchy instead of democracy. The way in which a part of humanity expresses its humanity by ordering itself or by maintaining an order is what gives a city its identity. This is how one makes a politically responsible assertion about cities whose parts are both a race of settlers and human beings. The question not answered in Aristotle's statement is whether the parts ordered need be identical to one another, but perhaps the way in which things are ordered depends on what things are ordered. This of course is the basis of the disagreement between democrats, who must argue that the parts are the same, and oligarchs, who argue that they differ. The disagreement between democrats and oligarchs is therefore not settled, but what is established is that it is reasonable for Athenian democrats and Athenian oligarchs to agree to disagree.

Our interpretation must be modified, however. Whereas a comic and a tragic chorus are said to be "other," cities are said to be "not the same." That a city can assume more than one form and still *be* is not clear. In the second examination Aristotle speaks throughout only of "serious" citizens, as if the city were a tragedy. But while in the first definition of the citizen the democratic citizen found it ridiculous to deny that his most sovereign magistrates were *archai*, properly so called, it seemed that the philosopher there spoke of the first principle or principles of being, and that the first principle of being simply is an Athenian magistrate is far from obvious. Antisthenes later finds it ridiculous to legislate for men of outstanding virtue—that is, philosophers. In other words, different men find different things ridiculous. If the city is being, and being is serious, then citizens and philosophers continue to understand being differently. If this is so, perhaps the more reasonable disagreement is still the one between citizens and philosophers, not between democrats and oligarchs. What Aristotle's teaching about forms accomplishes, however, is to allow one to speak of both kinds of being, both cities, in the same way.

A chorus is said to be similar to all other communities and compounds, the example of which is a harmony of sounds. A harmony is sensed only by being heard, as are speeches, and perhaps it is fully understood to be other only by understanding the differing mathematical proportions according to which the sounds are put together. The harmony we hear leads us to consider its possible correspondence to an intelligible mathematical nature of the whole, should there be one. That the city might be a compound more like a harmony than like a chorus is spoken by Aristotle but not asserted. In fact, he says that it is apparent that what must be spoken is that the sameness of the city is known by looking at its regime, its visible order. Presumably, we can understand both what we hear and what we see in the same way.

The examples of harmonies used by Aristotle are Dorian and Phrygian. These are used by Plato to represent, respectively, the states of soul of warlike men and philosophers.[26] By Aristotle they are used to represent oligarchs, who are precise and masterful, and democrats, who are open and soft.[27] Ultimately they are *thymos* and *erōs*, parts of the soul. The forms of human being are other, as are the orders in men's souls. That the being of a city can be known by looking at its regime is an analogue of the teaching that one knows a soul by knowing which part predominates, and this one knows best by listening to its speeches, for one cannot see a soul. Any other order there might be can be understood in the same way. Reflection upon the order of visible things may lead one to consider whether that order is truly an order—that is, intelligible as an order—and what the cause of its being an order is. In the case of a city, a chorus, or a harmony, the form seems to represent an order, and the being of that particular city, chorus, or harmony might be said to be its form or order.

Asserting that the city is like a river is to speak of it as if it were simply natural. This is not unlike the citizen's usual understanding of his city and of his regime: it simply is. But sometimes citizens dispute about the regime as if it were changeable by human intention. In attempting to speak of the city as a natural being, one cannot speak of both body and rational soul as a whole. One cannot even speak of the city as a whole, because each body is already one and a being, and not obviously a potential part of a whole. Furthermore, one cannot fully integrate man's specifically human being into his city; the city seems unconnected to human intention. Saying that the city is like a harmony is to speak as if the city had no bodies and consisted not of ones and beings, but of potential parts of an intelligible order. This is not unlike the philosopher's understanding: The city is a city in speech whose being is in an ordering of sounds heard by a man, or perhaps in an underlying order that makes possible a sharing of thought through speech. The harmony is itself made by a musician, though there may be a natural order underlying harmonics that makes a harmony identifiable as such by maker and hearer. In attempting to speak of the city as intelligible being, however, one still cannot speak of both body and intellect as a whole. But Aristotle makes no *assertions* about the harmony; rather, he *asserts* that the city is like a chorus. The chorus is both seen and heard, and the order of its parts reveals some poet's intention to the viewer informed by the conventions. The chorus combines two kinds of being, although its own being is its form. Through the form the two kinds of being, properly so called, might be known. In speaking and making assertions about the chorus, whose being is in its visible form, Aristotle seems to rest knowledge of being on what might be said to be the basis of a universal common sense: sight. Although how one sees may be informed by speech, and what we are in the habit of saying about what we see may depend on a theoretical defense, political judgments are made to seem to rest on a kind of knowledge that transcends the citizen's horizons but does not yet require any peculiar faculty. Knowledge gained by sight is accessible to man as man.

Aristotle's intention seems to be, first, to speak of the kinds of being in the same way, if not to make them one. The city is like a river, a chorus, a harmony. Natural (physical) wholes, man's artificial wholes, and intelligible (spoken) wholes are all known as the wholes they are by knowing the form they assume when their parts are ordered. Aristotle's intention seems to be, second, to speak of being in such a way that political knowledge can be asserted to rest on the discrimination of the man with the common or universal sense and, therefore, "common sense." Ultimately, judging by seeing will be shown to be insufficient, but the purpose of Aristotle's present argument, we suggest, is to free political judgments from any apparent dependence on theoretical natural science, like that of Heraclitus, or on mathematical metaphysics, like that of Pythagoras. The city's being is not its physical being, but neither does it seem to be human being simply. The city is its forms, its laws; and its justice presupposes these forms. Aristotle's teaching about forms respects this requirement. But if the forms differ according to the purpose they serve, and if there is more than one end the city might serve, then one can look at the forms in terms of the maker's intention. In any case, if the city is like a chorus, its regimes cannot be distinguished into those that are by being strong and those that are by being for the sake of the benefit in common—unless one can explain how bodies are governed without strength. Therefore, those who wish to dissolve their contracts, alleging that such a distinction can be made, have not yet made an argument that would counter Aristotle's assertion on behalf of common sense. To what form will the philosopher or the political man appeal to make assertions about what is more just?

In asserting that the city is like a chorus, Aristotle seems to have reverted to Gorgias's position that the city is an artifact. The city, however, is now made, according to Aristotle's dispensation, by a poet or maker who may or may not have the musical art and the science of harmonies. If the artisan's making is not limited by a theoretical science, it is limited by dramatic conventions; and whether he even has the option of making the city either a comic or a tragic chorus has been left unclear. Man's making is thus circumscribed. Furthermore, what is made is not many useful artifacts, but some whole. The chorus members are aware of their being parts of a whole, and of a still larger whole, the play, which has been created according to someone's intention. For whose benefit the chorus exists is unclear, because its work is to be something beautiful to behold. If the city is the chorus, who besides the poet is in the audience to behold it?

The difficulty we have just raised indicates that neither man's arts nor his capacities for perception are simply within the whole. The city is like a river, a chorus, a harmony. Water *is* without man, but it is known as a river by man, and similarly perhaps the sounds of a harmony. Yet the chorus, whose being is its form, has no being as a whole rather than as the men composing it, without being made a chorus by a poet. If human bodies are included within the whole, man's arts, especially the ones that make parts into wholes, are not included. Perhaps ultimately there cannot be a whole without reference to some external ruling part or first principle that resembles man's capacity for making wholes. Is the form made by this "former" the one to which the man choosing to break his contract must appeal?

Now some political men might be made to perceive that the search for this first cause is necessary, if they did not see that earlier. The reasonable man who takes politics seriously, who deliberates about whether or not to keep a contract, must understand politics as rational and serving some intended purpose. He must choose and give arguments for his choice. He cannot understand the city as a river, or as a race of men, as did the democrat who made citizen birth the chief criterion for citizenship. Rather, he sees a chorus, a whole made with intention and requiring the efforts of its members to make it beautiful or noble. From his point of view, that of the political man who understands himself as a free man, it is necessary to find a first principle by which at least the political order can be defended as intelligible; and his necessity is for the sake of justice and political freedom.

Aristotle next examines the question of whether the virtue of the serious citizen and the good man are the same or not the same. At the beginning of Book III, he gave three reasons for examining the city in its relation to the city, the second of which was that we see the statesman and legislator being wholly busy with the city. In order to do their work, the statesman and legislator would have to see the city as a chorus or a harmony in precisely the way a citizen serious about justice needs to see it and only a man can see it. In the second examination Aristotle speaks only of the statesman, and of as much of his business as we see; he is silent about the legislator and his business, the making of the speeches of which law consists. His silence about the legislator corresponds to his silence about the poet who makes the chorus.

We wonder whether Aristotle fails to describe the legislator's speech because he himself gives it, by founding in speech a city that makes possible the city's justice and moral virtue. Justice as law-abidingness and justice as an expression of true being seem to become one in the virtue of the good man who rules as a statesman, but Aristotle is the first man to state the law of moral virtue. When one speaks of being and its cause as previous philosophers did, and of citizenship as citizens do, one cannot also speak of a city which is a whole whose parts are men. But Aristotle attempts now to speak of a whole city of men—that is, of political being. In order to speak of political being, or human being "settled down," Aristotle does not at first speak either of the cause of there being a whole, or of what a part is; he begins with how the parts of being are ordered in regimes and forms. The being spoken about is the very ordering of things into a whole. Being, therefore, is justice, if justice means some order among parts. But to know the cause of being, to know that being is intended, and to understand man's arts and sciences, which have been left outside of the whole, it is well for us to keep in mind that the legislator is not simply a part of the city he makes.

Aristotle continues to speak to and about a man who makes sensible distinctions on the basis of what he sees. In the next section, while he proceeds to educate this man, Aristotle makes possible for him an understanding of serious citizenship and human goodness commensurate with his capacities. His assertions, as distinguished from his reasonable speeches, are directed not toward serious students of natural philosophy, but to men serious about themselves as men and citizens—political men and politic philosophers—because the wholeness of man's city lies in their being. The philosopher's question is whether the whole of being also lies in their being.

4. To Be and to Be (1276b16–1277b32)

The philosopher takes seriously the quest for being and the cause of all things; the citizen takes justice seriously. At first it seemed that the citizen was the part of the whole that made the nature of the whole manifest. If not every citizen of nature were the same, perhaps one could take one part, man, seriously, for man is unique among beings in combining physical and intelligent being in one being. Furthermore, man seems naturally to be a part of a whole, for he is born a citizen. But this first formulation now seems inadequate: The whole has been said to be the order of its parts, its form, rather than the parts themselves. And not all of man's being, in particular his intentional making, that is, his arts, and his perceptions, his sciences, is within the whole of citizenship. The philosopher's study of nature becomes the study of the order in nature, not only the study of each natural being. But even this is a study of the whole of being only if from the study of that order one learns about something resembling man's arts and sciences, as if from the order of the whole of nature one could make inferences about its maker's intention and intelligence. If the whole of nature were not an analogue of man's being, then by knowing all of nature, the parts and their order, one would not thereby know all of being. Nor would man's humanity have anything to do with nature. If, however, the whole of nature were an analogue of man's being, then by knowing the parts of human being and their order, one would know the natural order. The science of man, political science, would be the master science; the science of man's best order, that is, the science of man's virtue or excellence, would be tantamount to a theodicy.[28]

Similarly, if man's excellences do not belong to politics proper, then in knowing man's perfection one does not know the city and its just order. Nor does man's citizenship in a polity have anything to do with his humanity. The man who nonetheless takes the political seriously can have no nonpartisan reservation against any law. But if there is some analogue of man's excellence in his polity, then by knowing man's being, how the parts of his being are ordered, one knows the just order of things. The law that articulates man's virtue is the just law against which all other laws can be judged. If the cause of man's being is not natural or political, man's being is nonetheless "according to nature" and in accordance with justice, and the good man can be like a serious citizen. Both philosophy and obedience to just laws are reasonable.

The second examination has two sections, in which two questions are posed. The first is whether the virtues of the good man and the serious citizen are the same or not the same; its conclusion is that their virtues are both the same and other. The second is a closer consideration of who might be counted as a citizen; its conclusion is that that according to which a man is good and a citizen serious is the same only in the person of the statesman, and that in certain circumstances. The alternative theme for the second examination, we have suggested, was the being busy of the statesman and legislator. Aristotle speaks only of the statesman, however. The statesman is a man who rules the city as its chief citizen and who, in having occasionally to impose a rule on the city in situations where the law provides no absolute guidance, must rely on his common sense, or prudence; he must resort to some principle external to the law. This of course is the situation of any citizen who wants to appraise the justice of his city's laws, for he must judge them according to some standard. If the statesman is a serious citizen who measures the city's laws, its form, against some more authoritative law or form, where does he find this law? Aristotle's apparent answer is that he finds it in himself, in his own goodness or moral virtue. But political men know their virtue not as a law that they have been habituated to obey, but as a choice in each instance, as an assertion of their freedom. That the universal principles of moral virtue might be codified in a law—for example, in the Decalogue or in Hobbes's laws of nature—is known, rather, by political scientists or legislators. In showing how moral virtue is a law, and in teaching political men that moral virtue is the law against which the laws of actual cities must be measured, Aristotle himself does the work of a legislator.

But to defend his law as *the* form of law, it would seem that Aristotle must argue that this law articulates human being in completion. Man must have a nature that can be the object of some science, and the legislator must have recourse to political science, the science of the nature of political beings. But the men the political scientist examines already live under the law of some city, and it has formed their natures. Even if one wishes to argue that man is naturally a political being, that he is naturally suited for politics and not accidentally born in the city, one must still speak of man's nature. To know the nature of a thing, must not the political scientist look to a simply natural being? His ability to do so would presuppose that the natural, nonhuman beings he can examine are in fact knowable in the same way men are, even if their natures are not the same as men's. Compound beings, men, cities, and natural wholes, we have learned, are known by knowing the order of their parts. It seems that to defend the moral virtue of the good man as the form of law, someone must know what the natural order is, or how the whole composed of natural beings is ruled. This is the work of the natural philosopher.

Perhaps, ultimately, one cannot understand man and man's cities in the way one understands natural beings and natural wholes. Perhaps, ultimately, one can only understand natural beings and natural wholes by looking at them in the light of what one can know about political beings and political wholes. (This is a boast political scientists of late have forgotten how to make for the study of comparative government.) The philosopher would have to take politics very seriously indeed. But insofar as political scientists and philosophers are also born citizens under some law, they must somehow learn to distinguish what is peculiar to their cities from what universally belongs to the city. One begins to do this by disputing with a citizen who holds an opinion different from one's own or, even better, by disputing with a citizen of another city, a stranger who does not even share one's Athenianism. Hence the importance of the dispute between the democrat and the oligarch and the interruption by a stranger like Gorgias. Political science, it seems, necessarily begins with comparative government while presupposing the possibility of a science of comparative government. But if political science is a science, then it would seem to have to be like other sciences, which are all of natural beings. Therefore, contrary to what we have just said, it appears that the political scientist must at the same time become a natural philosopher in order to learn what a science is and how political science is possible. He must question his own presuppositions, or someone else surely will.

How these problems emerge and are resolved in Aristotle's text we shall see as we proceed. But we begin with a consideration of Aristotle's more immediate concern: How and why can moral virtue, or goodness, be said to be the form of law, the standard for the city's justice?

Aristotle's political intention in the argument that follows is, first, to attach the citizen to his regime and its laws, while at the same time showing him the kind of man he should respect at least as much as his laws. Serious citizens are necessary in any regime, and the virtue of a citizen pertains to his regime; one can and must be a serious citizen even if one does not have the virtue of the good man. But the good man should rule, and the citizen should know his place. In the best case the citizen does know how to rule, but in any case he must know how to be ruled. The second intention is to raise the status of the man capable of goodness and therefore of ruling, while at the same time teaching him how to be good and especially how to be moderate. The good man has a virtue that is one and complete, whatever his work as a citizen is. He may have a special education, although this appears to be an education in public service. His virtue is exercised essentially in ruling, but he, too, must know how to be ruled. Only if he is prudent as well as just, moderate, and courageous does he properly rule. Prudence, however, is an intellectual and not a moral virtue, and it is unclear to us that any amount of moral virtue is a sufficient substitute for prudence, or that it issues in prudence if the requisite intellect is lacking.[29] Furthermore, the good man has goodness and prudence, but the statesman is *necessarily* prudent; his prudence is a science, and he does not need goodness. If it is unclear that moral virtue brings prudence in its train, it is also unclear to us that moral virtue is simply necessary. Why, then, is the good man superior to the serious citizen? We must examine carefully the argument with political men in order to grasp what they learn about moral virtue and with political scientists in order to ascertain why they are taught about moral virtue. And with philosophers, we must consider what there is to be learned about being from the being of serious citizens and good men.

To understand the serious citizen and the good man we begin with an attempt to grasp the outline, or visible form, of a citizen. A citizen, a form, is asserted to be one in a community, and the citizen is compared to a sailor. Does Aristotle use this comparison because men living in a democracy are most likely to associate public service with serving in the navy? In being like sailors, citizens are both dissimilar and similar. Their capacities differ; one is suited to being a rower, another a pilot, another a lookout man; but in actualizing his particular capacity, each nonetheless does his common work, which is saving the voyage or the regime. Citizens, the citizen now learns, are defined by their work, not their birth; and their work is saving the particular regime in which they share, not their native city however governed.

Devotion to the good of the whole is as necessary as it is necessary that a ship's crew do its work to keep the ship afloat. But the ways in which citizens show this devotion will differ, because men have different capacities. Not everyone is capable of being a pilot, and presumably those who are capable should not be relegated to the ranks of rowers. Rowers are no less necessary, however. Both democrats and oligarchs learn that the regime, as does a ship, sails more smoothly because of the dissimilarities manifest in it. But oligarchs also learn that even then, the greatest differences among men will not become manifest, for the virtue of each is said to belong to a "private argument." Furthermore, if serving the ship is necessary for every citizen, a ship is in motion to reach some destination, and the city is only a vehicle. As no sailor ultimately desires a safe voyage for the sake of the ship or for his own voyage, neither is a citizen who makes his end saving the voyage at the same time concerned about his end as a man. Yet from all other points of view but necessity, that private end would be more important.

If political partisans, as serious citizens, do think of the city as a particular regime worth saving, their partisan seriousness will nonetheless be diminished, first, by the requirements of seaworthiness. Serious citizenship must mean seriousness about the common good, and what is beneficial to the city might be a moderation or mixture of partisan demands, unacceptable to serious partisans as partisans. Thus serious citizenship as devotion to a regime is diminished, on the one hand, by a consideration of the good for which the regime is intended. Consequently, an oligarch who might well be a serious pilot in an oligarchy would row in a democracy were he forced to do so, but he might then be less willing to take sailing seriously. Serious citizenship is diminished, on the other hand, by a concern for one's own good. If a citizen's virtue is dependent on the regime, a man can be good in any regime if his excellence belongs to a "private argument." What must be ensured is that he is not therefore a bad or disloyal citizen rather than an unserious one. Political moderation is necessary if concern for a man's good is to take precedence over his serious citizenship; political expectations must be moderated. A man must have a goodness that is neither simply identical nor incompatible with law-abidingness.

Aristotle's political argument reflects or points to the following reasoning. The visible whole consists not of similar parts, but of parts dissimilar in capacity. The excellence of a citizen, a part, is doing well its work, the work of the class of things to which it belongs. Each in a class desires to do the work of its form (*eidos*), or that which it potentially is. Citizens are the intelligible forms, the parts that do their work, and the forms themselves constitute a community. Their being, not only their capacity, is said to be dissimilar. Each serious citizen in a class is at work striving to be its form, to actualize its capacity; and to the extent that it does so, it has its own virtue.[30] The excellent citizen has no desire for himself because he is what he is meant to be; he strives to maintain the whole as a whole. The forms, although dissimilar, constitute their own regime as an order and as a fuller kind of being in actuality, and thus are presumably the best regime. But if there are several forms of regimes, with regime understood as a class of beings, then the virtue of a serious citizen cannot be one because the being and therefore the virtue of each form still differs. If there are several forms, and if all things subordinate to forms and at work becoming virtuous are to be called serious citizens, then for both these reasons no serious citizen can be as the whole of being, having one and complete virtue. The citizen as citizen is no longer the first principle or the being that makes all things a whole, and it appears that one cannot understand the whole by understanding what one citizen is. If all things are spoken of as partaking in the forms that constitute their being, one cannot continue to speak of being as either simply body or intellect, or as both in one. Yet the virtue according to which a man is good is both one and complete, Aristotle asserts. Man's specific excellences, his arts and his sciences, are not simply within the whole. It seems that man is not at work striving to be his form as the other citizens are; his virtue is not one member of the community of forms, but is itself a whole. Relaxing the criterion for citizenship, or being, is accompanied by an assertion of stiffened requirements for being a man. But does Aristotle mean to say that man's excellence is superfluous to the whole, and that the city and the visible whole are still wholes without man? Or is man's specific excellence necessary to the whole?

Aristotle continues by considering the problem specifically with respect to the best regime, the community of forms. In the best regime, the work of each citizen is to make or do well according to his work (or according to the same work), which is from virtue. The intelligible forms are both similar to each other in being intelligible forms, and dissimilar in being what each is. These forms are in matter, for it is said (1277al-3) that in order for the city, the whole, to be best, it is necessary that serious citizens *be* from the beginning. That is, as we learned in the preceding section, the forms are in visible matter, and formed matter must be said to be eternally. For the sake of politics, the first cause is not to be understood as the efficient cause. The whole's goodness consists simply in each thing's being in its proper place at its work. From this perspective, the whole is complete without man. Yet the argument rests on a contingency: The capacity of the good man is superfluous if there is no necessity that all citizens in the serious city be good. The serious city is the city in which capacities are being actualized, the one in which imperfect man dwells. The capacity that will not then be actualized is man's capacity for goodness, or moral virtue, if man can be said to have such a capacity. But if moral virtue is not necessary for the rest of nature, or for a city ruled by perfect artisans, goodness may be necessary to man as we know him. The defense of goodness, therefore, requires an explanation of a whole that is good. Nature is complete in itself without being one and good, but justice and virtue may depend on a demonstration of the unity and goodness of the whole.

Aristotle therefore restates what he has referred to as a grave difficulty in still a third way. The city is composed of dissimilars, exactly as a creature is from soul and body, a soul from reason and desire, a household from man and woman, and property from master and slave. The city is put together in this way from other dissimilar forms, and the virtues of its citizens are not one, exactly as among dancers those of the lead dancer and his assistant are not. The city is only an animal, less than a man, or it is a soul without intellect and without spiritedness and, therefore, less than a wise or a free man. The household has no offspring, and property is possessed but not said to be used. The chorus has neither poet nor audience. The whole, in lacking man's perfection, lacks a reason for being. The whole is a whole without man, however. Only to a being who needs to know how to use things does this whole seem incomplete, for nothing in it answers to man's necessities.

There is also a theoretical difficulty in understanding the whole in this way. In the comparison to the chorus, the "other dissimilar forms" from which the city is put together are like lead dancer and assistant lead dancer. These forms differ from each other perhaps in nothing more than in being more or less visible, or perhaps in being more or less sure of the steps in the dance. They are dissimilar in a way that the other parts of the city are not, because they are of the same kind. But this is the same ambiguity we found in the discussion of the citizens of the best regime: each does or makes well according to its own or to the same work, which is from virtue. The forms must then be both opposed to one another, as are soul and body, reason and desire, man and woman, despot and slave, and comparable to one another, as are lead dancer and assistant in a chorus. The city is composed of citizens whose work is both dissimilar and similar. Thus, how the forms might be understood as a whole is a grave difficulty. Perhaps in understanding how a good man's virtue can be asserted to be one and complete, we can understand how a whole is one and complete.

The virtue according to which man, not the citizen, is good seems to transcend the capacity of any one part of the whole itself. Yet man, insofar as he does not possess this virtue in completion, is himself a citizen, a part of a whole like a household, for example. If the good man's virtue brings the whole, one and complete, into being by the addition of the capacities absent from it, can this virtue somehow be understood as offspring as well as a user of the whole? Does man's work as a citizen contribute to his virtue as a man? Aristotle asks whether the virtue of some serious citizen and some serious man will be the same. Perhaps man's proper work for the whole as a citizen, that is, as a part of nature or of the city of his birth, is the same as the work he does for himself. Then the good man's completion of the whole is in accordance with some intended place for man within the whole. Correspondingly, the political argument based upon this reasoning would be that a man who takes his own goodness more seriously than his citizenship is nevertheless a citizen, and can be the best citizen.

In order to approach the question of whether the virtue of some serious citizen and the serious man might be the same, Aristotle immediately begins to speak of rulers. Two kinds of ruler are specified: the serious ruler, who is asserted to be both good and prudent, and the statesman, who is necessarily prudent. The serious ruler seems to be substituted for the serious citizen as the part of the whole that might complete the whole by beginning or ruling it or being its first principle. The statesman is substituted for the serious man, the man who strives for human being in completion. Man's work as man, it appears from what is said, is prudence, the wise use of things. Why only the serious ruler is good and the serious man, or statesman, is necessarily prudent becomes clear from what follows.

The relations between the serious ruler and the statesman and between the virtues of the citizen and of man are apparently understood by considering the education of rulers, of which Aristotle proceeds to speak. Some say the education of rulers is different, and a visible example of this is that the sons of kings are educated in horsemanship and in the warrior's art, "polemics." What we see is supported by the assertions of the poets, or of Euripides in particular, who is characterized as saying that the education of the ruler is in learning to do what is necessary for the city.[31] The line in Euripides' play preceding the line quoted by Aristotle makes clear that the rulers' skills include the art of speaking in the assembly, as well as skill in arms on the battlefield. The addition of this line might serve to make more obvious the ambiguity in the word "polemics," but in doing so, Aristotle would have made obvious the incompleteness of the manly political man who has only the military arts. Why he does not want to make this obvious we shall soon learn. But it now appears that in omitting the line, Aristotle implies that Euripides fosters an excessive concern for the manly, or military, arts. Aristotle also omits Euripides' next line, which says that these skills are necessary for those who wish to be great in the city always. The "sophisticated things," or subtleties not strictly necessary to the city, which are neither the military arts nor the art of speaking in the assembly but perhaps inquiries into non-political things and into ways of speaking about them, might be cultivated by those who do not wish to be great in the city. By his omission, Aristotle accuses Euripides of not allowing for this possibility.

What one sees and what one hears from Euripides might lead one to con-clude that if the serious ruler, taking the needs of the city wholly seriously, has learned any art, it is the warlike art, allowing him to become great by acquiring for the city. No wonder the serious ruler needs goodness in addi-tion to prudence. If he is prudent in acquiring, then his prudence without moral virtue, without justice toward his fellow citizens, is a danger to them as well as to his enemies. Unless an education in the subtleties said to be un-necessary to the city is nonetheless necessarily beneficial to the ruled as well as to the ruler, there must be additional education in moral goodness. This Aristotle provides by making it appear at first that even Euripides supports good citizenship. He makes it seem as if Euripides said that if one desired to rule and were skilled in acquiring, he would need a special education which had as its end serving the city's needs. Yet at the same time, Aristotle less obviously criticizes Euripides precisely because he fails to teach this. In truth, Euripides fails to defend a concern for the common benefit not because he takes political acquisitiveness seriously, but because he asserts that the ruler's education is necessary to the city, or that the city does not constitute a whole unless the wise man rules.[32] Euripides makes it obvious, as did Gorgias, that what is necessary is, if not military virtue, wisdom or art without moral virtue. It may be true that the wise man needs no moral virtue in addition to his prudence because the philosopher has no desire to acquire the kinds of things over which men do battle. But perhaps one should not assert this before men who do desire these things, and who are therefore likely to misunderstand why the philosopher's acquisition can be unlimited and why moral virtue is not necessary for everyone. Aristotle speaks hereafter of the good, not the serious ruler: of the man who acts as if he had moral virtue. Whatever the education of the ruler, moral or philosophic, its effect, if not its intention, must be good, and that it is good must be asserted.

As if to counter Euripides' truncated assertion that what the city needs is a ruler educated in military skills but not in subtleties, Aristotle provisionally identifies the virtue of the good ruler and the good man and distinguishes the good man who rules from the citizen who is ruled. If the virtue of the ruler and of the citizen is not same, perhaps this is why Jason said that he was a hungry man whenever not tyrant, as if he did not have the science of being a private man. We suggest that Aristotle here refers not to Jason, tyrant of Pherae, but to Jason the Argonaut, who in Euripides' *Medea* said, when deserting his wife and children for a new kingdom, that he would otherwise be a poor man, without nobility.[33] The change from poverty to hunger (*penēs* to *peinēs*) in Jason's excuse may well be connected to Aristotle's identification throughout the *Politics* of nourishment with wisdom.[34] In his explanation of Jason's excuses, Aristotle substitutes Jason's lack of science for what would seem to be a deficiency of moral virtue. According to Euripides, there seems to be no first principle in nature to guide man's limitless craving for wisdom and to order his quest toward some finite end. Hence, Euripides' Jason knew no science of being a private man. He lacked the moderation that could serve as moral virtue for the same reason that Euripides' teaching about nature fails to provide any foundation for moral virtue.

Aristotle's improvement upon Euripides is to teach about a good for man which has a ground in nature and can be asserted to be the intended end and ruling principle of both nature as a whole and of man's education. The whole is complete when its order is understood as intended for man's goodness, so that in knowing the "what" of man's virtue man knows the first principle of the whole. But the mention of Jason and what follows suggest that the end as good can be taught in either of two ways. Either the political man is provided some new understanding of what is noble in order to moderate the tyrannical tendency of political manliness, but without destroying this manliness, or some science of being a private man must be taught him.

Aristotle apparently does not intend to assert that the good is knowable only by some science, for he addresses political men as well as philosophers and it is political men, uninterested in science, who need the teaching about moral virtue. In order to defend to them moral virtue, and especially moderation, as good, he speaks to them in terms of what is praised. They must be made to see that Jason's deed was not noble, but ignoble. What is praised is the capacity to be ruled as well as to rule, and the virtue of the citizen somehow seems to be the capacity to rule and be ruled nobly. Aristotle wishes to bolster precisely this beneficial opinion which finds moderation praiseworthy. He wishes to assert neither that there is no support in nature for the opinion that moderation is good, nor that what is good can be known only with the completion of philosophy. Both for the sake of the city's justice and for the sake of preserving the respectability of the morally good man, Aristotle obscures the extent to which the science of the private man may not be a science at all, because it corresponds to nothing necessary in nature but is in any case a sufficient substitute for both the ruler's and the ruled citizen's virtue. The citizen who rules and is ruled is praised differently than the good man whose virtue is skilled rule. Such inconsistent praise reflects the citizen's inconsistent admiration of the acquisitive man whom he deems good, and his concern for justice so that the good man not acquire unjustly from him. Aristotle must preserve both the opinion that the good man's virtue is skill in ruling, and the opinion that the citizen has the virtue of being ruled as well as of ruling, while making the opinions consistent.

Aristotle distinguishes between two first principles or rules: skilled despotism and political rule. Citizens are said to have the science, and to partake of both. The despotic rule, we suggest, is exercised over citizens of nature, natural beings and the natural philosophers who seek the science of being. The despotic ruler must know the science not of making, but of using "the necessary things." The necessary things, we suggest, are not only the low things for which gentlemen employ slaves, but all natural things studied by science. Whoever rules according to despotic rule need not know how to make natural beings, because they have just been said to be eternal, though one might wish to know for the sake of theory how they could be made. But if the first principle is what reveals how things are to be used, rather than how to make them, then man, in knowing this, could be a master. What is "other" to the master is slavish. By the other, Aristotle says he means the capacity to assist in serviceable deeds, although being a slave should also mean "partaking," since it is said that the citizen must both know and partake. What the serviceable deeds are is not specified, but several forms of slave, differing as does their work, are distinguished. Thus, for partaking in a first principle is substituted each thing doing its work. Of the forms of slavery, only one example is given: that of handworkers. But the etymology used to prove that these workers, among whom are banaustic artisans, are indeed handworkers is at best dubious.[35] Men may well be at work learning some science, using their brains instead of their hands. Man as a citizen of nature is a master insofar as he has the science of using nature, but he is enslaved insofar as he cannot simply use all of nature, either for lack of the science or because of nature's intractability to his rule.[36] For example, man cannot yet control the motions of the heavenly bodies nor even explain them fully, and closer to home, he cannot even keep his own body from getting hungry occasionally. To the extent that man cannot master nature, he is a slave to nature. Furthermore, nature consists of other beings at work, and their work is necessary in order that all of nature be. In speaking of the demiurges who could not partake in the ancient rule, Aristotle suggests that there is a new rule, which he identifies with the extreme democracy, in which beings who have arts partake. But men at work in the arts are imperfect masters. Nature has two kinds of incomplete citizens: man, with his capacity for arts and

sciences, and bodies. Man himself is also both. Thus, even if his science of
use, prudence, were complete, man would remain a slave to nature in two
ways: he has an as yet unactualized potential for theoretical wisdom about
all necessary things, and he has a body to whose needs he must cater.

Praise of citizens who know how to be ruled as well as to rule is then
universally correct as long as even the wisest men remain enslaved. In order
to convey this truth, Aristotle speaks of forms of slaves, not of participating
in some first principle or substance. But he also wishes to support the argument that the good is the highest for man; to that end all things in nature
and all the sciences may be used. To give this support, it seems necessary to
assert that the man who is good or who knows the good is a free man, not
a slave. Therefore, Aristotle says that the good one, the statesman, and the
good citizen need not learn the slavish works; they need only know how
to use them. The good one, it would seem, has prudence as a completion
of his virtue, the statesman has it as a science, and the good citizen has it
by being part of a good city. Having the science of prudence is, of course,
different from having the moral virtue of goodness. Moreover, prudence is
made to seem an adequate substitute for a knowledge of that which might
make nature a whole. Man's whole, as a part of the whole, is completed by
prudence as political science if theoretical science remains subordinate to
prudence. The science of the statesman is the study of the good—that is,
the science of using the necessary things for man's good. But one could not
yet say that the need for slaves is obviated, or that prudence is higher than
slavery for Aristotle himself.[37] What Aristotle does say is that the knowledge
necessary to man as man is knowledge of the good, and that from the point
of view of man this knowledge is superior to natural science. It is dependent
on natural science only as a master is dependent on his slaves; he uses them
for the work he chooses.

This is why Aristotle proceeds to speak of man as a free man. The first
principle according to which free men are ruled is political rule. This rule,
Aristotle says, must be learned by having been ruled, as a military man
makes his way up through the ranks of the army until he is a general. As in
the first example of the ruler's education, the example is military. When the
man who thinks about military affairs is reminded that discipline is needed
in any army, he can see how it might be noble to speak of being ruled as
well as ruling. But Aristotle means not only what the military man thinks
he means.

The good citizen, who dwells among men similarly free, must have
the science and capacity of being ruled and ruling. The citizen as distinct
from the good citizen need only know the science of the rule of free men

the political community does become a whole in a way that differs from the way in which nonhuman beings become one. When one looks beyond the household, one will admit that for bodies that do not rule themselves, to be slaves to one master is not wrong. On the contrary, this is what makes nature well ruled. But the political man seems to be correct about how political beings should not be ruled.

Oligarchy is now said to be the sovereignty in the regime of those who have substance (*ousia*). The change made is from those who have resources (*euporoi*), which can also mean those who have answers. If the regime is also a soul, the possessions, or substance, of a soul are its opinions. In the third revision, democracy is said to be "in opposition," presumably to oligarchy, when those who do not possess a multitude of substance, but are "at a loss" (*aporoi*), are sovereign. The change is from rule for the benefit of those who are at a loss. Why the original formulation might not be a deviation is perhaps explained by the following consideration. The present passage includes one of the three mentions of philosophy in Book III, and in this passage Aristotle speaks three times of *aporiai*—"difficulties raised," "impasses in argument," "being at a loss in speech." If being at a loss is the mark of a philosopher, then the sovereignty of those who have resources— meaning solutions, as in the first definition of oligarchy—is no deviation. The democrat lacks a multitude of substance as well as solutions; he has no property. Or, the democratic soul has no opinions, not even the opinion that philosophy is the greatest good for man. But, of course, oligarchy as the sovereignty of men with property and unexamined opinions is a deviation. Democracy differs from oligarchy in being the sovereignty of those who lack property and do not know how to go about acquiring it. Democrats have too few opinions instead of too many, and they are completely "unarmed."

When the philosopher generalizes from his soul, he finds that it is a deviation from the right order for human beings to be made one like the rest of nature (tyranny), or for the soul to be surfeited with its opinions (oligarchy), or for it to have no opinion about how to acquire the nourishment it craves (democracy). All the deviations are deviations from the souls that philosophize. It is not clear that the good political man had in his mind this understanding of a right regime, instead of the rule of wealthy, warlike freemen. Nor is it clear to us that the political community can become one, that a political "one" differs from a natural "one," that there is anything besides opinion, and that the alternative to opinion is not skepticism. Aristotle reveals the presuppositions of his science to us, but he has yet to demonstrate their reasonableness.

Aristotle says there is some difficulty even with this division. But there were in fact two divisions; and there are two difficulties, one with each division. If the political man and the philosopher speak of the "whats" of regimes, immediately preceding was a numerical division of regimes. The first objection is that the division does not seem noble. Two possibilities are offered to make the point clear. What if many who have resources should be sovereign in the city, yet it is a democracy whenever the multitude is sovereign? In other words, why is the sovereignty of a multitude called a democracy regardless of the quality of the multitude? Classification by number does not tell us as much as we need to know. Second, what if somehow those at a loss, though few, should be superior or stronger than the wealthy and therefore be sovereign in the regime, and yet assert that the sovereignty of a few is an oligarchy? Again, the criticism is directed to those who speak of multitudes in terms of their quantities, not their qualities. The classification of multitudes by their quantities, as by a mathematician, is not said to be incorrect but only perhaps ignoble. Perhaps noble regimes are not right according to nature, and perhaps political men require them nonetheless.

If the first difficulty is with the assertions of the mathematicians, the second is how to speak aloud, or how to speak in the agora (*prosagoreō*), about the regimes. The political man also distinguishes between few and many, classing himself as one of few. He, too, associates goodness with fewness and incomplete virtue with manyness. He may be correct in assuming that these qualities are usually found in multitudes of their respective sizes. But no more than the mathematician can he speak intelligibly about the exceptions. Whatever our expectations of human multitudes, surely there are some manys that would have all the "answers" that nonhuman beings would need in order to be what they should be. And is it not possible that the behavior of some few who are at a loss, who have no answers but always seek them, is very different from that of most men, who have no answers but do not seek them? In other words, can one distinguish philosophers from lawless democratic citizens? If so, how does one speak of them, and how does one make clear the basis of the distinction? Is there not some way to speak intelligibly about "nonhuman" multitudes, men who live in cities and have opinions, and philosophic souls all at the same time?

This Aristotle attempts to do in his summary of what the argument "looks like it makes clear." Multitudes are properly defined by their "whats," not their numbers. Quantity is accidental; quality, essential. The reason that political men speak so facilely of "few" and "many" is that it is virtually always the case that the wealthy are few and the poor are many; one never finds the hypothetical case of there being many wealthy and few poor. Thus, the political man's understanding is more or less correct, and his mistaking accident for essence does not lead to incorrect political opinions. The mathematician's understanding, that the essence of a multitude is its number, looks incorrect.

Similarly, if the reader mistakes the appearance of the argument for its reality, he will not reach generally unsound political conclusions. He will surmise that democracy and oligarchy differ not in the size of the multitude that rules, but in the first principle according to which the multitude rules. But what an argument "looks like" is also its accidental, not essential, quality, and we must understand what the argument is. If, as we have suggested, *euporia* and *aporia* mean having answers and raising difficulties as well as having *obols* and not having *obols*, then it is correct to say that the men who have answers, wise men, are few indeed. That nonhuman beings have all the resources or answers they need to be what they are, and that only some few men think of themselves as being at a loss for what they need are both more than mere hypothetical possibilities. The argument can look as it does only if Aristotle maintains silence about nonhuman beings and the few human beings who philosophize. Aristotle makes and repeats a statement that the resourceful happen to be few and those at a loss, many everywhere; but in the repetition he does not say "everywhere." For it is reasonable to suppose that somewhere, though not in politics proper, those with resources are many and those at a loss are few. The political *logos* that "looks like" a *logos* is an incomplete *logos*.

It may still be an image of the truth, however. The difference between democracy and oligarchy, Aristotle says, is a difference between poverty and wealth (*ploutos*). Democracy is poverty, not having *obols*, not having answers, not having opinions. But where either many or few rule either for the sake of or by virtue of wealth, this is an oligarchy. To the extent that the philosopher makes wealth, understood as wisdom, his first principle, he is as much an oligarch as any other man. To the extent that knowing the necessity of philosophy constitutes his wisdom, he is one of the few with answers to whom Aristotle refers at the end of this passage.[13] To the extent that he remains partially ignorant, he is one of the all who are said to partake of freedom. The truth in the oligarch's claim to rule by virtue of his wealth is that man has needs of various sorts, for which he must provide by his own efforts. Wealth is therefore the end, or the first principle. The error in the oligarch's claim is that money might not be the only "wealth" a man needs.

Aristotle is less critical of the oligarch than we might expect. But if the oligarch's only opponent in the city is a democrat, then the oligarch might have the best claim to rule. The claim of the poor, when they dispute for a share in rule, is that the first principle of the city is freedom and that all men, including themselves, partake in freedom. Their end may be wealth as much as it is the rich man's, but one does not fare well by arguing that he needs to rule in order to get his hand in the public till. Rather, one emphasizes what he understands to be an attribute of his humanity: his freedom. The difficulty in the democrat's claim is that even if being a free man were the proper title to rule, "partaking" in freedom is hardly being a free man. Indeed, the democrat is not even as free from his bodily necessities as is the wealthy oligarch. The city may therefore deem oligarchs who contribute wealth to the public till to be freer than democrats. Furthermore, it is not clear that being free is more desirable than being wise. The democratic citizen's boast about his freedom is a distorted image of the philosopher's shame of his ignorance. Nevertheless, as we shall see, freedom, not wealth, is the principle according to which men both partake and share in the bringing together (1279a31).

The assertions of the mathematicians must be silenced if those assertions are truly ignoble and man needs to live nobly. But when the political man attempts to speak of the "whats" of the regimes, he does so only more or less adequately. With Aristotle's clarifications, it becomes clear that he associates being with doing good and with having substance, or wealth. Whatever his professions about concern for the common good, the first principle by which he orders his life is the desire for wealth. The inconsistency might be remedied if he could be taught about some wealth that is essentially common or sharable. The oligarch distinguishes himself from the poor without knowing what wealth is. He identifies himself as a man of the few, and to the few he opposes all multitudes, regardless of their size and quality. Therefore, he would not be at home in a democracy. He is a man who needs to learn not only what kind of wealth is worthy of being desired, but also how to live among democrats while maintaining one's distinctiveness. He will be publicly criticized by Aristotle as a lover of lucre, and shown that the city must be democratic. But he will also be taught about noble friendships that are possible for virtuous men and superior to the city's justice.[14] His democratic opponent will be taught that the free man is the wealthy and virtuous man, or the noble man. Aristotle seems to take the side of political men against natural philosophers, and the side of oligarchs against democratic citizens; but in doing so, does he bring to light or obscure the truth about all things?

3. Ignoble Division (1280a7–25)

If neither mathematicians nor political men can say all that should or must be said about the regimes, why do they speak so authoritatively? If they are both right, why do they disagree? If they are wrong, what is the cause of their errors? And in the light of what wisdom do we, Aristotle and his reader, pass judgment on democrats and oligarchs? We must clarify our judgment by understanding the errors of others, for Aristotle tells us that we must grasp what "they say" the boundaries of oligarchy and democracy are, and what the just favorable to oligarchy and democracy is.

Even before we grasp this much, we must reiterate our understanding of whom Aristotle speaks about when he refers to oligarchs and democrats. We can infer from his opening statement here that oligarchy and democracy must differ if they have different boundaries. Yet oligarchic and democratic *justice* do not differ; one just is favorable to both. It is well to recall, then, as we have previously surmised, that all human beings, the few among beings, could be said to be oligarchs insofar as they seek to acquire some sort of wealth, to make something of themselves. Within the city, oligarchs can be distinguished into oligarchs and democrats as ordinarily understood, men who have acquired money and those who have not. And we have also argued that among the many men who lacked *obols* were a few who sought not *obols*, but wisdom about the whole of nature. At the conclusion of the last passage, Aristotle seemed to announce that he would continue to think of these men, who are not yet wise, as democrats. They are similar to democratic citizens in their understanding of what a "one" is, and therefore in what the just as a measure is. But in agreeing with democrats, in giving support to democratic politics with their theories, these natural philosophers forget that they themselves are also oligarchs who dwell in a sea of democrats. They forget what Aristotle stresses: the being who philosophizes.

All men, we are told, grasp the meaning of justice to some extent, but they fail to say all of "the most sovereign just." Some men say justice is equality, but justice should be equal shares to equals only; some men say justice is inequality, but justice should be unequal shares to unequals only. They fail to make these distinctions for two reasons: They abstract from the "for whom," and they judge badly. Both errors, abstracting from the "for whom" and judging badly, are traced by Aristotle to one cause: The judgment is about themselves, and most men are base judges of "the household things," or their own things. What is meant seems to be the following: The men who abstract from the "for whom" remind us of the mathematicians who count bodies and then abstract from the bodies to understand the very numbers by which they count.[15] If it is reasonable for them to abstract from the "for whom" or the "what" when they examine numbers, it may not be reasonable for them to do so when they speak about the household things, the human things. The scientist who is not a political scientist does not know how to judge about himself. He judges the household things as he judges all of the other things he knows, and that is basely. Some men, however—for example, the political man who has attempted to speak about the "whats" of the regimes—may simply judge badly because they have not yet learned to judge well or nobly.

The more obvious meaning of Aristotle's text is that the errors of "democrats" and "oligarchs" are not simply errors in judgment—that is, intellectual failings. Rather, they judge as they do because it is in their self-interest to do so. Aristotle tells us that they divide the "for whom" and "the things" or "the businesses" in the same way. Philosophers know that their business is to philosophize, not to lord it over others. Nature is full of the bodies that the philosopher comprehends with his intellect, and the city serves men's bodies. Just as the philosopher's intellect is outside of the whole of being he studies, philosophers think they need not be a part of politics. They forget about their own bodies, and so they do not care about politics.

What inconveniences this *hybris* may cause for philosophers we shall see in the next section. But what of political men? We have already learned that the assertions of the mathematicians are ignoble and a possible support for man's bad political judgments. Indeed, their assertions support the opinion that justice *is* the justice favorable to oligarchy and democracy. By this we mean oligarchy and democracy as opposed to aristocracy. Aristotle says that most, and therefore not all, men judge basely about the household things. He now refers us to his discussion of justice in the *Ethics*, his book of assertions about the household things, addressed to men who are noble or potential noble judges. In briefly comparing the discussion to which we are referred and its context in the *Ethics* to the explanation of justice at this point in Book III of the *Politics*, we come to understand something about what kind of philosophic assertions are necessary to support noble judgments.

In the *Politics*, Aristotle says that men divide the things (or businesses) in the same way as they divide the "for whom." They agree on equality in the thing, but dispute the "for whom." Those who dispute about the "for whom" are only political men, we may surmise. In the *Ethics*, Aristotle does say something similar: that the "for whom" and the thing are divided similarly.[16] But we must consider the context in which the statement is made in the *Ethics*. The justice of which Aristotle speaks here is distributive justice. In the *Ethics* we learn that distributive justice is only one part of justice; and even then, Aristotle is at pains to argue that there is such a thing.[17] He first distinguishes distributive justice, which he calls a part of justice, from the whole of justice, which is roughly the same as law-abidingness. If law-abidingness appears as the primary meaning of justice, it does so reasonably, because the law attempts to command all the virtues and forbid all the vices.[18] Legal justice means to be prudence. Aristotle opposes the simple identification of law and justice because the law is only more or less what it intends to be, yet because it is at least more or less what it intends to be, he does not want to destroy that identification for the citizen. He therefore opposes the opinion that there is only the whole of justice, and he makes a part of justice the standard for the whole of justice by placing all of his substantive discussion of justice under the explanation of the parts—not under the whole of justice, which is law-abidingness.

More precisely, particular justice consists of two parts: distributive and commutative.[19] The second kind is said to be appropriate to private transactions, examples of which are business agreements, but also criminal penalties. It does not take into account the "for whom." Aristotle will soon make an argument in the *Politics* that the city is not a contract; he needs to stress this point in order to argue that distributive justice does properly take into account the "for whom." The other part of justice, distributive justice, means giving equal shares to equals. The shares given are shares in the regime; the distribution is of honors and useful things.[20] Persons are divided in the same way as things, not businesses; the regime is the whole. Furthermore, in the *Ethics* the discussion of justice is in terms of equality only; inequality is identified with injustice.[21] One reason for the identification in the *Ethics* of justice with equality is that justice is there said to be a proportion, involving four terms. The proportion would be A:B::C:D, person:share::person:share. Presumably one knows that $A \times D = B \times C$ by knowing how the things as well as the persons are commensurable. In other words, we may assume that the proportion in the *Ethics* is based on a knowledge of how philosophy and politics are related in a regime, not on an absolute separation of the two as is implied in the division of persons and businesses in the same way. The regime that distributes justice in the *Ethics* combines the economic and the legal with the philosophic to make the political.

For the present, Aristotle promotes the opinion that justice is the unequal as well as the equal. He must do so, it would seem, because he cannot speak of an "equal" in terms of which bodies and intellects, economics and philosophy, can be compared. Yet at the conclusion of Book III Aristotle will present the argument of the *Ethics*, showing that justice is a mean between bodies and intellect. Therefore, we should consider an additional reason for Aristotle's not stating that the just is the equal at this point in the argument. One might say that in the *Ethics* Aristotle educates the man he now attempts to make manifest: a serious political man. In the *Ethics* he moderates the claim of the serious political man on politics by exposing him to other pleasant and noble ways to spend his life, for example, with dear friends or in getting a PhD in political science instead of running for office.[22] But at this point in Book III of the *Politics*, where Aristotle wishes to bring to light the nature of the political man and explain why the education of the *Ethics* can be said to be his proper education, Aristotle must first distinguish him from both philosophers and the demotic many. He therefore begins by promoting the political man's claim in such a way that his distinctiveness can be made apparent both to others and to himself. And in order to make his teaching attractive to this potential student, Aristotle must first take the political man's claim seriously before he can teach him what should be taken more seriously than politics.

This educable man is, despite his desire to be public-spirited, an oligarch. He thinks those who provide useful things for the city should be proportionately rewarded with offices. If the city's justice were economic justice, his argument would be reasonable. But Aristotle says that citizens dispute about the "for whom" first, because they judge badly about their own things; and second, because they believe they speak the just simply. The oligarch does not yet know what is most useful to men and cities, and perhaps he does not reflect sufficiently on the fact that the democrat can present a seemingly unreasonable argument and yet believe it correct.[23] The partisans who dispute without speaking "the all of the most sovereign just" do not speak of the law that purports to be identical with the whole of virtue. Aristotle must explain to the oligarch both why virtue as well as money is useful to men and cities, and why the form of the city's justice must be law. These explanations will be given in the next section.

Oligarchs judge badly because they think that by having useful things they are wholly unequal. Democrats judge badly because they think that by being free they are wholly equal. Democrats forget their own needs for useful things, almost as if they have forgotten that they have bodies. Similarly, taking their freedom for granted, democratic philosophers make judgments about nonhuman bodies without considering how their own bodies and the bodies of other human beings affect their ability to judge. If the philosopher wishes to understand being, he needs to know how body and intellect are connected. The measure of equality and inequality between these cannot be like the just favorable to oligarchy and democracy, for that "just" presupposes the separability of body and intellect. It is beneficial neither to philosophers or philosophy, for it brings nothing together, neither political men and philosophers nor the kinds of being. If the most authoritative "just" about which citizens do not speak is the law that commands the whole of

metics as well as to citizens. The philosopher who lives as a metic, teaching political science, is also free to defend himself, unsuccessfully, for impiety and corrupting the young. Philosophers are not well received by the law-abiding many in the cities, and perhaps rightly so; their good names, if not their very lives, are in need of defense in the city's courts. The philosopher seems unjust because he calls into question the city's legally ordained beliefs about what is good and just. Because the city determines the just and the unjust, it is not sufficient to win a few friends. The philosopher's apparent need of a guard explains his cultivation of manly political men; it explains his rhetoric defending the possibility and superiority of the rule of morally virtuous men in an aristocracy. But these men are few, and the fact that the rest of the city may sit in judgment necessitates that the philosopher no longer be understood as unjust. Socrates lacked thirty votes for acquittal.

Aristotle's point is not limited to any particular city. Even if existing city boundaries were destroyed, any city would necessarily reconstitute the boundaries within which human life is made possible. There is no city for the philosopher to escape to, not even any barbarian nation. Carthage and Etruria, Aristotle says, would have conventions about what can be imported (*eisagogimoi*),[32] encounters concerning not being unjust, and statutes about alliances. Philosophers with mortal bodies cannot avoid taking the city's laws and justice seriously. Whether they take justice seriously for any other reason is left open for the moment. Curiously, the very defense of the philosopher before the city will be a demonstration of his ability to justify the city's laws.

Indeed, precisely why cities do need laws and legal justice has not been established. As Aristotle has indicated, men understand the city to be an association of men for the mutual service of the needs and desires, especially the bodily needs, of each man. Aristotle does not deny that this is correct, but neither will he assert that it is correct, as does the sophist Lycophron. In fact, Aristotle does not show that the function of the city is to secure the good life rather than mere life, nor does he show that it is not an alliance against other cities and a system of exchanges and mutual uses. What he does deny is that the city can be anything thus understood. The political, as distinct from the economic, cannot be made intelligible in terms of an association of bodies only. Justice as anything other than free-market price cannot be defended, and no particular configuration of buyers and sellers can be defended as natural or necessary. It is difficult to imagine any bodily need or desire that cannot be filled as well by an Etruscan or a Carthaginian as by an Athenian. The political beginning seems to be one's own good, yet what good citizens share is immanifest. The city is nothing other than its laws and conventions, but these laws are necessary only to keep the military-industrial complex working well. Hence, the city is still nothing.

Yet Aristotle also speaks of good laws, and in doing so he indicates both how the city might be said to be something and how the philosopher and the city might be reconciled. He proposes that the conventions and laws making citizens of one city those who were originally citizens of the two great commercial empires, Carthage and Etruria, would be inadequate for the following reasons: They do not have common rules or offices, they do not think about "making something of one another," and they do not think about rectifying each other's injustice and other wretchedness. Their city would not be a whole because they do not make their first principle man's possible perfection, the principle of Aristotle's hypothesis by which man is a citizen, and because they do not teach that justice means the completion of a man's virtue and is therefore good for a man. The city *is* when it takes for its principle the citizenship of whole human beings and demonstrates that the city's justice is necessary to this end. Only if the city is shown to be in the service of the good life, understood as philosophy or as philosophy and moral virtue, can it be defended to its citizens.

Yet even for the city to function well as a military-industrial complex, a minimum of virtue is necessary. Citizens must at least not do injustices to one another. The political man seems to understand virtue as the ability to acquire, although not from his fellow citizens if possible. Therefore, he is now advised to examine "political virtue and vice" from different points of view (*diaskopeō*). Political beings are characterized both by an ability to acquire and the need to form a community; the excellence of which the oligarch speaks, acquisitiveness, seems to prevent men from constituting a true community. Ultimately, a concern for acquisition for oneself conflicts with the opinion that the justice which requires a limitation on acquisitiveness can be good.

But when the political rule was first introduced (1277b7), those under it were likened to a household of man and woman. The virtues and works of each part differed; and womanishness, we suggested, was connected to philosophy. Its consequence was apparent unmanliness, an unwillingness to acquire politically because of a greater craving for wisdom. Our present point is that half of what makes man political is his ability to commune in speech, for political virtue is skill in speech as well as skill on the battle-field. As the philosopher must care enough about the safety of his body, so the political man must broaden his understanding of what is political. The connection between the two meanings of political virtue, acquisition and speech, will be made through good law, for law at its best combines force with reason. Force and reason are also combined in self-compulsion, that is, in the moral virtue that befits free beings with both bodies and intellects. Aristotle says that in the city truly so named, not the city in speech, one must care about virtue. The parts of political virtue, military and philosophic, combined in a form that is a bit of both yet neither and more, is the virtue of a Solon or a Lycurgus, a Pericles or a Brasidas.[33] The good law that makes the city's virtue coextensive with a man's virtue as far as possible is the most sovereign thing about which citizens and philosophic men fail to speak. Good law embodies the statesman's prudence. The political man who seeks a standard for justice, who "worries about good law," is about to become a legislator, and in formulating the speeches that comprise the law, he will be made to examine political virtue from another point of view. By making this man a legislator—that is, a political scientist—one moderates or at least modifies his political acquisitiveness and uses him to teach virtue to others.

Law or virtue is necessary precisely because the city is an alliance of bodies serving each other and defending themselves. Each man's body is essentially private, and there is nothing in the city to overcome the natural prior concern of each man for his own needs and desires. Thus, the physical propinquity of bodies does not make a city. Not even Socrates' City of Pigs, with its carpenter, its farmer, and its shoemaker, an association of artisans meeting the basic needs of all bodies, would be a city.[34] Mutual needs cannot be the basis of a city as a whole, for all needs seem to be private. To repeat, Aristotle does not deny that the city originates in these needs and serves them, but they cannot be said to be that for the sake of which the city exists, for they do not point to the necessity of the political as distinguished from the economic. Nor would the mere addition of the good households, which remain somewhat separate from the city, make the city a whole, for there is no common end. Hippodamus's city of ten thousand, in which philosophy in the service of the city's prosperity is lawfully rewarded, would not be a city.[35] Philosophers *might* survive among other men, but there will be no community that embodies man's humanity.

Virtue or justice is necessary, then, to overcome the natural preference of each man for what is useful to himself, especially if he deems unsharable wealth most useful. If self-preference cannot be overcome by the praise of justice for its own sake, care for the public must be fostered by providing a benefit to each that could not otherwise be obtained, and this benefit must be made to seem more choiceworthy than all others. The city needs a first principle, an end of its own, which must be neither acquisition of riches nor wisdom. The city not only is *like*, but *is*, some put-together whole. It is a whole put together of political animals who are characterized by a concern for their own good, but also by some desire to constitute a community. A city is a whole if the city has as its end a common good that is the greatest good for each political being qua political being. A community is achieved "down" in the cities only when the concern for the good of each is overcome by a concern for what transcends each and is "possessed" by none. Aristotle speaks of funerals, brotherhoods, sacred rites, and the pastimes of living together. The first of these is to make it seem as if the city has cared for men throughout their complete lives, and the others to make it seem as if the city has been the guarantor of sufficiency in all facets of life. These institutions cannot be ends in themselves, however; they are for the sake of the city's being a whole. They might be sufficient to produce a semblance of virtue, for if the city did this for each man, it would be reasonable to care for it. But such things do not make the city intelligible as a whole. The conjoining of the city of Megarians, the temples (*megara*), and Corinth, the city reputed for its wealth, does not make the city a one, Aristotle says. The divine added to the economic does not result in the city's having an end in which the parts as parts might share. The true end is the good life, Aristotle *says*, and he *asserts* that it is the happy or noble life.

The reason why Aristotle must say one thing and assert another is as follows. What constitutes a city is a community in the good life for the sake of the complete and self-sufficient life. This community in the good life is said to be the work of friendship, and it is composed of the "households" that engage in speaking about the good. But if the good life is for the sake of the complete and self-sufficient life, it is not a complete or self-sufficient life itself. The philosopher is not complete in remaining unwise, and not self-sufficient in needing someone to care for the body in which his speechful soul is housed. The first problem might be solved by philosophic friendship; the villages, which are groups of households, are said to live the complete life.[36] This would issue in the greatest good for political beings, achieved by each but only in common. But this is an association of philosophic souls, and the philosopher's bodily insufficiency requires him to live in a city.

The city tries to overcome the incompleteness and insufficiency of its parts through the institutions that we might call "culture," in which the city has its own version of the good life. The city looks up toward what seems to transcend each man, the divine things, and its citizens associate in a community that offers a pleasure no man could have without there being a city. But in order that the city's end be *the* end, not merely necessary to these supra- and subpolitical ends, the city's end must be specifically political. The political community is for the sake of noble deeds, not for culture, and the end of a political man is living nobly by doing nobly. Odysseus and Diomedes have a friendship for the sake of doing noble deeds;[37] they could not live noble lives without each other's help and without the city, yet each lives a noble life and the city needs their nobility. The city's defense of the public over the private is intelligible as a reflection of philosophic friendship, though the reflection differs from the reality. Aristotle will later speak of a beautiful *painting*; the city's being an image is intelligible if one takes into account men's bodies.

Thus Aristotle's "just" speech before the city is a defense of the city to its citizens. In it there is no defense of the city's justice, but neither is there an assertion that the philosopher is the most just man. Rather, it is a defense of the virtue and nobility of which political men are capable.[38] The offspring of the "intermarriage" of philosophy and politics is the teaching of virtue.

Aristotle has not refuted the three arguments he proposed to defeat in this section: (1) that the city exists for life only, (2) that it is an alliance for the sake of not being done an injustice by anyone, and (3) that it is for exchanges and the use of one another. These were the arguments of ignoble political men and ignoble philosophers. Instead, Aristotle has replaced them with even stiffer demands upon political men, and then has shown that even meeting these demands is not quite enough. He claims that he has made apparent that there is no city if there is a community in place, if men are merely not unjust to one another, and if the end is giving shares. Thus, he has made men care about others besides themselves, the gods and clansmen who constitute a community which is not simply physical; he has made men think about being just rather than merely avoiding injustice; he has made them think about giving rather than taking. Aristotle raises the standard for political justice to friendship,[39] and then defends what is obviously an inadequate political substitute for true friendship, but which nonetheless must be made to seem adequate to political men. The city requires that men think of living not among friends but among clansmen, that sacrifice to the gods replace the ability to be perfectly just, and that the pastimes of living together replace philosophizing and sharing together. What is even more problematic, the city's necessity seems to require that its opinions about the good or noble life not be examined to reveal their inadequacy, whereas philosophy, of which the good city is an image, is precisely this examination of opinions about the good. The incompleteness of philosophy, as well as its weakness, makes impossible a bald assertion that only in philosophizing are the good, the just, and the self-sufficient lives one. The city's *end* is the good life, a life that cannot be lived in the city proper. The city *is* when it makes human perfection a possibility.

The oligarchic *logos* is the *logos* of political beings, the few among many beings. That *logos*, Aristotle tells us at the beginning of this passage, *seems* to have bodily strength and supposes that acquisition or possession is the end. Thus stated, the argument must be defeated precisely because it does not describe political beings, for the distinction between political beings and others does not lie either in their bodies or in what they possess. In criticizing the oligarchic understanding, Aristotle calls our attention to the contributor of one *mina*, either at the beginning or later. Man's "being" may well be more the end he seeks or the work he does in seeking that end than what he presently is. Perhaps man's being cannot be understood without appreciating that one *mina* which is man's end. The man who wants to maintain the distinctiveness of human beings wants to show that man is naturally political because the parts of human being come together to comprise the whole of human being in a way that the other beings, who do not appear to come together of their own volition, do not. Furthermore, if man is naturally political, then political being is a kind of being. The political man who attempts to make the city intelligible as the military-industrial that serves the physical well-being of each citizen is unable to explain how man is political. Only the good as an end makes man's communities intelligible; political being cannot be explained as simply being for the sake of being what it is, existing for mere life. What is yet unclear is precisely why and how man's cities, rather than his other associations, contribute to this end.

The oligarchic *logos*, with its bodily strength, also purports to explain how bodies, nonhuman as well as human, constitute a city. In this passage, Aristotle begins by speaking of beings coming together and associating; the concluding arguments make reference only to beings who associate. Near the end, Aristotle mentions a multitude of ten thousand that does not become a city because each does not associate, and he speaks of some "each" that do not form a city because each remains the same having come together as when separate. The multitude of ten thousand represents, both in the discussion of Hippodamus and in the *Metaphysics*,[40] forms understood numerically, as a mathematician understands the numbers with which he works to be more real than the things they are counts of. Aristotle attacks the understanding that all of being can be explained through mathematics in both those discussions and, as we have argued, in Book III of the *Politics*. The difficulty he finds here is that not even by abstracting from the "for whom," that is, by considering the "households" or pure integers as separate, can it be explained how numbers can be said to form a community. In the Aristotelian conception, each number stands for a specific multitude of specific things seen and counted.[41] Even if what is counted is disregarded, numbers can have something in common only by breaking down each number itself into the units composing it. A number comprised of units *is* the number, not many units; but the numbers cannot be worked with except by understanding them as mere collections of units. If units can be added together, "married," to form a number, as they are within Megara and Corinth, yet one cannot make Megara and Corinth into one city by conjoining their walls. When we add six and seven to make thirteen, what we do is to break six and seven down into six units and seven units, respectively, and then count the total of units: thirteen. In other words, one cannot make a whole through the numerical forms; nor are those forms necessary to account for the sum of all the multitudes they represent. The independent being of each pure number seems superfluous. Nature is democratic: It is units; it is each body.

When Aristotle began to examine the regimes, he asked whether those who did not share in the bringing together could should still be asserted to be citizens (1279a31–32). The forms with which the mathematician works "share in the bringing together," according to Plato but not according to Aristotle, by sharing in the genus of numbers.[42] Hence Aristotle's mention here of the city consisting of villages and genera. That he speaks of genera suggests that the mathematician's forms do not bring things together. Perhaps one cannot assert that nonhuman beings are "citizens." That one can say that they are not beings is less clear; perhaps the inference to make is that there is no "city," no whole, by nature.

Aristotle concludes the passage by saying that all who dispute speak a part of the just. The "all" are philosophers who speak of being, and oligarchs and democrats who dispute about citizenship. The philosopher, in attempting to speak of nature as nonhuman being, can neither make sense of it nor explain to others why he desires to make sense of it. Perhaps when he speaks of human being he can make sense of it, and need not even offer to explain to other men why it is important to make sense of it. Hence Aristotle's assertion that those who contribute most to the political community which exists for the sake of noble deeds have a greater share in the city. Even if it seems unjust that man have a seemingly disproportionate share in the whole, his being may be more valuable not only to himself, but for the sake of understanding what being is.

The democratic citizen, claiming a share in rule for no other reason than that he is a free-born citizen, means to say that the city aims to be a community of friends, and that the deeds of friendship required by the city, worshipping the city's gods together and being clansmen, are precisely the deeds of which all citizens and only citizens are capable. One who opposes democracy must argue that the city's friendship is a friendship in noble deeds, and that those who have political virtue and are therefore capable of noble deeds must have a greater share in the city. The oligarchic citizen, who claims a share in rule because he contributes to the city's wealth, is told that not wealth but virtue is the greatest contribution one can make to the city.

Yet, beginning with either the ignoble mathematician's or the ignoble oligarch's understanding, Aristotle cannot provide us with a convincing explanation of why it is natural for men to live in cities and to take virtue seriously for its own sake. What Aristotle needs to show is that the city which does the work of the economic community, but nonetheless aspires to be the philosophic community, is according to nature. The economic community is undoubtedly necessary, and philosophic friendship may be good for man if we have reason to hope that wisdom is possible. But we cannot assume that wisdom about the whole is available, any more than we can assume that cities are natural, not put-together, wholes or that nature is a whole. Yet Aristotle must make this demonstration about the wholeness of the community dedicated to noble deeds, if for no other reason than to defend in speech the noble man who might in turn defend him should he come to rule in a city. Perhaps he must also make this demonstration because it is correct to say that it is according to human nature for men to live in cities. If we cannot yet assume that it is correct for him to live in economic communities, or actual cities as they understand themselves, we can assume that it is natural. If we examine men's behavior in these communities, perhaps we can find something in man that makes political communities necessary and good for man, thus "according to nature," if not "by nature."[43] In doing so, we will discover how the oligarchic *logos* can be said to have *logos*.

5. Unreason Is the Reason (1281a11–39)

Let us suppose that man's city is as Aristotle has just described it: It appears to be essentially an economic community. And let us also suppose that Aristotle is correct in arguing that to this economic community it would be necessary to add what we call culture: music and poetry, religion, friendships, and association. We would then have a "city" which is comprised of the elements of what we might call liberal society. What is missing from it is a sovereign, a government, for we do not suppose that man is necessarily political. Presumably there is commutative justice in this "city"—the justice of the marketplace and of criminal penalties. But there is no distributive justice because there is no regime; who gets what, where, when, and how is unsettled. There is no political rule because the city has no first principle of its own; if the end is not the physical well-being of each, man's possible perfection as an end seems to mean philosophizing, not lording it over others in cities.

If the political man with whom Aristotle converses has learned his lesson thus far, he has understood that one cannot assume that the sovereignty of wealthy men, even if for the benefit of others, is just. Whether it is reasonable for him to worry about politics, he nevertheless continues to do so. To the extent that he grasps that politics may differ from economics, and political justice from economic justice, he is ready to consider with Aristotle what the alternatives to the sovereignty of the wealthy are. To the extent that he proves to be more interested in reasoning about politics than in ruling, he can discern, as we do, that Aristotle's consideration of the question of who should be sovereign gradually becomes the question of what is to rule or be a first principle, and that both questions are left unresolved for the present.

If the political scientist has followed Aristotle's argument thus far, he receives in this passage an emphatic answer to the question that should be on his mind: Why, if at all, can one rightly say that man is a political animal? What in his nature makes it natural for him to live in cities that are neither simply economic communities nor philosophic friendships? He also begins to understand what culture is for, and therefore why it must be set down that the political community exists for the sake of noble deeds.

If the natural philosopher with whom Aristotle seems to dispute is prepared to take a turn in listening, he will discover or be reminded of a kind of being that he does not seem to find in nonhuman beings or in philosophers overwhelmed with a yearning to know the whole. Perhaps in considering this element, he will eventually be able to do what he has failed to do thus far, which is to comprehend how the parts of being form a whole and what the cause of their being a whole is.

We stress that this mysterious x of which we speak is not identified by Aristotle; what it is can only be inferred from the form of the discussion. We nevertheless identify it as *thymos*, which means "spirit," "anger," "will." That Aristotle does not yet speak of it by name should not surprise us too much. The political man exhibits it without being able to explain it; the philosopher who has looked at nonhuman beings and at philosophic souls cannot yet speak of it because it seems to be found primarily in public men, whom he has not yet made an object of study. Finally, that it is to be found only in the form of the discussion will no longer surprise us when we learn that *thymos* is the source of forms, or at least of the philosopher's positing of forms.

Our understanding emerges from the following analysis of the passage: Aristotle begins by giving a list of candidates for sovereignty in the city. In contrast to the original double list of regimes according to their numbers and according to their "whats," this list combines quantities and qualities. Furthermore, it seems to reflect a greater clarity on the part of the political spokesman, and a greater self-awareness on the part of the scientist. Finally, the list could reasonably be said to be ordered. The five candidates presented are the multitude, the wealthy, the respectable or reasonable,[44] the one best of all, and the tyrant. We might surmise, first, that the political spokesman has not overcome his antipathy to the multitude, for he attributes no quality to them, whereas he does make a distinction among "fews" and "ones," which are listed according to their qualities. Presumably the few are either wealthy or respectable. Thus, the oligarch has learned that one cannot claim to be sovereign simply on the basis of wealth. The respectable man would seem to be the political man Aristotle has been striving to educate. The man distinguishes between "ones" as he did before, but he no longer speaks of a king who merely looks on (1279a33–34). The king might be sovereign as an aristocracy of one. We might further surmise that the mathematician has realized that speaking of "fews" is no help to him. There is no specific mention of "fews." Rather, manyness and unity are opposed, as if Aristotle's criticism of pure integers has been taken into consideration. In accordance with another suggested criticism, two "ones" are specified, as if in recognition of the problem of establishing what the "one" with reference to which other things are "many" is.

However reasonable this list may seem to us, when the candidates present themselves or are presented, the list is expanded from five to seven and the order is changed. The new order is the poor, the majority, the tyrant, the few, the wealthy, the respectable, the one most serious, and the law. In the new list, the many poor are distinguished from those who constitute a majority "when all are taken into account," the one best is now said to be the one most serious, and the law is added. What these changes mean we shall consider as we proceed. As for the change in order, we offer the following explanation. After the initial list is given, Aristotle comments that all the alternatives cause "peevishness." The list that follows is a list in order of decreasing degrees of peevishness, beginning with the poor who not only speak but swear on their own behalf, and ending with the law which is said to be noblest in lacking the passions of the human soul. Whoever gave the first list failed to take into account the anger of political men.

We note a further complication in the list of seven. After the poor defend their manifestly unjust actions with an assertion about their justice, with Zeus as their witness, Aristotle asks what must be said to be the extreme of injustice. The word he uses for "must" (*chrē*) is not his usual "ought," but one that has a connotation of cosmic necessity, as if he sought an answer to Zeus. The next three candidates discussed are discussed as a set, for they are said to be no more just than one another. Furthermore, the discussion of these three is prefaced with "again" or "on the contrary" (*palin*), which we understand to be a way by which Aristotle often signifies his switch from a consideration of political to natural things, or vice versa.[45] In other words, Aristotle's response to the democratic justice sanctioned by Zeus is an attempt to discern what is by nature just. After concluding that all of these alternatives appear to be base and unjust, he speaks of the rule as well as the sovereignty of the respectable and serious, as if to suggest that human dignity and reason would have to serve as the first principle and standard for justice because there seems to be none other.

We consider the candidates in greater detail: The first in the original list was the "multitude," and this the political man apparently understands to mean the poor, for someone says, "Well, if the poor, because they are a majority, divide up the things of the wealthy, is this not unjust?" The answer to this is emphatic: "No, by Zeus, for it seemed just to the sovereign." We have learned thus far that the city ought to sacrifice to some god, and that democratic citizens believe they are just; but what kind of a Zeus sanctions the expropriation of the property of fellow citizens? We now see that if "culture" is necessary to complete the city, not all cultures make cities wholes; a Zeus who sanctions such expropriations does little to reconcile the rich and the poor. But if the democrat is correct in his opinion of what is just according to Zeus, then the oligarch must learn a thing or two about justice and friendship. Indeed, equality of property seems just to many people who have never professed a high regard for Zeus.

When citizens support their opinions with a "By Zeus," what they mean to say is that their understanding of justice is universally correct. The democrat's Zeus is the equivalent of the scientist's "nature." Therefore, in order to defend or challenge any particular understanding of justice, one would have to speak of what is right by nature. But to what nature does one look? Aristotle's second, third, and fourth candidates for sovereignty, we suggest, represent alternative formulations of what nonhuman nature is. The conclusion is that they are all equally just or unjust; nature is indifferent to justice. If, when all are taken into account, the things of the few are distributed to the majority, this law *is not of the sort to be just*, that is, neither just or unjust, nor capable of being either. But does not Aristotle teach that the forms, the few, are in matter the many beings? And the deeds of the tyrant were all necessarily just. Perhaps the whole was brought into being, or is ruled by a tyrant. Do not many people learn that the world was created when one very excellent and very strong being made a cosmos out of chaos? And if the few were said to rule, they would do what the multitude does and abstract from their possessions. But have not some notable men, the Pythagoreans and Platonists, taught that the few forms were the causes of being? It is apparent, Aristotle says, that these alternatives are all base and unjust. But the truer point seems to be that they are neither more nor less just than one another, because they are not of the sort to be just. All these explanations could describe a nature that is well ruled. The forms are in matter; if one abstracts from body and its multiplicity, the few forms can be understood as responsible for the many in each class of things being what they are, and all things are what they are according to the design of one creator or ruler.

Yet if one should look to nonhuman nature as we now do in order to find an argument for how a human city should be ordered, it is far more than "apparent" that all these things are base and unjust. The distribution of the goods of the few by the poor will indeed destroy a city of democrats and oligarchs, and therefore it is unjust; for if justice is the virtue that pertains to the city, Aristotle says, and a virtue cannot be understood as something that destroys its possessor, then this democratic deed cannot be just, no matter what Zeus says. The poor, whatever they say, act as they do because they are strong and able to get away with being unjust. Neither the nature nor the cause of their deed differentiates them from one tyrant who acts for his private good. We do not therefore conclude that the tyranny of one is preferable to the tyranny of many, however. Nor, for the same reason, is an oligarchy of wealthy men who take the fruits of their labors from the poor any more just. It seems that all the regimes that are right by nature are deviations according to politics.

Aristotle seems to have been contending that human beings are as much a part of nature as is anything else. What seemed to differentiate the political community from the rest of nature was its ability to associate in thought, even if this were done only imperfectly and never visibly. Thus, two more candidates for sovereignty are considered: the respectable and the one most serious, that is, men of good political judgment and the philosopher. Aristotle speaks of their rule as well as their sovereignty, because looking to man's peculiar excellence as "nature" seems to require the acceptance of the hypothesis by which men are citizens. To make the possible perfection of man the first principle is as much an abstraction from nonhuman being as it is an abstraction from human being to seek the first principle in the cause of all bodies. It is as "oligarchic" as the first is "democratic," favoring the few at the expense of the many instead of the many at the expense of the few. It is necessary, Aristotle says, that all others be dishonored if they are not honored in the political first principle. Is this an admission that the "one" to which Aristotle looks as a measure, the possibility of the wise soul, is no more an all-inclusive "one" than the one to which the mathematical physicist looks? Can either be the ground of a full account of being, rather than a "regime," a part?

The rule of the respectable or the one most serious would seem to be objectionable for other reasons, however, even if Aristotle could demonstrate to us that political being does comprehend all of being. Their rule is not said to be either unjust or base as the other alternatives are, but their rule dishonors many and causes peevishness. The men most worried about being honored are, we recall, such as the angry Achilles, whose anger will not be reasoned away, and who can be ruled only by what they hold honorable. Achilles, the man who shares in honors, was most truly said to be a citizen (1278a35–37), and Aristotle now makes a similar statement in his own name: We say that honors are the first principles. Achilles epitomizes the political man who is not a philosopher but who lives in political communities that might exist for the sake of noble deeds. In the last section Aristotle said that the economic community in which men "settle down" must make part of itself loyalties to the clan, worship of the divine, the pleasures of living together, and the doing of noble deeds—in sum, the part of man expressed in these activities. He now speaks of men's peevishness, worship of the divine, political and economic factions, unjust deeds, and competing for honors. He will soon record an oath, a vehement response to the democrat's "By Zeus," which is a noble oath, reflecting Aristotle's hypothesis about man's citizenship. What is authoritative in the city is what is honored, and what is most honorable is usually called divine by men, or is an imitation of what they believe is divine.[46] What is honorable must also be spelled out in laws that proclaim themselves to be just, for, as the democrat reveals, righteous indignation on behalf of "justice" belongs no less to the base than the noble. Indignant, angry men cannot be reasoned with; they can at best be tamed by being habituated to use the energy behind anger in the service of what they believe to be noble.

If men must be habituated, if things must come to be believed, then opinions about the just, the noble, and the good must remain relatively fixed.[47] But the respectable (reasonable) man corrects the just, and the serious man questions what the city holds to be good. If they are sovereign, their superiority to the law makes manifest the insufficiency of what men presently honor, and may lead them to hold nothing sacred. It does not seem that the reasonable ought to rule unless it can be explained how they will manage unreasonable men without maintaining the honorable and sacred as sacred, and without maintaining a distinction between noble and ignoble wrath.

Nor do we understand why reasonable men should rule if we do not know in the light of what the use of reason could be deemed reasonable. The seventh candidate for sovereignty is the law, which might be thought to be nobler than the sovereignty of any men or man because law lacks the passions that souls have. Law is what the reasonable and serious aim to be in order to distinguish themselves from the angry poor. "Someone" makes this assertion on behalf of law. Aristotle does not make it in his own name, but he does seem to object to it in his own name: The law will be favorable either to democracy or to oligarchy. What the law should be is no clearer than who should be sovereign or what should be the first principle. In this passage, Aristotle speaks of what we understand to be a law of nature, and this law is not of the sort to be just. If law seems noble because it is reasonable, we must still ask what reason reasons about, for some reasonings lead neither to noble politics nor to a proof that philosophy is beneficial to man in any way.[48] The someone who makes the assertion about law knows that reason is a fine thing, but he has not thought about the possibility that political beings have or need laws of their own.

Perhaps there are laws of human nature. We cannot presuppose their existence, but that there are such laws Aristotle will attempt to demonstrate to his and our satisfaction. He seems to have shown that if men need to live in economic communities, they need to live in cultures that turn anger into public spiritedness, and this is done by making something publicly honorable, which men then emulate. Evidently, Aristotle wants to argue that laws of human nature can be known by knowing whether there is something universally honorable to which all the various understandings or misunderstanding of honor are directed, and in the light of which each particular misunderstanding can be made intelligible.[49] For example, the oligarch honors wealth. Can it not be reasonably argued that the wealthiest man is not the man who has the most things, but the man who never lacks for "things" because his desires for them are few? The democrat honors freedom. Can it not be argued that the freest man is not he who has lawless desires, but he who freely chooses to live in an orderly, lawful way? The would-be statesman is a serious citizen, but perhaps one's private virtue is the only thing that can reasonably be taken seriously. Aristotle says that honors are the *archai* not only because what any society or any man makes honorable serves as the first principle, but because honors are the beginnings for an examination of the first principle that allows us to speak of a law befitting political beings.

If we are to attach any significance to the changed order of the list of candidates for sovereignty, we must surmise that Aristotle wishes to show that politics is the realm in which men are anxious to assert themselves regardless of how much they know. Sovereignty is exercised by assertive men. Men's anger makes them political, not merely economic, beings; and their assertiveness as well as their desire to know differentiates them from other beings. The assertions they make are about justice, but that their opinions about justice are anything more than statements about what is beneficial to a part is unclear. Aristotle contrasts the philosopher's behavior to the citizen's. The philosopher is the man always at a loss, always raising difficulties. In this passage, virtually every sentence is a question, not an answer. In seeking the whole, the philosopher forgets to assert himself; the "reasonable" and "the serious" lose their places in the line of candidates.

If "the desire to live together" leads to philosophic friendship, assertiveness, the demand of each to stand apart, makes it necessary that men who live in economic communities be "put together" into a whole and that their anger be tamed or ruled. The philosopher learns about this anger or assertiveness only from examining political men, it seems. If anger is natural to man, and if it is ineradicable, or if it is undesirable that it be eradicated, then politics is natural to man. If politics is natural, then one can rule political men either by convincing them that their anger is really a kind of desire, misunderstood, or by trying to guide them to express their humanity in noble wrath.

If the philosopher has something to teach political men about calming their anger in order to examine their assumptions and about being reasonable, perhaps the political man has something to teach the philosopher about making assumptions. And perhaps he has something to teach the philosopher about taking himself and his own good more seriously. Other parts assert that their good is the just, and they assimilate the whole to themselves. Perhaps the philosopher's good is the just and he is the whole. Or perhaps not.

6. The Multitude, the Demos, and Free Men (1281a39–1282b13)

That it is probably true that the multitude, rather than the few good, should be sovereign does not at first strike the modern reader of the *Politics* as a problematic assertion. We now live in democracies that for all their imperfections surely seem more just than the old aristocracies or monarchies they have replaced. We democrats might be said to subscribe to the following opinion:

If you think it profitable to turn man's intellectual and moral activity toward the necessities of physical life and use them to produce well-being, if you think that reason is more use to men than genius, if your object is not to create heroic virtues but rather tranquil habits, if you would rather contemplate vices than crimes and prefer fewer transgressions at the cost of fewer splendid deeds, if in place of a brilliant society you are content to live in one that is prosperous, and finally, if in your view the main object of government is not to achieve the greatest strength or glory for the nation as a whole but to provide for every individual therein the utmost well-being, protecting him as far as possible from all afflictions, then it is good to make conditions equal and to establish a democratic government.[50]

Furthermore, we live in a world which we know to be "the whole masse of all things that are," and we know that "every part of the Universe, is body, and that which is not Body is no part of the Universe."[51] Science, or philosophy, we know to be "the knowledge acquired by Reasoning, from the Manner of the Generation of any thing, to the Properties; or from the Properties, to some possible Way of Generation of the same; to the end to be able to produce, as far as matter, and humane force permit, such Effects, as humane life requireth."[52] Being is body, and the scientist is somehow outside of the whole he examines. Nature, which is "God's art," is remade by the scientist, who sets down hypotheses and must consider them verified if they produce the anticipated results. Philosophy is not a "Knowledge of Fact," that is, of "whats," but a knowledge of cause and effect.[53] Because the scientist can test his hypothesis only by what it produces, the man who loves the truth has the appearance of a lover of technology and of a benefactor of mankind. Thus, the modern philosopher seems to be a partisan of democracy, first, because his teaching about nature seems to provide an argument that political democracy is according to nature; for democracy too is a city made into a whole of many equal beings. (We shall consider the difficulty with this simple identification later.) Second, even as he pursues his science, he appears to have the same interest as do democrats, that is, making the poor wealthy. Both modern politics and modern science are fundamentally "democratic."

If Aristotle's argument in favor of democracy does not offend us, it is because we have been prepared by men like Hobbes to find it sensible. But what of Aristotle's political friend, or reader, who, even after having been disabused of his facile identification of a few of wealthy men with a few of virtuous, public-spirited men, now seems to be told that even the virtuous cannot be sovereign in cities? How will he agree that the base should lord it over the respectable? And what of the philosophers prior to Aristotle who thought that being lay in the few intelligible forms whose existence might mean that there was a necessary connection between the many bodies contemplated and the hypotheses made by the scientist?[54] The necessary workings of the human mind could be said to correspond to the very being of things in nature, or of nature as a whole; science could be a finding, not a making. Furthermore, that science might appear to support not democracy but aristocracy, which his reader's "common sense" told him was more beneficial to cities than democracy. Nevertheless, because the verification of his science need not be in technology, the philosopher would appear to others to benefit only himself, and, because others could not understand how wisdom could be beneficial, to benefit no one.[55] According to the ancient understanding, natural science was theoretical and politics practical, whereas we moderns could be said to have a practical physics and a theoretical politics.

We wonder, then, about the meaning of Aristotle's assertion that it is probably true that the multitude is sovereign. The argument he presents is manifestly a teaching well suited to reconciling an aristocrat to living in a democracy, and to showing a democracy how to utilize his virtue for the public benefit without allowing him to utilize that virtue to undermine the regime. Yet Aristotle says that this teaching is "probably true," and we therefore cannot assume that it is meant to be merely salutary, regardless of its truth. Furthermore, we have understood the argument immediately preceding this one to be chiefly concerned with the question of who is to be authoritative in political communities. But Aristotle says that this is "another argument," and we are induced to suppose that the present argument is not primarily political, regardless of its political effects. Indeed, we suggest that it is a criticism of the Platonic teaching that being lies in the forms, the "few good." Only a man in the habit of thinking politically, as we no longer seem to be, will without hesitation identify a "multitude" with a *dēmos*, and the few good with would-be aristocrats.

To illustrate the truth of his proposition about multitudes, Aristotle gives three examples of how multitudes surpass good fews in their ability to constitute wholes. Our contention is that each of the examples refers to the three different multitudes that we seem to have distinguished thus far: nonhuman bodies, political beings, and pure intellects. The last are referred to as "serious men."

The first is a multitude who are specifically distinguished from serious men. Once these many have come together, they form an all. All can be better (presumably better than the few good), in the same way that a potluck supper is better than a feast provided by one. The standard of comparison of the many to the few is a one that is a total, and the contention is that the many become a complete one. If, as we suggest, the many spoken of are the nonhuman beings that comprise nature, then the argument seems reasonable. Indeed, the "few good," the forms that exist independent of body, might provide much food for thought, but nothing as substantial as the sum of each of the bodies. Nor, apparently, does it matter that these bodies, like each of the pots at the supper, have not emanated from one kitchen. The visible whole is simply the total of its parts, with no necessary order in it.

The second example in support is that when each of the many has a part of virtue and prudence, the multitude becomes one human being. The human being will have many hands, many feet, and many senses, and it will be similarly endowed in habits and intellect. This argument does not seem completely reasonable, unlike the first. Granted, the problem with the few good was precisely to explain how the parts of virtue and prudence became a whole,[56] and the problem is perhaps not more insoluble if each of many similarly possesses a part of virtue. The few good seemed to reduce to two, courage and moderation. The human being produced by the multitude is visibly a monstrosity, whereas if the few are two, they will produce a quite comely human being. Does Aristotle mean to say that there can be a courageous multitude and a moderate multitude in a democratic city, just as the few combine in a "household"? Or does he mean to call our attention to the inferiority of democracy to aristocracy as a political solution?

The third point is that the many are better judges of the works of music and of the poets (makers). This is so because one judges one part and another judges another, and thus all judge all. If the second argument was difficult, this argument seems even less reasonable. Works of music are wholes whose very being is the order of their parts, and knowing each and every part would surely not enable one to judge the whole as a whole.

Our criticism presupposes, of course, that there is a whole, similar to those made by the Muses and by poets, and that this is the whole it is necessary for men to judge. Perhaps in the light of Aristotle's next observation we must question this assumption. "But in this way the serious among men differ from each of the many, exactly as they assert that the noble do from the not noble, and the painted by art from the true things, and the scattered separate, having been brought together into one . . . , since surely among separated things, this eye has more beauty than the painted one and another part more than some other." If for the moment we set aside the noble and the "painted by art," the praise of the many's ability to judge wholes as if they were "alls" is based on this understanding reported by Aristotle:

$$\frac{\text{serious man}}{\text{each of many}} = \frac{\text{scattered separate, collected in one}}{x}$$

The statement is left incomplete, through either delicacy or ignorance. A serious man, we may surmise, is a man who can become part of a one that is a whole; the scattered separate things, the forms. The serious man differs from each of the many, who are ones but not wholes. But from what do the scattered separate differ? Presumably the statement should be completed by the phrase "the scattered separate things that have not yet been collected into one." If each of the many things cannot be said to be a part of a natural whole, then the philosopher's attempt to speak of a whole through the forms cannot be said to be science instead of art, or finding instead of making. The philosopher's making of a whole corresponds to nothing necessary in nature, and his is not a "correct" judgment of wholes. His "one" or ordered whole cannot be defended as superior to the "all" that the many heap together when they judge. It seems that knowing the "scattered separated things" does not require or permit any necessary inferences about the nature of the whole. In the *Metaphysics*, Aristotle says:

> These thinkers came upon this doctrine of Ideas because they were convinced about the truth of the Heraclitean arguments which state that all sensible things are in a state of flux, so that if there is to be a science or knowledge of anything, there must exist apart from the sensible things some other natures which are permanent, for there can be no science of things which are in a state of flux.[57]

The Platonic theory fails to *prove* the possibility of a science of the whole. What is necessary is an argument about the one, not the few. The perhaps untrue abstraction from body required by the theory of separated forms seems to contribute nothing to this end; hence Aristotle's defense of the multitude.

Furthermore, the very teaching that the intelligible forms are being may lead to undesirable political interpretations. For this reason, the true ground on which Aristotle criticizes Plato is unclear. Aristotle too, later speaks of "abstracting" from body, although not of separated forms that are prior in being. At the same time, he speaks of the rule of the morally virtuous in cities not "for the sake of speech," whereas Plato teaches that philosophers must rule and that moral virtue is not a natural end for man. We have not yet considered a clause interjected into the comparison of serious men to collections of separated things. The serious differ from each of the many, exactly as "they assert that the noble do from the not noble and the painted by art do from the true things. . . ." The true things are each body, and these are not noble or beautiful.[58] Beauty in its proper sense seems to be an attribute of something with a body and of an ordered whole, like a painting or a virtuous man. If the true things are each body, putting together the parts of being is a making that corresponds to nothing that is; the noble, by which one makes a whole of human being and human cities, is not according to nature, but the work of an art. The artisan is more excellent than the artifact. The common-sense understanding that beauty and nobility belong to beings with bodies and to politics seems to be destroyed by the Platonic teaching, for according to that teaching, the intelligible forms *are* more than the things we see partaking in them. As Aristotle points out with irony, the forms must be more beautiful than painted, or visible, things.

If in this passage Aristotle means to identify the beautiful or noble (*kalon*) with the moral, then he seems to criticize the Platonic teaching for leading to the conclusion that there is no noble political solution on the level possible for political men. Philosophers would then be correct in not taking political men and what they call virtue seriously, and democrats and oligarchs would be correct in ignoring considerations of morality in their disputes. It might seem that the political multitude is in fact nothing more than a combination of the two multitudes, each of the many and the serious men. That is, the city will be composed of two kinds of multitudes with fundamentally different ends, without there being any real connection between the two.

This, we note, is essentially the solution attempted by modern political science. But is it really possible that the peculiar character of political beings, their spiritedness, can be explained away to us and to the men who exhibit it? What must be argued to us is that men need not be political after all, because their anger is or can be made to be simply subservient to some desire.[59] The alternative would be to make anger useful in two ways: to show how noble cities are superior to democracies, and to show how taking political being seriously as a kind of being allows one to offer a better explanation of the whole than does the materialism of Heraclitus or Hobbes and the separated forms of Plato.

Aristotle eventually will argue that political being is being. First, however, he must make a better case for his original point, which is that being lies in multitudes. To do this, he must argue that the philosopher can make as much sense of being as he could if the forms existed, and he must show that democracy can do the necessary work of a city as effectively, if not as the political community does become a whole in a way that differs from the way in which nonhuman beings become one. When one looks beyond the household, one will admit that for bodies that do not rule themselves, to be slaves to one master is not wrong. On the contrary, this is what makes nature well ruled. But the political man seems to be correct about how political beings should not be ruled.

Oligarchy is now said to be the sovereignty in the regime of those who have substance (*ousia*). The change made is from those who have resources (*euporoi*), which can also mean those who have answers. If the regime is also a soul, the possessions, or substance, of a soul are its opinions. In the third revision, democracy is said to be "in opposition," presumably to oligarchy, when those who do not possess a multitude of substance, but are "at a loss" (*aporoi*), are sovereign. The change is from rule for the benefit of those who are at a loss. Why the original formulation might not be a deviation is perhaps explained by the following consideration. The present passage includes one of the three mentions of philosophy in Book III, and in this passage Aristotle speaks three times of *aporiai*—"difficulties raised," "impasses in argument," "being at a loss in speech." If being at a loss is the mark of a philosopher, then the sovereignty of those who have resources— meaning solutions, as in the first definition of oligarchy—is no deviation. The democrat lacks a multitude of substance as well as solutions; he has no property. Or, the democratic soul has no opinions, not even the opinion that philosophy is the greatest good for man. But, of course, oligarchy as the sovereignty of men with property and unexamined opinions is a deviation. Democracy differs from oligarchy in being the sovereignty of those who lack property and do not know how to go about acquiring it. Democrats have too few opinions instead of too many, and they are completely "unarmed."

When the philosopher generalizes from his soul, he finds that it is a deviation from the right order for human beings to be made one like the rest of nature (tyranny), or for the soul to be surfeited with its opinions (oligarchy), or for it to have no opinion about how to acquire the nourishment it craves (democracy). All the deviations are deviations from the souls that philosophize. It is not clear that the good political man had in his mind this understanding of a right regime, instead of the rule of wealthy, warlike freemen. Nor is it clear to us that the political community can become one, that a political "one" differs from a natural "one," that there is anything besides opinion, and that the alternative to opinion is not skepticism. Aristotle reveals the presuppositions of his science to us, but he has yet to demonstrate their reasonableness.

Aristotle says there is some difficulty even with this division. But there were in fact two divisions; and there are two difficulties, one with each division. If the political man and the philosopher speak of the "whats" of regimes, immediately preceding was a numerical division of regimes. The first objection is that the division does not seem noble. Two possibilities are offered to make the point clear. What if many who have resources should be sovereign in the city, yet it is a democracy whenever the multitude is sovereign? In other words, why is the sovereignty of a multitude called a democracy regardless of the quality of the multitude? Classification by number does not tell us as much as we need to know. Second, what if somehow those at a loss, though few, should be superior or stronger than the wealthy and therefore be sovereign in the regime, and yet assert that the sovereignty of a few is an oligarchy? Again, the criticism is directed to those who speak of multitudes in terms of their quantities, not their qualities. The classification of multitudes by their quantities, as by a mathematician, is not said to be incorrect but only perhaps ignoble. Perhaps noble regimes are not right according to nature, and perhaps political men require them nonetheless.

If the first difficulty is with the assertions of the mathematicians, the second is how to speak aloud, or how to speak in the agora (*prosagoreō*), about the regimes. The political man also distinguishes between few and many, classing himself as one of few. He, too, associates goodness with fewness and incomplete virtue with manyness. He may be correct in assuming that these qualities are usually found in multitudes of their respective sizes. But no more than the mathematician can he speak intelligibly about the exceptions. Whatever our expectations of human multitudes, surely there are some manys that would have all the "answers" that nonhuman beings would need in order to be what they should be. And is it not possible that the behavior of some few who are at a loss, who have no answers but always seek them, is very different from that of most men, who have no answers but do not seek them? In other words, can one distinguish philosophers from lawless democratic citizens? If so, how does one speak of them, and how does one make clear the basis of the distinction? Is there not some way to speak intelligibly about "nonhuman" multitudes, men who live in cities and have opinions, and philosophic souls all at the same time?

This Aristotle attempts to do in his summary of what the argument "looks like it makes clear." Multitudes are properly defined by their "whats," not their numbers. Quantity is accidental; quality, essential. The reason that political men speak so facilely of "few" and "many" is that it is virtually always the case that the wealthy are few and the poor are many; one never finds the hypothetical case of there being many wealthy and few poor. Thus, the political man's understanding is more or less correct, and his mistaking accident for essence does not lead to incorrect political opinions. The mathematician's understanding, that the essence of a multitude is its number, looks incorrect.

Similarly, if the reader mistakes the appearance of the argument for its reality, he will not reach generally unsound political conclusions. He will surmise that democracy and oligarchy differ not in the size of the multitude that rules, but in the first principle according to which the multitude rules. But what an argument "looks like" is also its accidental, not essential, quality, and we must understand what the argument is. If, as we have suggested, *euporia* and *aporia* mean having answers and raising difficulties as well as having *obols* and not having *obols*, then it is correct to say that the men who have answers, wise men, are few indeed. That nonhuman beings have all the resources or answers they need to be what they are, and that only some few men think of themselves as being at a loss for what they need are both more than mere hypothetical possibilities. The argument can look as it does only if Aristotle maintains silence about nonhuman beings and the few human beings who philosophize. Aristotle makes and repeats a statement that the resourceful happen to be few and those at a loss, many everywhere; but in the repetition he does not say "everywhere." For it is reasonable to suppose that somewhere, though not in politics proper, those with resources are many and those at a loss are few. The political *logos* that "looks like" a *logos* is an incomplete *logos*.

It may still be an image of the truth, however. The difference between democracy and oligarchy, Aristotle says, is a difference between poverty and wealth (*ploutos*). Democracy is poverty, not having *obols*, not having answers, not having opinions. But where either many or few rule either for the sake of or by virtue of wealth, this is an oligarchy. To the extent that the philosopher makes wealth, understood as wisdom, his first principle, he is as much an oligarch as any other man. To the extent that knowing the necessity of philosophy constitutes his wisdom, he is one of the few with answers to whom Aristotle refers at the end of this passage.[13] To the extent that he remains partially ignorant, he is one of the all who are said to partake of freedom. The truth in the oligarch's claim to rule by virtue of his wealth is that man has needs of various sorts, for which he must provide by his own efforts. Wealth is therefore the end, or the first principle. The error in the oligarch's claim is that money might not be the only "wealth" a man needs.

Aristotle is less critical of the oligarch than we might expect. But if the oligarch's only opponent in the city is a democrat, then the oligarch might have the best claim to rule. The claim of the poor, when they dispute for a share in rule, is that the first principle of the city is freedom and that all men, including themselves, partake in freedom. Their end may be wealth as much as it is the rich man's, but one does not fare well by arguing that he needs to rule in order to get his hand in the public till. Rather, one emphasizes what he understands to be an attribute of his humanity: his freedom. The difficulty in the democrat's claim is that even if being a free man were the proper title to rule, "partaking" in freedom is hardly being a free man. Indeed, the democrat is not even as free from his bodily necessities as is the wealthy oligarch. The city may therefore deem oligarchs who contribute wealth to the public till to be freer than democrats. Furthermore, it is not clear that being free is more desirable than being wise. The democratic citizen's boast about his freedom is a distorted image of the philosopher's shame of his ignorance. Nevertheless, as we shall see, freedom, not wealth, is the principle according to which men both partake and share in the bringing together (1279a31).

The assertions of the mathematicians must be silenced if those assertions are truly ignoble and man needs to live nobly. But when the political man attempts to speak of the "whats" of the regimes, he does so only more or less adequately. With Aristotle's clarifications, it becomes clear that he associates being with doing good and with having substance, or wealth. Whatever his professions about concern for the common good, the first principle by which he orders his life is the desire for wealth. The inconsistency might be remedied if he could be taught about some wealth that is essentially common or sharable. The oligarch distinguishes himself from the poor without knowing what wealth is. He identifies himself as a man of the few, and to the few he opposes all multitudes, regardless of their size and quality. Therefore, he would not be at home in a democracy. He is a man who needs to learn not only what kind of wealth is worthy of being desired, but also how to live among democrats while maintaining one's distinctiveness. He will be publicly criticized by Aristotle as a lover of lucre, and shown that the city must be democratic. But he will also be taught about noble friendships that are possible for virtuous men and superior to the city's justice.[14] His democratic opponent will be taught that the free man is the wealthy and virtuous man, or the noble man. Aristotle seems to take the side of political men against natural philosophers, and the side of oligarchs against democratic citizens; but in doing so, does he bring to light or obscure the truth about all things?

3. Ignoble Division (1280a7–25)

If neither mathematicians nor political men can say all that should or must be said about the regimes, why do they speak so authoritatively? If they are virtue, then the democratic philosopher fails to speak about the "just" according to which body and intellect can be spoken of as one.

4. The Oligarchic Logos (1280a25–1281a10)

The political man who distinguished the regimes listed as the right regimes the monarch who has a fond regard for the community, the rule of the wealthy for the community's good, and the political activity of a warlike multitude for the community's benefit. He objected to the rule of anyone for their private benefit. One might call this man a public-spirited oligarch. He respects men who acquire successfully, but he does not admire men who acquire at the expense of fellow citizens, especially at the expense of their freedom. It has seemed that this man's most formidable opponent in the city has been the democrat, who believes it just that all free-born citizens share in rule. But is he? Aristotle's definition of tyranny was the exercise of skilled mastery, the science of ruling all natural beings, over the political community. The natural philosopher who asserts that political beings are ruled like natural beings, without freedom, is no less an opponent of our oligarch than is the democratic citizen. Our oligarch, despite his preoccupation with acquisition, still considers himself a free and good man. He must therefore be purged of his love of wealth, if that is not beneficial, without destroying his love of freedom and manly virtue, if that is beneficial. And simultaneously, the philosopher, a lover of another kind of wealth, must have a lesson about acquisitiveness.

What follows is the apparent defeat of the oligarchic *logos*, which is said to have "bodily strength."[24] The emphatically antioligarchic tone of the argument is, although a reflection of the true argument, a tone adapted to the political man to be educated. The language of contracts and alliances is designed to attract the attention of and be intelligible to wealthy and warlike men. The oligarch is taught that there is a limit to acquisition; that the end is living well, happily or nobly; and that this life may or may not be accompanied by material abundance. But what follows is also a *logos* for the philosopher about the proper respect for "bodily strength."

The argument favoring oligarchy is that the city exists for the sake of acquisition or possession. One can infer from Aristotle's presentation that the argument is attacked and a contrary hypothesis defended by an apparent refutation of three premises. These are that the city exists (1) for the sake of life only, (2) for the sake of an alliance to avoid injustices, and (3) for the sake of exchange and the use of one another. In fact, however, these seem to be the only reasons for the sake of which cities do exist. Furthermore, these are the premises not only of the poor, the warlike, and the wealthy, but of the philosopher as well. The argument that the city is anything more than a military-industrial complex is indeed most difficult to make. To make it, Aristotle restates his hypothesis about man's citizenship, or the first principle of that hypothesis: The city exists not for life only, but more for the good life.

With respect to the second and third premises, Aristotle does not state the corresponding "but mores." Presumably, what one might want the city to exist for, more than an alliance for the sake of not having injustices done to oneself, is either that it make all men just or, in the secret thoughts of some men, that it allow them to do injustice without suffering retribution.[25] What one would want more than that men make use of one another is that men be self-sufficient. Stating these "but mores" is unnecessary if living the good life means being just and being self-sufficient. Stating them is imprudent if one cannot demonstrate that living the good life means being perfectly just or unjust and self-sufficient, for then one admits that even the city that exists more for the good life cannot satisfy all of man's aspirations. It may be the case that being perfectly just or unjust and being self-sufficient have nothing to do with living the good life or with living in cities, but this admission will not make living the good life in cities seem an attractive life. What is most difficult is to argue that men should be just in the sense of having all the virtues that the law commands, precisely because justice seems to be virtue for the good of others, not for oneself.[26] At the conclusion of this passage it is said that the end of the city is the good or the self-sufficient life; nothing is said about justice. In a passage framed by speeches about justice, Aristotle gives a speech that omits a praise of justice.[27] The men addressed, political men and philosophers, are men interested in their own good, not the just, and they think, perhaps reasonably, that justice is not the greatest good for men.

As we shall see, however, they also err in thinking that the good for men is "possessed" by men. The premise of the oligarchic argument is that acquisition, or possession, is the city's end, and, therefore, that men who have acquired ought to partake in the city to a degree proportionate to the amount that they have acquired. If the end were possession, the oligarchic argument would be strong, because "it would not be just for someone bringing in one *mina* to partake equally in 100 *minae* with someone giving all the rest, whether of the things from the beginning or those coming after." The contributor of one *mina* reminds us of the first principle or cause of being.

In the case of political beings, we suggested, the cause of their being might be late rather than prior in time, hence "coming after." The oligarchic *logos* has bodily strength because it is held by many men, and because it is true with respect to beings who possess their being in completion. But Aristotle will argue that in the case of human beings, the one *mina* that completes the whole is the good at which men aim, but which they never possess; and that the very desire for that one *mina* is the cause of men's being just. He will thereby show that the oligarchic *logos* lacks strength in speech. In so doing, he will also show, however, that present cities are not in accordance with nature as men usually understand it, that is, bodies. If Aristotle wishes to assert that man is by nature political, then he will have to offer an explanation of how man's cities can still be said to be according to nature. The contributor of that one *mina* must *be* nature.

Aristotle does not deny that man begins with a paltry amount. Whatever wealth he acquires is the result of his own efforts; whatever is good or sweet enough to cause men to cling to life is almost completely the result of their own making.[28] But what is the end of man's making, the first principle that either preordains his doing and being or inspires his hopes? Man's needs and desires seem limitless. But one can reasonably argue that man's possessions are meaningful to him only if they are useful to him, and what is useful is for the sake of what is or seems good for him. Not only is what is good for man the limit to his acquisition, but the good provides a principle of order for what is desired and acquired. Every man must accept this argument; his activities presuppose it. The first sentences of both the *Ethics* and the *Politics* reflect this human necessity: All of man's works are intelligible as a whole only if they are understood to be for the sake of some good.[29] Man's having many things or knowing many things is of no profit to him unless he knows that for the sake of which they are good or useful.

Aristotle indicates that this reasoning applies to democrats as well as oligarchs. Democrats and philosophers try to make partaking in freedom their first principle, and they do so because they understand freedom to be that which distinguishes a citizen or an excellent man from a noncitizen or a nonhuman being. But is not the distinctive human freedom to live happily or to live a choiceworthy life, as we suppose neither slaves nor animals do? The completion of man's whole, his good, is the happy life or the life according to choice—that is, the life a man would reasonably choose if he had full awareness. Choice requires both desire and a knowledge of the end and the means to it; only the prudent man could choose well.[30] The philosopher, as a man, must also give some thought to his humanity. Both oligarchy and democracy, then, point to the necessity not of philosophic wisdom, but of prudence, human wisdom. From the point of view of man as man, unlimited acquisition and undefined freedom are unintelligible.

Only the belief that the whole or its first principle is knowable by man and useful to him can make the life devoted to the acquisition of knowledge the good life for a man. Yet the philosopher as philosopher rests content with no belief, not even this one. That the city exists more for the sake of the good life than for mere life is only a hypothesis for Aristotle. In order to justify to himself and others his activity, the philosopher must confirm that his way of life is useful and have others deem it good, even as he understands his living the good life, doing the work of a good man, as being for the sake of the complete life. While the philosopher questions the good, he must hold that good and speak of it to political men. He must be a political scientist and make assertions about happiness and nobility.

Why the philosopher should be concerned about the other men who live in cities, and show this concern by teaching about justice and defending moral virtue, is a problem. Any use he makes of other men, any benefits he gains, seem to come from exercising and examining other men like himself.[31] Yet we have just supposed that some men may deem the philosopher's way of life good. Insofar as he desires companions and offspring in order to reproduce his kind, the philosopher must make himself attractive. He needs students, so he must take care that the best men think his way of life worthy of emulation. Furthermore, the philosopher has a body that must be protected and nourished by someone else's labors. The philosopher lives in a city and benefits from it, even if he does not wish to take politics seriously. Indeed, the truth that the philosopher lives off the city and steals its juiciest lambs is not denied or obviated by Aristotle's attempt to differentiate himself from the sophist Lycophron, whose name means "wolf-minded." The philosopher's preying upon the city is justified by his demonstrating that he pays for his lambs or returns them unharmed. Hence his teaching citizens about justice, his making philosophy politic, and his moderating grasping men.

There is, then, reason for the philosopher to take the city's justice seriously. If his original theft is unjust, he cannot do injustice without retribution. Perhaps it is useful at this point to recount the first discussion of the citizen. The citizen simply was distinguished from metics and slaves who also shared in making their homes in some place, and who partook of the just things in such a way that they could undergo trials and be brought to law. This privilege was said to belong to those who share in contracts and to metics as well as to citizens. The philosopher who lives as a metic, teaching political science, is also free to defend himself, unsuccessfully, for impiety and corrupting the young. Philosophers are not well received by the law-abiding many in the cities, and perhaps rightly so; their good names, if not their very lives, are in need of defense in the city's courts. The philosopher seems unjust because he calls into question the city's legally ordained beliefs about what is good and just. Because the city determines the just and the unjust, it is not sufficient to win a few friends. The philosopher's apparent need of a guard explains his cultivation of manly political men; it explains his rhetoric defending the possibility and superiority of the rule of morally virtuous men in an aristocracy. But these men are few, and the fact that the rest of the city may sit in judgment necessitates that the philosopher no longer be understood as unjust. Socrates lacked thirty votes for acquittal.

Aristotle's point is not limited to any particular city. Even if existing city boundaries were destroyed, any city would necessarily reconstitute the boundaries within which human life is made possible. There is no city for the philosopher to escape to, not even any barbarian nation. Carthage and Etruria, Aristotle says, would have conventions about what can be imported (*eisagogimoi*),[32] encounters concerning not being unjust, and statutes about alliances. Philosophers with mortal bodies cannot avoid taking the city's laws and justice seriously. Whether they take justice seriously for any other reason is left open for the moment. Curiously, the very defense of the philosopher before the city will be a demonstration of his ability to justify the city's laws.

Indeed, precisely why cities do need laws and legal justice has not been established. As Aristotle has indicated, men understand the city to be an association of men for the mutual service of the needs and desires, especially the bodily needs, of each man. Aristotle does not deny that this is correct, but neither will he assert that it is correct, as does the sophist Lycophron. In fact, Aristotle does not show that the function of the city is to secure the good life rather than mere life, nor does he show that it is not an alliance against other cities and a system of exchanges and mutual uses. What he does deny is that the city can be anything thus understood. The political, as distinct from the economic, cannot be made intelligible in terms of an association of bodies only. Justice as anything other than free-market price cannot be defended, and no particular configuration of buyers and sellers can be defended as natural or necessary. It is difficult to imagine any bodily need or desire that cannot be filled as well by an Etruscan or a Carthaginian as by an Athenian. The political beginning seems to be one's own good, yet what good citizens share is immanifest. The city is nothing other than its laws and conventions, but these laws are necessary only to keep the military-industrial complex working well. Hence, the city is still nothing.

Yet Aristotle also speaks of good laws, and in doing so he indicates both how the city might be said to be something and how the philosopher and the city might be reconciled. He proposes that the conventions and laws making citizens of one city those who were originally citizens of the two great commercial empires, Carthage and Etruria, would be inadequate for the following reasons: They do not have common rules or offices, they do not think about "making something of one another," and they do not think about rectifying each other's injustice and other wretchedness. Their city would not be a whole because they do not make their first principle man's possible perfection, the principle of Aristotle's hypothesis by which man is a citizen, and because they do not teach that justice means the completion of a man's virtue and is therefore good for a man. The city *is* when it takes for its principle the citizenship of whole human beings and demonstrates that the city's justice is necessary to this end. Only if the city is shown to be in the service of the good life, understood as philosophy or as philosophy and moral virtue, can it be defended to its citizens.

Yet even for the city to function well as a military-industrial complex, a minimum of virtue is necessary. Citizens must at least not do injustices to one another. The political man seems to understand virtue as the ability to acquire, although not from his fellow citizens if possible. Therefore, he is now advised to examine "political virtue and vice" from different points of view (*diaskopeō*). Political beings are characterized both by an ability to acquire and the need to form a community; the excellence of which the oligarch speaks, acquisitiveness, seems to prevent men from constituting a true community. Ultimately, a concern for acquisition for oneself conflicts with the opinion that the justice which requires a limitation on acquisitiveness can be good.

But when the political rule was first introduced (1277b7), those under it were likened to a household of man and woman. The virtues and works of each part differed; and womanishness, we suggested, was connected to philosophy. Its consequence was apparent unmanliness, an unwillingness to acquire politically because of a greater craving for wisdom. Our present point is that half of what makes man political is his ability to commune in speech, for political virtue is skill in speech as well as skill on the battlefield. As the philosopher must care enough about the safety of his body, so the political man must broaden his understanding of what is political. The connection between the two meanings of political virtue, acquisition and speech, will be made through good law, for law at its best combines force with reason. Force and reason are also combined in self-compulsion, that is, in the moral virtue that befits free beings with both bodies and intellects. Aristotle says that in the city truly so named, not the city in speech, one must care about virtue. The parts of political virtue, military and philosophic, combined in a form that is a bit of both yet neither and more, is the virtue of a Solon or a Lycurgus, a Pericles or a Brasidas.[33] The good law that makes the city's virtue coextensive with a man's virtue as far as possible is the most sovereign thing about which citizens and philosophic men fail to speak. Good law embodies the statesman's prudence. The political man who seeks a standard for justice, who "worries about good law," is about to become a legislator, and in formulating the speeches that comprise the law, he will be made to examine political virtue from another point of view. By making this man a legislator—that is, a political scientist—one moderates or at least modifies his political acquisitiveness and uses him to teach virtue to others.

Law or virtue is necessary precisely because the city is an alliance of bodies serving each other and defending themselves. Each man's body is essentially private, and there is nothing in the city to overcome the natural prior concern of each man for his own needs and desires. Thus, the physical propinquity of bodies does not make a city. Not even Socrates' City of Pigs, with its carpenter, its farmer, and its shoemaker, an association of artisans meeting the basic needs of all bodies, would be a city.[34] Mutual needs cannot be the basis of a city as a whole, for all needs seem to be private. To repeat, Aristotle does not deny that the city originates in these needs and serves them, but they cannot be said to be that for the sake of which the city exists, for they do not point to the necessity of the political as distinguished from the economic. Nor would the mere addition of the good households, which remain somewhat separate from the city, make the city a whole, for there is no common end. Hippodamus's city of ten thousand, in which philosophy in the service of the city's prosperity is lawfully rewarded, would not be a city.[35] Philosophers *might* survive among other men, but there will be no community that embodies man's humanity.

Virtue or justice is necessary, then, to overcome the natural preference of each man for what is useful to himself, especially if he deems unsharable wealth most useful. If self-preference cannot be overcome by the praise of justice for its own sake, care for the public must be fostered by providing a benefit to each that could not otherwise be obtained, and this benefit must be made to seem more choiceworthy than all others. The city needs a first principle, an end of its own, which must be neither acquisition of riches nor wisdom. The city not only is *like*, but *is*, some put-together whole. It is a whole put together of political animals who are characterized by a concern for their own good, but also by some desire to constitute a community. A city is a whole if the city has as its end a common good that is the greatest good for each political being qua political being. A community is achieved "down" in the cities only when the concern for the good of each is overcome by a concern for what transcends each and is "possessed" by none. Aristotle speaks of funerals, brotherhoods, sacred rites, and the pastimes of living together. The first of these is to make it seem as if the city has cared for men throughout their complete lives, and the others to make it seem as if the city has been the guarantor of sufficiency in all facets of life. These institutions cannot be ends in themselves, however; they are for the sake of the city's being a whole. They might be sufficient to produce a semblance of virtue, for if the city did this for each man, it would be reasonable to care for it. But such things do not make the city intelligible as a whole. The conjoining of the city of Megarians, the temples (*megara*), and Corinth, the city reputed for its wealth, does not make the city a one, Aristotle says. The divine added to the economic does not result in the city's having an end in which the parts as parts might share. The true end is the good life, Aristotle *says*, and he *asserts* that it is the happy or noble life.

The reason why Aristotle must say one thing and assert another is as follows. What constitutes a city is a community in the good life for the sake of the complete and self-sufficient life. This community in the good life is said to be the work of friendship, and it is composed of the "households" that engage in speaking about the good. But if the good life is for the sake of the complete and self-sufficient life, it is not a complete or self-sufficient life itself. The philosopher is not complete in remaining unwise, and not self-sufficient in needing someone to care for the body in which his speechful soul is housed. The first problem might be solved by philosophic friendship; the villages, which are groups of households, are said to live the complete life.[36] This would issue in the greatest good for political beings, achieved by each but only in common. But this is an association of philosophic souls, and the philosopher's bodily insufficiency requires him to live in a city.

The city tries to overcome the incompleteness and insufficiency of its parts through the institutions that we might call "culture," in which the city has its own version of the good life. The city looks up toward what seems to transcend each man, the divine things, and its citizens associate in a community that offers a pleasure no man could have without there being a city. But in order that the city's end be *the* end, not merely necessary to these supra- and subpolitical ends, the city's end must be specifically political. The political community is for the sake of noble deeds, not for culture, and the end of a political man is living nobly by doing nobly. Odysseus and Diomedes have a friendship for the sake of doing noble deeds;[37] they could not live noble lives without each other's help and without the city, yet each lives a noble life and the city needs their nobility. The city's defense of the public over the private is intelligible as a reflection of philosophic friendship, though the reflection differs from the reality. Aristotle will later speak of a beautiful *painting*; the city's being an image is intelligible if one takes into account men's bodies.

Thus Aristotle's "just" speech before the city is a defense of the city to its citizens. In it there is no defense of the city's justice, but neither is there an assertion that the philosopher is the most just man. Rather, it is a defense of the virtue and nobility of which political men are capable.[38] The offspring of the "intermarriage" of philosophy and politics is the teaching of virtue.

Aristotle has not refuted the three arguments he proposed to defeat in this section: (1) that the city exists for life only, (2) that it is an alliance for the sake of not being done an injustice by anyone, and (3) that it is for exchanges and the use of one another. These were the arguments of ignoble political men and ignoble philosophers. Instead, Aristotle has replaced them with even stiffer demands upon political men, and then has shown that even meeting these demands is not quite enough. He claims that he has made apparent that there is no city if there is a community in place, if men are merely not unjust to one another, and if the end is giving shares. Thus, he has made men care about others besides themselves, the gods and clansmen who constitute a community which is not simply physical; he has made men think about being just rather than merely avoiding injustice; he has made them think about giving rather than taking. Aristotle raises the standard for political justice to friendship,[39] and then defends what is obviously an inadequate political substitute for true friendship, but which nonetheless must be made to seem adequate to political men. The city requires that men think of living not among friends but among clansmen, that sacrifice to the gods replace the ability to be perfectly just, and that the pastimes of living together replace philosophizing and sharing together. What is even more problematic, the city's necessity seems to require that its opinions about the good or noble life not be examined to reveal their inadequacy, whereas philosophy, of which the good city is an image, is precisely this examination of opinions about the good. The incompleteness of philosophy, as well as its weakness, makes impossible a bald assertion that only in philosophizing are the good, the just, and the self-sufficient lives one. The city's *end* is the good life, a life that cannot be lived in the city proper. The city *is* when it makes human perfection a possibility.

The oligarchic *logos* is the *logos* of political beings, the few among many beings. That *logos*, Aristotle tells us at the beginning of this passage, *seems* to have bodily strength and supposes that acquisition or possession is the end. Thus stated, the argument must be defeated precisely because it does not describe political beings, for the distinction between political beings and others does not lie either in their bodies or in what they possess. In criticizing the oligarchic understanding, Aristotle calls our attention to the contributor of one *mina*, either at the beginning or later. Man's "being" may well be more the end he seeks or the work he does in seeking that end than what he presently is. Perhaps man's being cannot be understood without appreciating that one *mina* which is man's end. The man who wants to maintain the distinctiveness of human beings wants to show that man is naturally political because the parts of human being come together to comprise the whole of human being in a way that the other beings, who do not appear to come together of their own volition, do not. Furthermore, if man is naturally political, then political being is a kind of being. The political man who attempts to make the city intelligible as the military-industrial that serves the physical well-being of each citizen is unable to explain how man is political. Only the good as an end makes man's communities intelligible; political being cannot be explained as simply being for the sake of being what it is, existing for mere life. What is yet unclear is precisely why and how man's cities, rather than his other associations, contribute to this end.

The oligarchic *logos*, with its bodily strength, also purports to explain how bodies, nonhuman as well as human, constitute a city. In this passage, Aristotle begins by speaking of beings coming together and associating; the concluding arguments make reference only to beings who associate. Near the end, Aristotle mentions a multitude of ten thousand that does not become a city because each does not associate, and he speaks of some "each" that do not form a city because each remains the same having come together as when separate. The multitude of ten thousand represents, both in the discussion of Hippodamus and in the *Metaphysics*,[40] forms understood numerically, as a mathematician understands the numbers with which he works to be more real than the things they are counts of. Aristotle attacks the understanding that all of being can be explained through mathematics in both those discussions and, as we have argued, in Book III of the *Politics*. The difficulty he finds here is that not even by abstracting from the "for whom," that is, by considering the "households" or pure integers as separate, can it be explained how numbers can be said to form a community. In the Aristotelian conception, each number stands for a specific multitude of specific things seen and counted.[41] Even if what is counted is disregarded, numbers one that has a connotation of cosmic necessity, as if he sought an answer to Zeus. The next three candidates discussed are discussed as a set, for they are said to be no more just than one another. Furthermore, the discussion of these three is prefaced with "again" or "on the contrary" (*palin*), which we understand to be a way by which Aristotle often signifies his switch from a consideration of political to natural things, or vice versa.[45] In other words, Aristotle's response to the democratic justice sanctioned by Zeus is an attempt to discern what is by nature just. After concluding that all of these alternatives appear to be base and unjust, he speaks of the rule as well as the sovereignty of the respectable and serious, as if to suggest that human dignity and reason would have to serve as the first principle and standard for justice because there seems to be none other.

We consider the candidates in greater detail: The first in the original list was the "multitude," and this the political man apparently understands to mean the poor, for someone says, "Well, if the poor, because they are a majority, divide up the things of the wealthy, is this not unjust?" The answer to this is emphatic: "No, by Zeus, for it seemed just to the sovereign." We have learned thus far that the city ought to sacrifice to some god, and that democratic citizens believe they are just; but what kind of a Zeus sanctions the expropriation of the property of fellow citizens? We now see that if "culture" is necessary to complete the city, not all cultures make cities wholes; a Zeus who sanctions such expropriations does little to reconcile the rich and the poor. But if the democrat is correct in his opinion of what is just according to Zeus, then the oligarch must learn a thing or two about justice and friendship. Indeed, equality of property seems just to many people who have never professed a high regard for Zeus.

When citizens support their opinions with a "By Zeus," what they mean to say is that their understanding of justice is universally correct. The democrat's Zeus is the equivalent of the scientist's "nature." Therefore, in order to defend or challenge any particular understanding of justice, one would have to speak of what is right by nature. But to what nature does one look? Aristotle's second, third, and fourth candidates for sovereignty, we suggest, represent alternative formulations of what nonhuman nature is. The conclusion is that they are all equally just or unjust; nature is indifferent to justice. If, when all are taken into account, the things of the few are distributed to the majority, this law *is not of the sort to be just,* that is, neither just or unjust, nor capable of being either. But does not Aristotle teach that the forms, the few, are in matter the many beings? And the deeds of the tyrant were all necessarily just. Perhaps the whole was brought into being, or is ruled by a tyrant. Do not many people learn that the world was created when one

very excellent and very strong being made a cosmos out of chaos? And if the
few were said to rule, they would do what the multitude does and abstract
from their possessions. But have not some notable men, the Pythagoreans
and Platonists, taught that the few forms were the causes of being? It is apparent, Aristotle says, that these alternatives are all base and unjust. But the
truer point seems to be that they are neither more nor less just than one another, because they are not of the sort to be just. All these explanations could
describe a nature that is well ruled. The forms are in matter; if one abstracts
from body and its multiplicity, the few forms can be understood as responsible for the many in each class of things being what they are, and all things
are what they are according to the design of one creator or ruler.

Yet if one should look to nonhuman nature as we now do in order to find
an argument for how a human city should be ordered, it is far more than
"apparent" that all these things are base and unjust. The distribution of the
goods of the few by the poor will indeed destroy a city of democrats and
oligarchs, and therefore it is unjust; for if justice is the virtue that pertains
to the city, Aristotle says, and a virtue cannot be understood as something
that destroys its possessor, then this democratic deed cannot be just, no
matter what Zeus says. The poor, whatever they say, act as they do because
they are strong and able to get away with being unjust. Neither the nature
nor the cause of their deed differentiates them from one tyrant who acts for
his private good. We do not therefore conclude that the tyranny of one is
preferable to the tyranny of many, however. Nor, for the same reason, is an
oligarchy of wealthy men who take the fruits of their labors from the poor
any more just. It seems that all the regimes that are right by nature are deviations according to politics.

Aristotle seems to have been contending that human beings are as much
a part of nature as is anything else. What seemed to differentiate the political
community from the rest of nature was its ability to associate in thought,
even if this were done only imperfectly and never visibly. Thus, two more
candidates for sovereignty are considered: the respectable and the one most
serious, that is, men of good political judgment and the philosopher. Aristotle speaks of their rule as well as their sovereignty, because looking to
man's peculiar excellence as "nature" seems to require the acceptance of
the hypothesis by which men are citizens. To make the possible perfection
of man the first principle is as much an abstraction from nonhuman being
as it is an abstraction from human being to seek the first principle in the
cause of all bodies. It is as "oligarchic" as the first is "democratic," favoring
the few at the expense of the many instead of the many at the expense of
the few. It is necessary, Aristotle says, that all others be dishonored if they

are not honored in the political first principle. Is this an admission that the "one" to which Aristotle looks as a measure, the possibility of the wise soul, is no more an all-inclusive "one" than the one to which the mathematical physicist looks? Can either be the ground of a full account of being, rather than a "regime," a part?

The rule of the respectable or the one most serious would seem to be objectionable for other reasons, however, even if Aristotle could demonstrate to us that political being does comprehend all of being. Their rule is not said to be either unjust or base as the other alternatives are, but their rule dishonors many and causes peevishness. The men most worried about being honored are, we recall, such as the angry Achilles, whose anger will not be reasoned away, and who can be ruled only by what they hold honorable. Achilles, the man who shares in honors, was most truly said to be a citizen (1278a35–37), and Aristotle now makes a similar statement in his own name: We say that honors are the first principles. Achilles epitomizes the political man who is not a philosopher but who lives in political communities that might exist for the sake of noble deeds. In the last section Aristotle said that the economic community in which men "settle down" must make part of itself loyalties to the clan, worship of the divine, the pleasures of living together, and the doing of noble deeds—in sum, the part of man expressed in these activities. He now speaks of men's peevishness, worship of the divine, political and economic factions, unjust deeds, and competing for honors. He will soon record an oath, a vehement response to the democrat's "By Zeus," which is a noble oath, reflecting Aristotle's hypothesis about man's citizenship. What is authoritative in the city is what is honored, and what is most honorable is usually called divine by men, or is an imitation of what they believe is divine.[46] What is honorable must also be spelled out in laws that proclaim themselves to be just, for, as the democrat reveals, righteous indignation on behalf of "justice" belongs no less to the base than the noble. Indignant, angry men cannot be reasoned with; they can at best be tamed by being habituated to use the energy behind anger in the service of what they believe to be noble.

If men must be habituated, if things must come to be believed, then opinions about the just, the noble, and the good must remain relatively fixed.[47] But the respectable (reasonable) man corrects the just, and the serious man questions what the city holds to be good. If they are sovereign, their superiority to the law makes manifest the insufficiency of what men presently honor, and may lead them to hold nothing sacred. It does not seem that the reasonable ought to rule unless it can be explained how they will manage unreasonable men without maintaining the honorable and sacred as sacred, and without maintaining a distinction between noble and ignoble wrath.

Nor do we understand why reasonable men should rule if we do not know in the light of what the use of reason could be deemed reasonable. The seventh candidate for sovereignty is the law, which might be thought to be nobler than the sovereignty of any men or man because law lacks the passions that souls have. Law is what the reasonable and serious aim to be in order to distinguish themselves from the angry poor. "Someone" makes this assertion on behalf of law. Aristotle does not make it in his own name, but he does seem to object to it in his own name: The law will be favorable either to democracy or to oligarchy. What the law should be is no clearer than who should be sovereign or what should be the first principle. In this passage, Aristotle speaks of what we understand to be a law of nature, and this law is not of the sort to be just. If law seems noble because it is reasonable, we must still ask what reason reasons about, for some reasonings lead neither to noble politics nor to a proof that philosophy is beneficial to man in any way.[48] The someone who makes the assertion about law knows that reason is a fine thing, but he has not thought about the possibility that political beings have or need laws of their own.

Perhaps there are laws of human nature. We cannot presuppose their existence, but that there are such laws Aristotle will attempt to demonstrate to his and our satisfaction. He seems to have shown that if men need to live in economic communities, they need to live in cultures that turn anger into public spiritedness, and this is done by making something publicly honorable, which men then emulate. Evidently, Aristotle wants to argue that laws of human nature can be known by knowing whether there is something universally honorable to which all the various understandings or misunderstanding of honor are directed, and in the light of which each particular misunderstanding can be made intelligible.[49] For example, the oligarch honors wealth. Can it not be reasonably argued that the wealthiest man is not the man who has the most things, but the man who never lacks for "things" because his desires for them are few? The democrat honors freedom. Can it not be argued that the freest man is not he who has lawless desires, but he who freely chooses to live in an orderly, lawful way? The would-be statesman is a serious citizen, but perhaps one's private virtue is the only thing that can reasonably be taken seriously. Aristotle says that honors are the *archai* not only because what any society or any man makes honorable serves as the first principle, but because honors are the beginnings for an examination of the first principle that allows us to speak of a law befitting political beings.

the "painted by art," the praise of the many's ability to judge wholes as if they were "alls" is based on this understanding reported by Aristotle:

$$\frac{\text{serious man}}{\text{each of many}} = \frac{\text{scattered separate, collected in one}}{x}$$

The statement is left incomplete, through either delicacy or ignorance. A serious man, we may surmise, is a man who can become part of a one that is a whole; the scattered separate things, the forms. The serious man differs from each of the many, who are ones but not wholes. But from what do the scattered separate differ? Presumably the statement should be completed by the phrase "the scattered separate things that have not yet been collected into one." If each of the many things cannot be said to be a part of a natural whole, then the philosopher's attempt to speak of a whole through the forms cannot be said to be science instead of art, or finding instead of making. The philosopher's making of a whole corresponds to nothing necessary in nature, and his is not a "correct" judgment of wholes. His "one" or ordered whole cannot be defended as superior to the "all" that the many heap together when they judge. It seems that knowing the "scattered separated things" does not require or permit any necessary inferences about the nature of the whole. In the *Metaphysics*, Aristotle says:

> These thinkers came upon this doctrine of Ideas because they were convinced about the truth of the Heraclitean arguments which state that all sensible things are in a state of flux, so that if there is to be a science or knowledge of anything, there must exist apart from the sensible things some other natures which are permanent, for there can be no science of things which are in a state of flux.[57]

The Platonic theory fails to *prove* the possibility of a science of the whole. What is necessary is an argument about the one, not the few. The perhaps untrue abstraction from body required by the theory of separated forms seems to contribute nothing to this end; hence Aristotle's defense of the multitude.

Furthermore, the very teaching that the intelligible forms are being may lead to undesirable political interpretations. For this reason, the true ground on which Aristotle criticizes Plato is unclear. Aristotle too, later speaks of "abstracting" from body, although not of separated forms that are prior in being. At the same time, he speaks of the rule of the morally virtuous in cities not "for the sake of speech," whereas Plato teaches that philosophers must rule and that moral virtue is not a natural end for man. We have not yet considered a clause interjected into the comparison of serious men to collections of separated things. The serious differ from each of the many, exactly as "they assert that the noble do from the not noble and the painted by art do from the true things. . . ." The true things are each body, and these are not noble or beautiful.[58] Beauty in its proper sense seems to be an attribute of something with a body and of an ordered whole, like a painting or a virtuous man. If the true things are each body, putting together the parts of being is a making that corresponds to nothing that is; the noble, by which one makes a whole of human being and human cities, is not according to nature, but the work of an art. The artisan is more excellent than the artifact. The common-sense understanding that beauty and nobility belong to beings with bodies and to politics seems to be destroyed by the Platonic teaching, for according to that teaching, the intelligible forms *are* more than the things we see partaking in them. As Aristotle points out with irony, the forms must be more beautiful than painted, or visible, things.

If in this passage Aristotle means to identify the beautiful or noble (*kalon*) with the moral, then he seems to criticize the Platonic teaching for leading to the conclusion that there is no noble political solution on the level possible for political men. Philosophers would then be correct in not taking political men and what they call virtue seriously, and democrats and oligarchs would be correct in ignoring considerations of morality in their disputes. It might seem that the political multitude is in fact nothing more than a combination of the two multitudes, each of the many and the serious men. That is, the city will be composed of two kinds of multitudes with fundamentally different ends, without there being any real connection between the two.

This, we note, is essentially the solution attempted by modern political science. But is it really possible that the peculiar character of political beings, their spiritedness, can be explained away to us and to the men who exhibit it? What must be argued to us is that men need not be political after all, because their anger is or can be made to be simply subservient to some desire.[59] The alternative would be to make anger useful in two ways: to show how noble cities are superior to democracies, and to show how taking political being seriously as a kind of being allows one to offer a better explanation of the whole than does the materialism of Heraclitus or Hobbes and the separated forms of Plato.

Aristotle eventually will argue that political being is being. First, however, he must make a better case for his original point, which is that being lies in multitudes. To do this, he must argue that the philosopher can make as much sense of being as he could if the forms existed, and he must show that democracy can do the necessary work of a city as effectively, if not as beautifully, as can aristocracy. The first step in the argument would be to assert that a multitude can be understood as one as much as if it were one by partaking in an intelligible form. This point Aristotle makes in his statement that if it is possible for every *dēmos* and every multitude to differ in the way that the few serious do from the many, this is immanifest.[60] The few serious (men are not specified) become one in intellectual being. The *dēmos* that might become one is, we suggest, that curious multitude of intellects, the philosophers, whose becoming one would be immanifest. Similarly, in speaking of a multitude's being one, we mean that the many things seen are intelligible as many of some one same thing, although they are seen as many ones. Therefore, their being one is certainly immanifest in the sense of being not visible.

What is manifest is well stated in another "by Zeus": "Perhaps, by Zeus, it is manifest that it is impossible for some, for the same argument would fit beasts, although how do some differ from beasts?" We understand this "by Zeus" to be a response to the poor man's "by Zeus," a response given by Aristotle's political friend. What has been revealed to him by Zeus differs little from what Aristotle hopes to demonstrate, and from what "common sense" and good political sense dictate. What is manifest is that multitudes do not become one, as anyone can see, and that the demotic often act more like beasts than like serious or good men. What is manifest is true, and we can begin not by doubting our senses but by trusting them.[61] Does Aristotle oppose the Platonic teaching in order to protect the right opinion of the political man who needs Zeus, only to assure him that neither his senses nor his sense deceive? Aristotle can complete this man's education without questioning his beliefs by explaining to him how the very thing that differentiates men from beasts is the source of the immanifest unity of some multitudes. The nature according to which this man's oath is sworn is not inconsistent with a teaching about the soul of the serious man, which sets some men apart from the rest of nature. It is a beginning that might make possible a full account of being.

Multitudes of bodies can become one immanifestly, by being thought of as one; serious men become one by thinking the same thoughts. Political beings are problematic, however, not only in having bodies, but in having the assertiveness that makes them stand apart. In having anger, human beings seem to have a bit of bestiality. Hence Aristotle's second example of a political animal: the many-footed and many-handed monster that did not properly become one human being. Political multitudes require further examination. Aristotle says that the difficulty of what things the free and the multitude of citizens should be sovereign over might be solved in the same way as the first mentioned difficulty. The difficulty seems to be whether one can speak of the political—the realm in which man's freedom, as distinguished from his bodily necessity and his science—is manifest, as if it were nothing more than a combination of those other two realms.

Aristotle's language in the passage that follows is unusually ambiguous. One reason for his obscurity might be that it is as unclear that there are "free" men as that there are the separated intelligible forms represented by the "few good." But the necessity that men think of themselves as free may be all the greater if the multitudes cannot be shown to be an adequate substitute for free men. Even if their moral virtue cannot be shown to be according to nature instead of painted by art, it might be necessary that they understand their virtue as natural. And perhaps the philosopher profits from taking that understanding seriously.

Ambiguities notwithstanding, we offer the following interpretation. Aristotle distinguishes the multitude of citizens from free men by three characteristics: they are not wealthy, not reputed for virtue, and not a one.[62] The free from whom the multitude is distinguished are thus wealthy and/or reputed for virtue and/or one. If any men had all these attributes, they would be everything a man could be from almost every point of view. But the description of the multitude of citizens seems to fit the small multitude of philosophers, for they, no more than demotic citizens, are wealthy, reputed for virtue, or yet one. Hence our contention that free men are, unbeknownst to themselves, made to live together with philosophers as well as the demotic.[63] And, as if the philosopher had learned something from the political man, he is told that he must assert himself, claiming his share and profiting the city at the same time. Free men are taught that they must give in to the forceful demands of the poor, but the free man whose judgment seems sensible is not made to see that common sense must be protected from theoretical assertions that make the opinions of free men sound like nonsense. The city appears to be a mix of the demotic and of gentlemen who are wealthy, reputed for virtue, and in agreement. But the mix is made possible by the immanifest addition of the philosophic multitude.

With the utmost unclarity, Aristotle states that some "they" cannot partake in the highest offices or first principles because through injustice and imprudence they are necessarily unjust in some things and erring in others. Yet that "they" neither be given a share nor partake in rule is fearful, because *this* city, with many dishonored and poor, is full of enemies. Therefore it remains for "them" to deliberate and to partake in judging. Because of this, Solon and some other legislators appointed "them" to choose rulers (*archairesis*), and to make corrections of the rulers or call them to accounts.

dom because there was a science of politics, then there would be no need for the moral virtue of the free man. Whatever knowledge is required for choosing is likened to geometry or land surveying, and to piloting. That a man have a science of choice would require, first, that he be able to survey, accurately measure, and explain the whole as precisely as a mathematician could and, second, that he be able to guide and command men as well as a ship's pilot could. The philosopher seems to lack both abilities, and therefore, Aristotle says that according to this argument the multitude should not be made sovereign. The philosopher is an *idiōtēs*, an ignorant or a private man, a knower of neither the whole nor practical politics. We cannot conclude, however, that the man who does in fact choose chooses well.

Aristotle proposes a way around what he calls an "ignoble" argument. Yet again he admits that someone might only think the problem solved in this way. First, he says that a multitude not too reduced to slavery judges better or no worse than the knowers. The multitude not too reduced to slavery reminds us of philosophers who still concern themselves with the human things, which philosophers have been said to know well enough. But now Aristotle speaks of judging, not choosing. Second, concerning some things, the maker is neither the only nor the best judge, but as many as come to know by mental perception, without having the art, can judge. Here again, Aristotle speaks of judging, not choosing, and he speaks of a different kind of knowing than previously, not of the seeing for oneself that is needed by those who exercise the art and choose. The philosopher can judge well enough without political geometry, but he still does not make choices as a pilot would. Thus, there is no political substitute for the free man. Furthermore, in Aristotle's examples of users who judge, there is no mention of skilled users. We are therefore led to wonder whether Aristotle's "noble" response does not go too far. If there is no art of using or judging, how are we to differentiate the judgments of philosophers and their students from the judgments of the demotic multitude? It seems that if philosophers do not toot their flutes a bit more about a science of judging, then there will be nothing more noble than democracy. There will be no choosing well and no judging well—that is, no prudence and no science.

Hence, Aristotle says that another difficulty follows upon the first. It seems out of place that the base should be sovereign over greater things than are the respectable (reasonable). The greatest things are said to be making corrections and choosing the rulers, or first principles. In a democracy one finds a sovereign assembly; and those of little estimate, the demotic, partake in the assembly, in deliberating and in judging the just. The wealthy, courageous free men seem to hold the treasurership, the generalship, and "the greatest offices." But there is a difficulty, it seems, because the greatest sovereignty is said to lie in choosing the men who hold the greatest offices, not in holding them. Aristotle must explain how it is fitting that the base be sovereign over greater things than the respectable, and how those of little estimate and those of great estimate exclusively can both be said to exercise the greatest rule.

Perhaps what Aristotle means becomes clearer when we observe that, although the assembly is said to be authoritative, Aristotle also speaks of a *boulē*, a smaller council that served as a check on or at least an advisor to the assembly in democracies. Aristotle said that in some regimes, choosing the rulers and calling them to accounts is given to the *dēmoi*;[70] but he thereafter speaks of the *dēmos* (singular), whose domain is the assembly, and of deliberators, whose domain is the *boulē*. He also speaks of judges, who are unidentified, but who, we may presume, differ from the *dēmos* sovereign in the assembly. We have just suggested that Aristotle defines the political work par excellence as choosing, and the philosophic work as judging. If "the highest offices" are memberships in the council, then the respectable are the deliberators or choosers, who may be more responsible than they would first appear for staying in office. They have as much of a say as the many will allot to the council. The *dēmos* is sovereign in theory, but perhaps the political men are sovereign in practice.[71]

Another argument is made for this solution's being "perhaps right," that is, according to nature. One must speak not of each judge, each deliberator, and each assembly member as a ruler, but of the jury and the council and the *dēmos* as rulers. Each is a part of these rulers. The rulers are partial wholes, defined by their political works. Similarly, it is perhaps reasonable to speak of a nature that consists of many bodies, yet consists of distinct multitudes. To speak of the "few" is unnecessary because by beginning with the multitudes, one can come to what amounts to the same thing: a multitude of similar things, one in the similarity of its parts. But why define a multitude by its work, as Aristotle seems to do here? It seems most reasonable to do so if the work is the being of the thing or the cause of its being. This definition seems most appropriate to the deliberators in the council, for whom choosing an *archē* is identical with being an *archē*.[72] Man, especially, can be the cause of his own being. If this solution is "perhaps right," it is right according to political being, it seems. The inconsistency is that the sovereignty of all in the assembly seems to be just according to the "one" that is the measure of nonpolitical beings, the "one" that is an "each." The understanding on which man's claim to freedom rests is not the same as that on which justice rests.

Democracy is perhaps right if there is a kind of natural being who makes his own being. With what nature gives him, and without presupposing politics, man is a free being. But then the rule of all is just for men not because each man is a one like a nonhuman "each." Rather, it is just because it seems that if men are the causes of their very being, and therefore that what they are cannot be predetermined, then it is not possible to maintain a distinction between choosing and choosing well. Prudence cannot rule, because one cannot speak of imprudence.

It seemed that substantiating Aristotle's hypothesis about man's citizenship required taking man's freedom seriously.[73] Man, as distinguished from the other parts of nature, must have no necessary end; otherwise, he could not be said to be a citizen in a different way. If one wishes to speak of man as free, then one cannot speak of his partaking in two necessary realms, of body and intellect, as was earlier suggested. If man is the cause of his being, his virtue and his arts and sciences must be an expression of his freedom as well. Man must be spoken of as free not only because it is politic to do so, but because it may be true that there are no Platonic forms that are prior in being and which make science necessary. In any case, from the perspective of man's freedom we can justify not only man's politics, his self-rule, but the "goodness" of natural necessity and man's own excellence as well. Or can we?

The political man and the political philosopher who has taken his side against natural philosophy know that it is right for men to rule themselves instead of being ruled by a tyrant. But following this premise to its conclusion seems to have led to consequences that the good man and his philosophic defender might find distressing. For if one posits "nature" as bodily necessity in order to assert that man is free, then it seems necessary to conclude that of the choices of political men, none can be said to be better, and of the judgments of scientists, none can be said to be truer.

The political solution reached seems more or less adequate. Justice appears to mean a democracy, not as the democrat would have it, as the rule of the poor over the rich, but a democracy in which all the factions have their fair say. The rich or respectable are assured a place by allowing only them to run for high office, and by teaching them about the importance of the council. Whether the courts are packed with philosophers is less clear.[74] If they are so packed, then democracy, oligarchy, aristocracy, and philosophy are mixed. Yet they are mixed primarily on the democrat's terms: a one is an each, and the many form an all, not a whole. Thus, democratic justice for political beings seems to presuppose a fundamental equality in moral and intellectual capacities, and this is because one cannot defend a particular use of these capacities. That all men are equal in these capacities is called into question by the need to speak of the council and the separate juries, but there can be no public questioning until the ground for defending superior choices and judgments of free men has been established.[75]

The inadequacy of this democratic solution seems to be theoretical rather than practical. The democrat attempts to establish a justice for political beings, who are free from nature, as if they were like the nonhuman parts of nature.[76] In conclusion, Aristotle says that the first difficulty mentioned makes apparent nothing so much as that rightly laid laws must be sovereign, the ruler being sovereign only when the laws cannot speak accurately. The first difficulty was not only to train "doctors," choosers, and judges, but also how to maintain a distinction between judging well and simply judging. We suppose that science is man's articulation of the laws that are in nature, not his legislating for nature. We must know that science is possible. But, again, "the ancient grave difficulty" crops up: What is nature? The democrat tries to assume that nature is the bodies in it, but this leads to a justice that is base, not "serious." Not only is it ignoble, but we cannot confirm the correctness of the scientist's judgment. The alternative seems to be to assume that the "one" that comprises the whole of man's possible perfection, the serious man, is nature.

There must be a science of political beings, and that there is such a science must be demonstrated by beginning with man's freedom from nature, and showing that this freedom has a necessary meaning. For example, as we have already suggested, if nature is bodily necessity, then freedom means resisting the demands of one's own body with virtue, not indulging every desire; and it also means attempting to overcome the limitations that the passions impose upon one's judgment, not abandoning the attempt to judge well. But as we shall see, this political science justifies kingship and aristocracy as well as democracy. The freest man is a king who "does everything according to his own intention," yet rules "according to" something. The king is a political scientist who justifies both politics and science.

We seem to have been incorrect in speaking of political being as a species of natural being. What is natural seems to be only that man asserts himself against nature. His assertiveness, his making his own first principle according to which he then lives, is what makes him a political being. Philosophy, too, seems to be an assertion of man's freedom from nature, if nature is bodily necessity. In looking at man as a natural being, all we can see is his baseness; but we need to know about his nobility or freedom, his virtue and his science. If we study man as a political being, we can study both the meaning of freedom, that is, of being the cause of one's being, and we can examine the scientist to see how science might be pssible. In order to speak about being at all, we must speak of all beings not as natural beings but as political beings. Natural beings who are not free as are human beings will be understood as defective political beings. What we must assume for the present is that through the study of political being, we can discover a kind of being which is both like visible nature, in that one might formulate laws describing its workings, and unlike visible nature, in that one might speak of a justice that is according to it and which takes into account man's freedom.

Studying man as a scientist might study nature allows the philosopher to see that it is reasonable to take the assertions of the political man seriously. But to democratic and oligarchic citizens who dispute about rule, it is the man who takes politics and virtue seriously for their own sake who appears ridiculous, not themselves. In pursuing their private gains, "living as one wishes," it is they who seem to live according to nature. Yet they forget that if the exceptional man does not understand his own good as virtue, he will nonetheless take his own good, however understood, as seriously as they do theirs. If they do not take politics, as distinguished from economics, seriously, they do take justice for granted. In fact, however, the base need politics and political science as much as do noble men and philosophers. For, as it stands, they have demonstrated the justice of their democracy according to a law that is "not of the sort to be just," and according to which the deeds of a tyrant are necessarily just. Democracy, or the mixture of regimes that we now call liberal democracy, requires a demonstration that it is just according to a "one" or an "each" that is a free man.

THREE

1. Political Philosophy (1282b14–1284a3)

> The hypothesis of the democratic regime is freedom. They are in the habit of
> saying this, as if only in this regime did they partake of freedom, for they assert
> that this is an element of every democracy. One freedom is to be ruled and to
> rule in turn. And the demotic justice is to have equality according to number,
> but not worth. . . . But one [freedom] is to live as someone wishes. They assert
> that this is the work of freedom. . . . Therefore, this is the second boundary of
> democracy. (1317a40–1317b17)

The democrat, we have just learned, is a bit inconsistent. He attempts to
argue that all men must rule according to a just or an equal that resembles
the measure by which bodies in nature should be judged. Yet the freedom of
a man seems to mean precisely a rebellion against bodily nature. The democrat thus attempts to combine two different if not incompatible meanings
of freedom. Either a democracy of human beings must have a better defense
than this, or it has no defense.

Democracy needs a defense, it seems, against the exceptional political
man, the free man who takes the second democratic principle seriously. As
Aristotle describes them, democrats seem to take politics and ruling in turn
seriously only to ensure their freedom to take other things, especially their
neighbor's wealth, seriously. In this, Aristotle has explained, democrats do
not differ significantly from most men, but they seem to differ from the
men for whom living as they wish means living as political, not economic,
men. Some men take politics seriously, either to satisfy their desires to be
honored or perhaps to bring great benefits to the community. What this free
man must be taught for the sake of democracy and his own good is how to
take himself seriously as a man, and how being a man requires ruling and

being ruled in turn. Ultimately, taking one's humanity seriously does lead to taking all of one's capacities, including philosophy, seriously; but Aristotle attempts to show that taking philosophy seriously need not result either in the philosopher's estrangement from the city or in his prosecution by it. Taking humanity seriously means making the political manifest and, for the philosopher, philosophizing about political beings.

We looked at man as a natural being in order to determine whether or not man was naturally a political being. What we seem to have discovered was that precisely if man is a political being because he is free from the nature that is a totality of bodies, we can learn very little about how a free man might wish to live his life. Political communities seemed necessary, but we could not demonstrate, despite our original wish to do so, that the end of politics, and therefore the standard for a just law, must be virtue. To be a free man means to owe one's being to oneself, not to nature; to be political means to assert one's independence from bodily nature and to come together in a community of free men. But man can choose to live according to bodily necessity as well as to strive to live according to human perfection. Choosing is man's "work" because it is how he makes himself man, and what he chooses is the first principle by which he is ruled. An examination of "natural" man reveals that this choice is a possibility for man; it does not make manifest the content of his freedom. From an examination of nature, therefore, we cannot learn about what is just or noble or good for free men.

Thus, when the citizen tries to say what is by nature just in the light of what philosophers say nature is, he cannot speak of a justice befitting free men. When the free man must choose how to live his life, he has no guidance for his choice. When the philosopher tries to understand being as each thing, he cannot verify his judgment. Aristotle has a hypothesis, however, that man is a citizen in a way that the parts of nature do not seem to be. As a free man, he makes himself a man and a citizen, but he intends to be a part of a whole that encompasses the fullest human possibilities. Man's capacities are given, but his being is the actuality of which he is a cause.

The philosopher desires to examine political beings because he wishes to know about being, in its multiplicity and variety and in its unity, and the cause of being. He profits from examining political beings instead of other beings for several reasons. As a free being who makes his own being, man is an example of a cause of being. When we speak of political being as being we speak of it as we might wish to speak of being itself: Each man is a man. But we also distinguish kinds of men—wealthy, good, serious—and group them together as similar in kind. And we speak of "man," as if we had some dim recognition that humanity, for all its various manifestations, is some one same thing or is judged against some one standard. Thus we speak of human being as each thing, as having kinds (regimes), and as one. When we examine a city of men, we find being in its multiplicity, variety, and unity. When we consider what makes a city a whole, we know what a whole might be like, and therefore whether nature can be understood as a whole, not an "all." And, finally, we might be able to call our judgment science if by examining the judge we can determine how his judgments can be said to be according to something necessary.

Hence Aristotle's assertion: "Since in all the sciences and arts the end is good, and the greatest and most final is (the end) of the most sovereign of all, the political capacity is this same thing, and the just is the political good, and this is the benefit (bringing together) in common" (1282b15–17). The just must mean not the measure of nonhuman bodies, but the measure that enables men to judge the comparable values of the things he deems good for him. This just is itself the good for man as man. But it should also be the measure by which we can bring all things together, and therefore the science of justice thus understood is of benefit to the philosopher. As we shall see, this just which is the political good and the one common thing into which all are brought together is the first principle of Aristotle's hypothesis about man's perfection. This just will bring together man's two excellences, his politics and philosophy, justifying the one before the other. The sciences and arts will be made defensible in human terms, for they are good. And politics will be shown as worthy of the philosopher's serious attention.

Aristotle's political science requires what we might call "mathematical ethics" and "ethical mathematics." The premise upon which the benefit in common is effected is stated as follows: "The just seems to all to be some equality and surely up to some point they agree with the arguments according to philosophy in which the ethical things are defined. The just is something for someone, and they assert that it must be the equal for equals. But equality in what sort of things and inequality in what sort surely should not be neglected. This involves a difficulty and political philosophy." In this statement Aristotle seems to tell us two things. First, in speaking of men's partial agreement with philosophical arguments about ethics he means, we suggest, not only that there is partial agreement with the philosophic conclusions about ethics, but that political men find a basis for agreement with philosophers only when speaking about ethical things. Most men concern themselves chiefly with their families and perhaps politics, and their hostility to philosophers may well be due in part to the philosopher's strange unconcern with those things. Philosophy takes seriously what most men find ridiculous, and finds politics as a whole a bit ridiculous.[1] Yet to the extent that political men and philosophers of necessity think as human beings about human affairs, it is not inconceivable that they can agree about what the habits of a good human being are. In order to make himself less of a stranger to men, the philosopher teaches about virtue and about justice, as does Aristotle in the *Ethics* and the *Politics*.

Nevertheless, Aristotle can proceed at the same time to communicate with philosophers about the matters with which he as a philosopher is concerned. He can do so precisely because political men do not think and read in the way students of philosophy do. The examples in the *Politics* are political, but an example is a specific case of a more generally applicable, hence not essentially political, principle. Many words have more than one meaning, as do *archē* ("first principle," "ruler") and *sympheron* ("bringing together," "benefit"). The reader is likely to forget that the most obviously appropriate meaning is not the only meaning. Similarly, a "multitude," more than one thing, immediately suggests the *dēmos* only to those preoccupied with the menace of the *hoi polloi* or with the justice of their demands. The significance of qualifying phrases like "so-called," which indicate that Aristotle uses the word in question in a way other than it is commonly used, is also likely to go unnoticed by a political man reading a book on politics. So also, the use of important philosophical terms such as *eidos*, form, and *aitia*, cause, is not disconcerting because these words are not simply philosophical jargon but everyday words as well. In our day, ordinary speech borrows self-consciously from philosophy, but Aristotle could and did take his philosophical terms from unsophisticated speech. Another point: The connection by "and" of two words, one obviously political in import and the other similar but not necessarily political, often suggests to the reader a closer connection in meaning than their mere grammatical conjoining warrants. Furthermore, the common Greek correlatives *o men* and *o de*, "the one" and "the other," when used as relative pronouns, can be used either in series, as we use "this" and "that" in English to mean "the former" and "the latter," or in inverted order, as in Romance languages, thereby meaning "the latter" and "the former." Thus in each case the Greek lends itself to two equally possible but very different readings. We can suppose that a man renowned for a concern for precise speech would have been aware that this would be a problem, if ambiguous readings are problematic.

In sum, the teaching about ethical things is meant no less seriously, but it is meant for political men and men insofar as they are political. Not all men wish to be chiefly concerned with politics; and according to Aristotle, man has two kinds of virtue, moral and intellectual.[2] Aristotle speaks to political men and philosophers about politics, and to philosophers about philosophy. By proceeding as he does, Aristotle can elaborate a political teaching that reflects as true a teaching about metaphysics as he knows, yet without teaching metaphysics. The philosophic doubts are expressed as political doubts: the manyness of bodies is a democracy, the one principle by which all things are caused and ruled is an absolute monarchy, a whole differentiated into classes of things whose forms do not become one is an aristocracy. In Book III of the *Politics*, Aristotle presents the arguments for all three without making unqualified judgments between them.

The second point in Aristotle's statement to which our attention is drawn is his reference to political philosophy, or philosophizing about political things. Aristotle attempts to speak of the whole of being; the political analogue of his query is how one speaks of a city's being a whole. For Plato, the solution to the ontological problem lay in speaking of the generic unity of the separated forms.[3] With this solution Aristotle disagrees, and the transition from his criticism of Plato to his own solution as we have it in the *Politics* is the present section, commencing with the mention of political philosophy. In this section we find an examination of the disputes about political honors and of what place the good must have in the city. The question that remains for us is whether only in philosophizing about political things Aristotle finds a solution he might otherwise not have found, or whether his correction of the Platonic teaching is for the sake of politics. Or is the significance of philosophizing about political things that it enables Aristotle to present his conclusions in a form more comprehensible to political men? If a more correct or a more convincing answer to the question of how being is a whole is found only by considering man and his city, then taking the political seriously would be for the philosopher far more than a concern for the safety of his body. Philosophy would need "ethical mathematics" as much as politics needs "mathematical ethics."

The explicit difficulty that initiated this discussion was the one of articulating a regime underlying the right laws that someone might lay down, and the conclusion reached is an answer to the question that some put forward about whether the rightest laws should be for the benefit of the better or the majority. Earlier we suggested that Aristotle himself acted as a legislator in articulating the law of moral virtue. He will now begin to train other legislators. Becoming a legislator should satisfy the political ambitions of Aristotle's political friend. If he cannot be sovereign as a deliberator in a democracy, is not the greater glory that of the legislator who does in a dramatic way and once and for all what both the democratic assembly and the private man must do every day?[4] Law should be the general rule for deliberations, and the legislator's work of deliberating and choosing is the political work par excellence. Thus, the training of a legislator is the education of a political man. But learning to legislate might also benefit the philosopher, for what the legislator does is to order the parts he is given into a whole. Among those who raise a difficulty about whether the benefit (bringing together) is of the better or the majority are the philosophers who continue to wonder whether the materialists who find being in each thing or the Platonists who find being in the forms provide a more satisfactory explanation of being as a whole. Perhaps the philosopher who attempts to speak of a whole has something to learn from constructing a whole whose parts are men.

As we shall soon see, however, the parts the legislator puts together are the parts of his own being, and the legislator is, like Aristotle, a legislator in speech, not in deed. Thus it was only said to be *apparent* that the solution of the difficulty of how to ensure good judgment from those who practice politics was to lay down right laws to ensure their choosing and judging well. Aristotle speaks of a regime underlying right laws not only because legislating would require a consideration of the ordering of first principles. The regime is in fact the ruling body also because cities do not run according to the intention of some wise legislator. This is not to deny the effectiveness of laws in determining who has access to political office, or the effectiveness of laws in the broadest sense in habituating men to hold specific political opinions that form their whole posture toward politics. But it is to deny that laws have any other source than political men. Men, here and now, in their political deeds continuously make their political order, and what laws there are remain in force by the grace of those who have force. Their force might be brute strength or the ability to command respect and thus be the source of opinions.

The discussion of the regime is important because who is authoritative is the cause of a political order, whatever factors contribute to his being authoritative. Unless the legislator himself rules as a statesman, legislators are at best poets, men like Homer or Aristotle who articulate an ethical law, persuading men, if possible, to imitate Achilles or Odysseus in living according to the principles the poet makes manifest. Hence, whatever its frame, the content of Aristotle's discussion must be a teaching about justice to political men who can act upon that teaching.

Democracy is just because it is the rule of all, or because Aristotle writes in a city where democracy is just by law. Consequently, Aristotle's teaching begins from the perspectives of the political men in a democracy: democrats, the rich, the well-born. In a democracy justice means equality, an equal place in the assembly and in the courts for every man. If this order is undesirable, one must give arguments intelligible to those who actually dispute about justice, for they in fact settle their own disputes. One must explain what different qualities men might have, despite the similarities democrats seem to find so easily, and one must explain why, for the sake of justice, the differences are more important than the similarities. To claim special honors in a democracy must be to claim that one benefits the whole disproportionately; one is rewarded for a contribution. The contributions of men might be of different sorts. But Aristotle mentions no contribution of the poor at all, and his intention is to remind the many of their need and the city's need for the contributions of the few, and therefore of the necessity that they be treated unequally. The few, however, are reminded of the strength of the many, and are allowed to see that the private rewards of wealth and of the practice of virtue might be sufficient compensations if they are not sovereign in cities. The rule of the many strong is not necessarily contrary to the private interests of the rich if the many can be convinced to permit the rich to retain their wealth, and if the wealthy can be convinced not to abuse their privileged place. That this is what justice is all about for most men is conceded by Aristotle, for Books IV through VI of the *Politics* are most obviously devoted to a reconciliation of poor and rich.[5] Polity, or so-called polity, which bears the name common to all regimes, is a mixture of democracy and oligarchy, the rule of the poor and the rich for their own benefits.[6] There is a sort of justice between poor and rich, and a moderate democracy—a democracy tempered with oligarchy, or a mean between the two—is Aristotle's best regime for most.[7]

But Aristotle speaks against the many on behalf of another few: the virtuous. His taking the side of democracy against oligarchy is to make clear that not having wealth but having a specifically political excellence is the proper basis for a greater share in rule. If the poor are mixed with the rich, both poor and rich are then mixed with another few. But who these few might be is most obscure. Aristotle again speaks of flute playing, which meant ruling with prudence (1277b28–30). To the art of flute playing, neither wealth nor good birth contributes. Then who are the flute players? The well-born, the free, and the wealthy contest for political honors, but Aristotle makes an assertion on behalf of the virtuous, new claimants who would dispute for honors. But they only *might* dispute. Aristotle sets the sights of political men beyond what is or is likely to be by speaking of a class of men whose being is their being good, not their being wealthy or honor-loving or well-born, and by making it seem as if they might rule. Aristotle makes of the fundamentally democratic "mixed" regime a true mixed regime by making the mix manifest in speech.

In order to make the mix in speech, Aristotle makes clear enough the case for the many without making it as clear as he could. The majority, taken all together, are better and wealthier than the few because they include the few, but they are also superior in strength. Indeed, strength is the peculiar claim of the many. The many are to be taken seriously only because of their strength, but this is reason enough. Aristotle makes it "look like it is apparent" that the sovereignty of the many is not right in principle. But force does seem to be a principle in fact in politics, so he can do no more than make it look apparent. As he reminds the many of their inadequacies, he reminds the few of theirs, and in this way would temper the demands of both. Yet in speaking about the mixture found in the city, he shifts the balance toward the few, for instead of the sovereignty of an indeterminate multitude being just, against the wealthy and the virtuous the multitudes would have "some just speech."

The political solution toward which Aristotle points the disputing partisans is the true mixed regime, a mixture of first principles, not the fundamentally democratic mix that makes each into all by disregarding their ends.[8] The democratic principle of freedom is not wrong, and the strength of each and all of the many bodies is not inconsequential. But the many who are strong and claim to be free lack wealth, reputable ancestry, education, and virtue—all the things men deem good for themselves. The city, we are told, is put together of the free and those who "bear estimates." The many bear no estimate (*timēma*). Honors (*timai*) are also a first principle or a beginning, because the claim of the free-born citizen has no substance. One moves beyond bodily necessities, which are ignoble, and beyond the just on which democratic justice rests, the equality of body as body, by taking seriously the claim to be free and to be honored as free. For being free and honorable means having some wherewithal to combat bodily necessities, as do the wealthy and virtuous. The mixed regime is a mix of human bodies with the boasts men make about the ways in which they are more than bodies. It is more just than the democratic mix precisely because it mixes *men*.

The mix is ultimately a mix of different first principles, and Aristotle neither elaborates a principle by which to mix the principles nor announces or explains his failure to elaborate one. Each of the claims is a measure of more or less of that claim, and strength can be measured, but none of the claims are commensurable with each other or with strength. The possibility of making all these commensurable in one regime is assumed by the disputing partisans pressed by necessity to live together, but it is far from obvious to the legislator or political scientist. To understand this difficulty we must examine Aristotle's argument in greater detail.

Beneath what Aristotle makes apparent is indeed the attempt to moderate democracy's base justice in order that democracy do justice to man's humanity. But how does one do this, and in the light of what possibility is the undertaking justified? Putting forth the claims of the few against the many must appear and be beneficial to the city as a whole. If one cannot teach men how to make a mix by giving them a formula for mixing, one ought to make them see which inequalities should or should not be taken into account, and to what principle recognition of these inequalities points. Men's demands to be honored represent various opinions about what a good man is, and the claims voiced differ from each other as claims. But the one claim men do not voice is that of strength, for mere strength has no voice. Aristotle distinguishes strength or superiority as the cause of men's actually being authoritative from the claims they make. He presents the many as strong, but in fact one or a few could also be strong. The antithesis between the claims and the fact of sovereignty will soon be shown to lead to the antithesis between superiority in reasonable speech and superiority in bodily strength, thus between a philosophic "tyrant," who personifies all of man's excellences, and a tyrant who personifies the strength of the *dēmos*. Basing the city altogether on inequality, whether inequality in strength or in the excellences indicated in men's claims, destroys the politics of free men. The justification for speaking of the mixed regime as a political solution lies in preserving men's understanding of themselves as free. Yet making the possibility of human perfection a first principle may be beneficial in a way that making possible the sovereignty of a demotic tyrant is not beneficial. If so, then inequality must be introduced into democracy toward this end and no other.

In order to do this, Aristotle must educate the few men of distinction even as he speaks on their behalf. The few he educates are the honor lovers, the so-called aristocrats, who in craving honors may in fact be no less desirous of private gains than economic men, but whose love of distinguishing themselves from the many and whose great-spiritedness might cause them to oppose the many for the sake of something they cannot fully appreciate. The few are also the men who become political scientists, the "legislators" who remain private men. With the intention of benefiting each in the fitting way, Aristotle now restates the principle of justice from the *Ethics* correctly: Justice seems to all to be some equality.[9] Earlier he spoke of justice as equal amounts to equals and unequal to unequals, as if to make the few take the city seriously by emphasizing the opportunity for political inequality. He will now teach the few that the city is worth taking seriously only on the proper terms, either when equality is properly understood, or for the very purpose of understanding what an equal is. In the meantime, he protects the city's justice by emphasizing the kinds of equalities and inequalities that even uneducated democrats and oligarchs, but not tyrants, are likely to appreciate.

Aristotle again takes note of an assertion, this time by someone who might say that offices should be distributed according to excesses in every good. He seems to be concerned with the men who, sensing their superiority in some respect, are likely to grasp for more. These are would-be oligarchs and tyrants. He does not seem to disagree with the opinion that justness and worthiness are not the same, although he does at first try to show that the opinion is wrong if by "worth" superficial qualities are meant. There are some qualities that are not superficial, and these are man's arts and sciences and capacities. Worth must mean having the art of ruling well, flute playing; and political men are told that none of the apparent goods that become the bases of oligarchic claims contribute to the exercise of the political art.

Aristotle is particularly critical of the claim of good birth, put forth by those who assume that they have inherited some virtue from their ancestors. Theirs too is a superficial good if political virtue is acquired not by habituation, but by the kind of education needed to acquire an art. But the claim of good birth is the claim for the self-sufficiency of the city without political science, a claim presupposed by all citizens who distinguish themselves from noncitizens. The well-born and the free dispute, we are told, because they are near to each other, but the justification of the free man's claim must be in the promise of his future perfection, whereas the well-born man's claim refers to the past glories of his ancestors. The good that is the *archē* is not the beginning but the completion by man's political art. The justification first offered for political inequality is that there might be a political art. We have heard this argument before, from Gorgias the rhetorician, but we must listen hard to hear it from Aristotle.

Those who assert that the just and the worthy differ include philosophers who assert that they are superior to politics, and all their arts and sciences superior to prudence. Aristotle does not deny that other goods might well be greater than that of flute playing. At the conclusion of the *Politics* he criticizes the playing of flutes by free men, and interprets Athena's throwing away her flute as her recognition that flute playing contributes nothing to intellect.[10] The philosopher does not profit from playing the flute himself, although he may learn something from examining flute players. But even political science may not be the highest science.[11] If Aristotle demotes superficial goods in favor of men's rational capacities before political men, he also reminds the philosopher that his worth may have nothing to do with political justice. Yet he does not wish to deny the worth of man's arts and sciences; so he speaks of the incommensurability of goods.

Aristotle makes the argument about incommensurability not only with respect to politics and philosophy, but also with respect to "magnitude" and "virtue," which suggest the distinction between bodies and souls, and between the *dēmos* and the few. His argument to political men is as follows: The argument for demotic justice as well as that of wealthy oligarchs rests essentially on a measurement of bodies or bodily goods, and these partisans suppose the city to be chiefly concerned with the body. Nevertheless, the claims of political men to be honored express various understandings of virtue for the use of the body and the city to overcome their necessities. The measuring of bodies reveals nothing about the amounts of various qualities inhering in a body, or of the worth of those qualities. Magnitude measures the quantities of bodies, not qualities; but in the case of men's claims, there is no abstracting from quality. The claims point to the importance of qualities or "whats." Quantity cannot make a whole for men. Similarly, virtue is a whole only in abstracting from that which has magnitude—that is, body—and the strength of the bodies that put forth the claims. That virtue could not make a whole Aristotle does not say, but virtue cannot be the only principle if bodies are taken into account, unless virtue can be made strong. In commending the statement that not every inequality is rightly disputed, Aristotle in effect compares politics to a race in which the slow runners come in first. The city, whatever its claims, does in fact take its bearings from body. While not attempting to rectify the error, he mentions that gymnastic contests are the proper place for the distribution of honors. If the city honors the wrong men because it measures by the wrong standard, then the fast runners must be kept busy with something more honorable than politics. Ambitious men must learn about a greater sport. If the city cannot judge races fairly, the few can lead good lives in private and the city remains an imperfect whole of bodies.

Yet demotic justice seems incomplete if it finds no fitting place for the good man who still desires public honors. Furthermore, this desire to be honored seems to be exhibited by all the claimants to honor; it is the essence of politics. Such spiritedness is unsatisfied in an economic community, though it may be discovered by listening to men who live in one. It suggests that men must be more than their bodies and that there may be some kind of being other than body. Men's claims to be honored are demands for formal recognition of their qualities, and as we have seen, the forms often exceed the substance of the boasts. Aristotle shows us that men's assertiveness is the cause of formal claims; does he also mean to show us that it is the cause of "forms" and of the opinion that they have being?

Leaving aside this question for the moment, we can say that spiritedness is the source of the public. In man, body and virtue are connected in his refusal to honor the necessities of his body, which is the source of the private. The city, therefore, is said to be put together from the free and those who bear estimates, that is, from the freedom to make something honorable and that which can be recognized as honorable. Overcoming demotic justice requires not the poverty and slavishness of the natural philosopher, but having the masterfulness to fight for honors, expressed in the opinion that one is most worthy of being honored or that one serves something more honorable than the body. Man's humanity depends on his making something more honorable than his body.

Yet if the being of the city's public emerges from the angry passions that defend an opinion about what is honorable, Aristotle nevertheless speaks of the necessity of justice and political virtue to manage the city as one would manage a household. In man, spiritedness would seem to be the seat of the moral virtues, though in the *Ethics* Aristotle speaks of a part of the soul that holds the appetites that can cooperate with reason or, alternatively, of the part of the soul that holds practical reason.[12] If spiritedness is the source of the public, spiritedness educated is the source of political justice, and spiritedness tamed and appetite rational are virtue. In speaking of managing the city, Aristotle raises the question of whether what is rational can somehow manage a city or another man without being a part of it. But he immediately seems to answer his question by suggesting that an approximation of what should manage the city can be made a part of it, perhaps in the way that reason is a part of moral virtue.

Thus the city resembling a good man would be brought into being. The habits and intellectual virtue of the man with the political art might be reproduced in the city in the form of virtue and education (*paideia*). As in the virtuous man, the appetitive part of the soul obedient to reason, when properly educated by having been given sound opinions, manages itself more or less nobly in being obedient to its own reasonable opinions or those of others, opinions supported by the philosophic speeches about the ethical things. Aristotle's apparent position is that he can create a city with a mixed regime that is "somewhat" just in exactly the same way that a political man with a body and a soul can be somewhat just in asserting his justness. But the somewhat just will be distinguished from the just that exists only in speech; it will be in cities where the angry passions are needed to manage the bodies of the unreasonable. Among those who dispute somewhat justly are those who *would* dispute justly on behalf of the good life, but they only might dispute. The education of spiritedness points to its taming or its use in support of that for the sake of which it strives to overcome the body. Aristotle brings the city closer to a more noble alternative to democratic justice by being silent about democracy and philosophy, while still making clear that there is some kind of a good life, a nonpublic life of education and virtue, that might remain superior to the political life. The city is taught to respect men of good character who know their own worth, and to what extent and in what way their goodness includes wisdom is left unclear.

Thus, the principle of the mixed regime and its justice rest on its resemblance to a man. Regimes that accord equality according to some one are necessarily deviations. Man consists of two "ones," a body and a soul. From the point of view of being a whole man, unmixed regimes are deviations. These deviant regimes are not necessarily wrong from any other point of view. Being equal only according to intellectual virtue is a deviation perhaps in being later in time and in being inadequate if the strength of unreasonable bodies must be taken into account. Aristotle speaks of deviations in order to protect the dignity of the mixed regime he creates to oppose the bodily regime that is truly a deviation from man's humanity. The two deviant regimes, with body and intellect as first principles, should in fact be right regimes according to nature, but in order that the preponderance of body be overcome, Aristotle must dignify the passions that are the source of that overcoming.

The essence of the city is in man's making manifest how a multitude of men differs from a multitude of beasts. How he does so is revealed in the claims. Goodness has an ambiguous position due to the fact that the greatest difference between men and beasts, reason or speech, is not manifest in the way other things are. Speech is manifest when it is public, and public only when it assumes the form of public dispute, accompanied by the force of the passions; thus, it is no longer reason devoid of passion. Justice now lies in the more or less just disputes, not in the speeches about the parts of the just (1281a8–10). The claims put the parts together more or less well, and they make more or less complete wholes of justice for various human multitudes. The claims are forms, self-imposed upon human matter of differing capacities, revealing the various ways by which free men can rule themselves as beasts cannot. The passions and spiritedness of men are managed or ruled by being subordinated to laws, by being educated in the culture preserved by ancestral traditions, by being made to cooperate in moral virtue with a principle of reason that is one's own.

Specifically, the somewhat just ways of disputing are as follows. The wealthy contend that they own more of the country, and the country is what is common. The country, the physical being of the city, is what is commonly honored by both democrats and oligarchs. The wealthy, however, also claim a virtue that exceeds the unshared "common" concern of all. They can be trusted to keep their contracts, for they can restrain their acquisitiveness according to some rule. Even if their being more virtuous than the poor is due only to having enough of what they desire, they are nonetheless more just in precisely the way the base city requires: keeping the contract not to do injustices to one another, which is law.

If the wealthy both claim a share and provide a benefit, the well-born and free put forth a claim that is most insubstantial. They are more fully citizens than the base-born because they are the best in the genus, or race. More precisely, the better look like they come from the better, or they lead one to imagine that the ancestors are good. Yet they are distinguished from the virtuous. Thus, their claim on behalf of the ancestral customary law is a purely formal claim, unless it should coincide with the substance of virtue.

The third just disputant, on whose behalf Aristotle makes an assertion in the future tense, is the virtuous man, who will personify the whole of human virtue. Whether he is the good man who has moral virtue for its own sake or is the philosopher who is incidentally just is again made obscure. His justness is his virtue in associating, which suggests the most complete association two men can have: shared thoughts. The just man offers a virtue but claims no reward; his virtue is its own reward, as is philosophizing. Nevertheless, Aristotle speaks here and in the *Ethics* of friendships which seem to be between nonphilosophic men,[13] and he attempts to argue that moral virtue is also its own reward.[14] Perhaps insofar as man's work is necessarily political, and the political consequences of philosophic and moral virtue are the same, the distinction between them need not be made. But this implies that art cannot be admitted as a title to rule.

The fourth who might justly dispute are the majority against the few, for they are stronger and wealthier and better. They are not better-born or freer. The peculiar claim added by the many is strength, however.

These political claims seem to represent the parts of human being; the desires, spiritedness, practical reason, and the body. Each of the claimants provides different benefits, as do the parts of a man. The model for a just city would seem to be a whole man; but then the city would seem to have to recognize all the claims. Yet the whole of justice is said to be in either all or some of the parts. As a man perhaps cannot dedicate himself to all things at once, his dedication to one well chosen thing might make possible the proper functioning of all of his parts.

The claims express what men make honorable or authoritative for themselves, and there are two fundamental judgments about what is good: wealth and seriousness. The judgments result in a life devoted to acquisition to satisfy the body and its needs, or a life devoted to acquisition to satisfy the mind and its desire to know. The one is the economic life, the other the private life of philosophizing. The claims, we see, do not correspond to the principles of rule. The well-born who claim honors are now linked to the wealthy; an old aristocracy is an old oligarchy. Of freedom, nothing is said because one is no longer free after one has chosen. Neither is virtue mentioned, however; it does not seem to be an end any more than freedom is. This problem we shall consider later.

The regimes, whose first principles are wealth and seriousness, do not seem to be reducible to one, although perhaps both could be found within one city. The problem would of course be how to combine them, and toward this end the claim of the virtuous is somewhat illegitimately reintroduced and seriousness assimilated to it. The argument on behalf of the virtuous against the wealthy and well-born is curious, for Aristotle argues that if one were wealthier than all, this one should rule according to the same justice. But this only shows that all citizens can be ranked according to this claim, that one can measure quantities of this quality, and not that there is anything unjust about the principle. The case of genus is similar, and the well-born are said to be commensurable according to the same just as the wealthy. Virtue is not put forth as a distinct ground of justice, yet Aristotle speaks of aristocracies, in which the virtues might be made commensurable, and this if one man is better than the rest in the body of serious citizens. By partially obscuring the distinction between moral and intellectual virtue and then defending the men who are both wealthy and morally good, perhaps one can resolve the city's difficulty in fact, if not in principle. For good men, we recall, agree with philosophers at least concerning the ethical things. Thus, Aristotle refers to a multitude who are wealthier and better, and who therefore have a somewhat just speech to make. The point would seem to be that the philosopher's taking the side of the few, distinguished on various grounds, makes philosophy authoritative in the city. Unfortunately, however, the multitude that is better and wealthier is not said to be stronger. Furthermore, there are *multitudes* that would have somewhat just speeches to make. Even if one could make the claims commensurable, politics would still have to take into account strength, and there seems to be no formula that Aristotle can provide in advance. This is the mix in the mixed regime made not by a legislator, but by political partisans in deed.[15]

This discussion was supposed to have resolved the difficulty of whether the rightest laws should benefit the better or the majority, and the conclusion is that equally right laws are for the benefit of the whole city and for the community of citizens. It is at first difficult to understand why Aristotle speaks of both a community of citizens and the whole city. The city is composed of free men who make claims; and thus understood, they are "ones" stripped of all qualities except what makes them parts of the city: their assertion of freedom. The whole is, as demotic justice wished to understand it, a city of men asserting their freedom, and each is an equal one. But one must abstract from the quality of the claim in order to find them equal and to speak of a benefit or bringing together of the whole city.

What gives the city its wholeness is only that all political beings share in the assertion of a purely formal, though not for that reason inconsequential, claim that they are free to make their own whole. There would be no dispute about honors if men did not presuppose their freedom. In this sense, freedom should be the political first principle, the beginning. But because the claim of freedom has no substance, it cannot be the end. If man's choices presuppose freedom, they imply some end or purpose as well. Man does not rest content with being "a dishonored wanderer." He makes a whole for himself by making some first principle authoritative, living for himself and with others on the basis of what is commonly honored (1279a37). The city seems to be incomplete without a regime. Man's choices are the causes of regimes. To speak of the city as a whole is to speak of the capacity, not the choice. To speak of the community of citizens is to speak of those who have chosen.

Thus, the whole also consists of regimes, and one can also examine the city by separating all into regimes. That regimes exist and what they are is inferred from men's claims, for the differences in the claims reveal the ends that men make their first principles. A citizen is one who partakes in ruling and being ruled, and citizens differ according to each regime. Thus, the consideration of regimes and of who is a citizen is a consideration of the parts of the whole qua different. This consideration is no less reasonable than the consideration of the parts as similar.

Yet when Aristotle speaks of regimes here, he specifically mentions only one: the best, in which there is the capacity and choice to live according to virtue. This seems to be the only regime not fully integrated into the city, and the only claim to honor worth considering separately. Similarly, it was said that the virtuous, or the just, only *might* dispute on behalf of the good life. The city has a just, and there is a just lying in speech or reason. Again, a citizen is said to be "in common" in the regime, but it would seem that only in the best regime, in which speech is common, are there citizens in common. Without doing so obviously, Aristotle returns to the understanding with which he has begun Book I: that man is political because what is his own is *logos*.[16] But this just seems to differ from the city's just; the resolution of the city's disputes is not made dependent upon the reasonableness of its citizens. The argument for a just other than the demotic just is made by taking men's speeches wholly seriously. This just is, then, a just in speech; but if men take speeches seriously, the best regime and its just have as much being as the city and its just.

A legislator in deed or a statesman could not abstract from the strength of bodies, nor should he neglect what is reasonable. The just should be what allows him to measure and compare both. Yet there seems to be no rule prescribing the proper mixture, even if in practice the problem does not seem insoluble. Insofar as the mixture is based on the presumed differences among men, human nature would seem to facilitate the mix. As we shall see, however, there are obstacles to this natural mix. What is necessary is a mix that is a mean. But it seems that this mixed regime, the model for the city that contains several regimes and therefore is a whole, has no being other than its seeming to the noble political man who honors both wealth and virtue by taking the city seriously and listening to reason. Not the rightest laws but the somewhat mixed-up opinions of the noble man are the ground of a just and noble city. The moral virtue of the man who does not know for what end to use his freedom is the basis of the mixed regime. What is then necessary for political philosophy is a theoretical defense of a virtue that is political yet that sees itself in the service not simply of politics, but of some suprapolitical excellence. Therefore, what is necessary for philosophy is an explanation not only of how moral virtue is in accordance with man's nature, but of how the political and the suprapolitical are necessarily connected. In order to justify a just that is equivalent to moral virtue, "mathematical ethics" must be an articulation of the "what" of the mean between the economic community and the few who philosophize. But "ethical mathematics" must also demonstrate that there is a "one" that makes quantity simply and quantities of different qualities comparable.

Hence, we are led to a consideration of "ethical mathematics," the measuring and comparing of quantities of different goods. Indeed, Aristotle says that *some* seek a difficulty with the intention of legislating; others raise another question. The philosopher's question is analogous to the legislator's:

How does one make a whole that takes into account the differences of the parts as well as their similarity in being an "each"? The question we raised earlier was whether the study of the political was in some way the same as the study of all things and, therefore, whether political philosophy meant more than politic philosophy. The philosopher's query is not so much whether the ethical teaching necessary for politics is true, but whether the philosophic arguments about the ethical things do not provide a model for a more satisfactory science than mathematics.

Aristotle criticized the mathematician's hypothesis about the "one" with which he counts.[17] According to Aristotle, although each body does appear to be a one, human bodies give evidence of being incomplete individuals in their apparent desires to associate in various ways on the basis of something honorable. Thus, perhaps there is another kind of "one" that is not an each but an all, a "one" made manifest only in the examination of political beings. Why is a one not an all, and each part a fraction? This defies common sense, because each thing we see is a one. Only if mathematics is modeled on psychology, which brings to light the incompleteness of a human "each," does "ethical" mathematics make sense.

We are now given a more thorough explanation of Aristotle's disagreement with the philosophers. His criticism seems to derive from a consideration of politics and to reveal a concern with political consequences. "They" assert that the just is the equal, but they do not specify in what quality beings like men might be equal and unequal. The natural scientist cannot speak authoritatively about the order and rank of political beings, while political men can neither defend nor oppose a democratic order in any way that does not seem arbitrary. For example, in Ethiopia they did distribute offices according to size,[18] and even now in some places it is done according to color. Is there not some good argument to make for or against a kingship of the tallest or an aristocracy of the fairest? The science on which democracy has been shown to rest is wholly incapable of refuting any would-be tyrant's argument. But the awareness that men are unequal, both visibly and in immanifest capacities, should remind the philosopher that the things he sees can be considered as different in quality as well as similar in quantity. The "superficial" differences seen are a reflection of the sources or causes of differences exhibited in the works of things. The models for these differences are man's works, his arts and sciences, but also his capacities. Capacities must be understood to be given by nature. Perhaps one should then assume that all beings have natural capacities, whose "whatness" can be inferred from their "works" as we observe them. Each being has a virtue, a completion that is somehow the cause of its being what it is said to be, giving each its definition and making it identifiable as belonging to a multitude of similar things. If the rest of nature does resemble man in this way, then a comparison of "whats" is as important as a numerical count. About the importance of "whats" we have learned from political men.[19]

The mathematician's study is the study of bodies and their magnitudes. Magnitude is the quality of body from the mathematician's point of view. But Aristotle comments that "if some magnitude were more, then magnitude would be wholly an equal match for freedom and wealth, thus if this one differed more in magnitude than this one in virtue, and if magnitude wholly exceeded virtue, then all things would be commensurable." We suggest that Aristotle's point is directed specifically against the Pythagoreans, who did try to explain the capacities or "virtues" of things. But they understood the being of things to mean their being number. Numbers they thought to have bodily extension, that is, "magnitude," hence the reference to the contest with freedom, which we understand to represent pure units, and with wealth, or bodily substance. Magnitude could be "nothing more" after the discovery of incommensurable magnitudes, or one could not explain the visible whole as numbers with extension, as the Pythagoreans attempted to do. The Pythagoreans attempted to use mathematics to explain the whole, and, political objections notwithstanding, they failed to do so.[20]

Aristotle's criticism is not so much that mathematics and the study of nature are either useless or hopelessly incorrect, but that natural science is insufficient. Man needs to live in a whole that has a first principle. This necessity of human nature is knowable, but whether natural science contributes to this end is questionable, and whether it does not in fact have something to learn from man's necessity is arguable. The first principle of politics is not dependent upon theoretical natural science. To the extent that Aristotle's criticism is a criticism of those who assert that philosophy is superior to politics, it should perhaps be understood as a criticism of Plato's explicit teaching that philosophers must rule in cities.[21] The example of slow runners erroneously being rewarded is once used by Plato to emphasize the importance of astronomy in the education of the ruling free man.[22] Also, Socrates compares himself to a slow runner and Protagoras to a fast runner.[23] Aristotle relegates a determination of who takes the honors to some contest other than politics. Even if nature is understood as it is by Plato, the explicit teaching of the Platonic Socrates that knowledge is of the virtues, but also that virtue requires knowledge, must be explicitly corrected. As politics might subsist if the philosopher is put out of the competition for honor, political philosophy perhaps must make authoritative not theoretical natural science, but theoretical political science, and then obscure the extent to which politics is dependent upon the protection afforded it by political science. Whether the authoritative science is rightly the highest science depends on whether all things can be made intelligible as political beings are.

If, however, what is according to nature is not what is fitting to politics, then man's making of cities is, as Aristotle indicates, a "putting together in battle order" (*synhistēme*), and his disputes about honors are "a making against" (*antipoieō*). But precisely if man's making is independent of nature and if nature as it is perceived is incoherent, one must refine one's understanding of what nature is by taking man's wholes as models of what nature might be. From men's disputes about honors we learn that the somewhat just claims to *be* the city are those of the wealthy, the free and well-born, the virtuous, and the many. The wealthy, who have a share in the country which is common, we understand to be forms of natural bodies. The free and well-born who are like the free, but of a superior genus, we understand to be the forms as numbers. Immediately hereafter, Aristotle connects the well-born to the wealthy and then drops all reference to the well-born, for we have seen that he finds the numerical forms superfluous. The virtuous, on whose behalf "we" make assertions, would be the forms as the perfected works of things, as are the human virtues, and as Socrates and now Aristotle assert that they are. If the examination of men's claims·leads one to infer that forms are the causes of things being as they are, then these are the ways in which one might speak of the whole of nature as if it had forms. Or one might still contend that is better to speak of the many instead of the few, for the many things embody as much "wealth" and "virtue" as the few forms, and they have the strength the few lack. How we speak of the whole should be determined by justice, that is, how to speak most truly of all the beings at the same time. Therefore, Aristotle next raises the question of whether there will be a dispute about who should rule if all are present in one city: the good, the wealthy and well-born, and a political multitude.

Justice notwithstanding, it seems that the announced results of the examination will be made contingent upon what is necessary to defend the few virtuous. "How will they thrust through?" Aristotle asks. In order to make a politic speech about how the whole is ruled, we will have to consider how the man or the city ruled by virtue is ruled. We must therefore examine the work of the few: Do they manage the city or *are* they the city? If the forms "manage" the multitudes of things identical in form as the virtues manage a man's body, then one can still speak of being as body, not as intelligible forms that are more like souls than bodies. This would seem more in accord with common sense. Yet the intention is not to protect common sense abstractly, but to protect the common sense of the sensible man, the good man, and therefore to protect the good man. If the few virtuous cannot thrust through without a teaching about forms, then it might be necessary to speak of their being, not simply managing, the city. If virtue can be protected in another way, then forms will not be said to be beings.

The gravity of the difficulty of giving a just account of being is revealed in Aristotle's last consideration of the dispute about honors in this passage. Those who claim to rule on account of wealth or genus make no just speech but, on the contrary (*palin*), we can measure bodily nature according to the just, or equal, represented by wealth or freedom through birth, that is, mathematical quantities. Perhaps, however, there is also a just or a measure of virtue in *aristocracies*. Aristotle speaks of aristocracies in the plural, as if to acknowledge that there are two kinds of virtue. The problem with attempting to make a whole through an understanding of political being is that the kinds of virtue exemplified by the good political man and the philosopher do not seem to be of the same kind, though Aristotle has just now asserted that justice makes the virtues a whole. Justice must show how the manly and moral virtue the city seems to need and the intellectual virtue the philosopher needs are at least commensurable in order that Aristotle speak of a just that brings the forms together. What would be necessary, he tells us, is that there be one man better than the others in the multitude of serious citizens. This sounds like one very wise and politic philosopher. He is justly authoritative according to the just that is the political good. But he, being superior in the political multitude, which is justly authoritative in nature, is then justly authoritative over nature. If we wanted to say that the best of the philosophers was justly authoritative, we would have to speak of a nature so ordered that it is ruled by some one good in the light of which all things good are good, and this good must be the same as the human good. If the natural order could be shown to resemble the best human order, then the sovereignty over nature of the man who personifies the best part of human nature would be just, as would the sovereignty of best part of man over man, and the best man over other men. If nature as a whole were intelligible in the light of some first principle that is the same as man's good, then the wise man is justly sovereign over the whole, because only man speaks or makes manifest the intelligible. The life of human excellence would be right according to nature as a completion of nature, and nature *is* man's perfection. The wise man confirms Aristotle's hypothesis about man's ruling citizenship.

For the present, Aristotle attempts to do justice to all, and this means doing two justices, or using two measures of equality. We want to speak of a nature that makes intelligible not only man's virtues but bodies, and it is not yet clear that we can speak of the rest of nature in the same way. The "rightest" laws must speak of how men, the better, are brought together and how nature, the many, is brought together. In attempting to speak also of the many, we must either speak as mathematical physicists in addition to psychologists or be prepared to demonstrate that the whole of nature can be seen as an examiner of souls, a political scientist, would look at things. The difficulty is that nature does seem to be brought together mathematically and men seem to be brought together by considering the ends for which they rule themselves. If there is some "equal" against which all things must be judged, it must be a one that is both a quantity and a "what." Otherwise we cannot truly say that the study of comparative government is simply superior to mathematical physics, or that there is an "ethical mathematics."

Nevertheless, in the immediate sequel we shall learn that one cannot do justice to either the many or the few human beings without doing a seeming injustice to the many. One must compensate for the superior force of the many bodies by taking advantage of one's superiority in speech. Continuing to do justice to nonhuman nature, as we have seen, does not benefit even the many human beings who might think nature is on the side of democracy. How to do justice to the better remains problematic, however. If the second right "one" against which all things must be judged is a wise soul, not the moral virtue of a being who makes a whole of body and soul, then body and intellect are still incommensurable. Yet it seemed necessary that the political solution be not a mix of the right extremes, but the mean embodied in the man who connects the political to the suprapolitical. Perhaps the "just" sought by the philosopher lies similarly in the mean between the bodies in nature that are judged and the intellect that judges them. This, we shall soon learn, is speech, which aims to, but may not, express wisdom about nature. Political philosophy is politic because it does not make clear that the good man who agrees with philosophical speeches about the ethical things is himself not the good man who speaks well. The two sets of betters are similar, not identical, though a comparison of the two betters may prove more beneficial than a comparison of the multitudes, the nonhuman, and the demotic.

2. Hares and Hermaphrodites (1284a3–1284b34)

Political philosophy means not only the politic teaching of philosophy, but philosophizing about political beings and perhaps considering all the beings as if they were political beings. Examining them as political seems to mean taking politics seriously for its own sake, as is the premise of Aristotle's political friend. The political man, we recall, revealed his principles to us when he distinguished the regimes. He is public-spirited, for his first division is between regimes that serve the common benefit and those that do not. He places a premium on men's freedom, for he knows that tyranny is wrong. He understands aristocracy to be rule for the common good by men who are wealthy, but who are nonetheless distinguished from the merely wealthy because their doing good makes their very being good. He also knows that the minimal characteristic marking out political beings is the ability to acquire something or other. All political beings should be free and should acquire, though not from their fellow citizens. Yet it also seems that the few good should rule, or should at least have a greater share in political honors. The political man still seeks some just that measures each as a free man in the city and also measures the differing degrees of virtue concentrated in the few good. We must examine the implications of his opinions to see if they are as noble as they seem, if he does indeed take politics seriously for its own sake.

Doing justice to the better and many means not only finding a political order suitable for mixing those who are capable of nobility and those who are not, but explaining the relation of forms like the Platonic forms, "the few good," to the rest of nature, which seems to be bodies. Aristotle, we recall, criticized the Platonic teaching about forms to the extent that Plato taught that these forms had an independent being, prior to and separate from matter. But Aristotle seams to show that in taking men's political claims seriously, we can see for ourselves or teach to others the reasonableness of taking forms seriously. Men's spoken claims to be honored surpass in beauty the ignoble necessities of their bodies, and the claims are as real to the men who make them as are their needs. Furthermore, we can group together multitudes into regimes, classifying them by inferring from their spoken claims the ends they make their first or ruling principles. Eventually Aristotle too will speak of the forms as if they were separated from matter, like Plato's. Thus he returns to a teaching about forms, although his forms are made by men as if they were natural, because nature failed to make them. How it is true to see all things in the light of the teaching about forms, and not as multitudes, remains to be considered. This consideration, as befits politic philosophy, is presented as a philosophic *logos* about the ethical things: The fate of the few good men in the city reflects the place of forms in the whole. Thus, while political men learn what kind of equality justice must be, and virtuous free men learn in what way being a free man means ruling, philosophers learn to speak of being as a whole and to defend their speeches as science.

Ultimately, then, doing justice to the few better and the many means refining the political opinions of the few men while at the same time speaking the truth about nature. Throughout our presentation we have contended that Aristotle was concerned about what a philosopher could assert. The problem is treated more or less thematically in this section of Book III. Neither the impolitic assertions of the philosophers nor their silence nor the old myths to which cities adhere make manifest the rightness of the good man who personifies the mixed regime. Aristotle's assertions do defend its correctness. His discussions of politics seem intended to make apparent to political men that the life of virtue is the best life for a man, and that democrats ought to obey the virtuous man as a king unless they themselves are capable of virtue. In these discussions he allows us to see how a politic writer should write about politics. But in them we must also expect to find a theoretical defense of how the life of virtue is a right regime according to nature, an accounting intelligible to those who demand it. And we should hope to find an explanation of how science is possible, or how nature and the intellects that judge it are brought together. Aristotle's full elaboration of a possible solution to these problems is found in his examinations of kingship. We learn in the present section why those examinations are necessary.

In the last section we learned that what to assert about nature was problematic because it did not seem to be the case that nature and political wholes were brought together in the same way. Now we shall learn that making assertions about how nature or political beings are brought together may be simply inadequate to the needs of a city of free men. The first assertion, if understood politically, would lead to a democracy that is a whole of equal parts, but not of free men. The second would lead to the natural right of the tyrant who unifies the virtues. Aristotle gives us no indication that these conclusions are incorrect or even incompatible with each other. Just as nature may be a whole of equal and unfree bodies "ruled" by the intellect that comprehends it, man could have a city of perfect equality and unfreedom with the exception of one who rules by virtue of another principle of right. If the philosopher cannot speak and make assertions about the regime that underlies just laws for free men, then there will be no reasonable defense of decent politics and no public defense of science before free men.

We begin with an explication of Aristotle's somewhat obscure, that is, politic, statement of the problem. The problem is, we repeat, how to make the better, the one or few of "incommensurable virtue and political capacity," commensurable with the many. Virtue we have understood to mean primarily moral virtue, although not necessarily only moral virtue without intellectual virtue. The political capacity would seem to be the capacity of a free being to deliberate and choose, or to legislate for himself, and this is "the same" as the most authoritative of the arts and sciences. It is thus the capacity to reason or speak well. The good human being, who has both these excellences, could not be part of the city, we are now told.

He could not be part of the city perhaps because there is yet no measure of equality between bodies and human excellences. More obviously, he is too good to be part of the city. He is an image of a god among human beings, says Aristotle. From knowing his excellence we, Aristotle's readers, might imagine what a god would be like; he is the being who allows us to make inferences about what the first cause and ruler of the whole might be. Thus, his being seems to be of a superior genus. His being is also law, we are told. He is what the legislator tries to make, and it is ridiculous for such a man to take seriously the city that strives to be what he already is. Yet the city needs to take him seriously, it would seem. We wish to articulate a law of human nature that might serve as a standard for the legislator's law. The law the legislator makes intends to be a reasonable speech about how men should lead their lives, as if the legislator could choose well for them, and if the law is fully what it intends to be, it is based on a knowledge of the nature or natures of human beings. The difficulty in speaking of laws of human nature that does not arise in speaking of the rest of nature is this: When we formulate laws that describe the working of nature, we generalize from the average case. But man's very nature is the capacity to make more of himself, and therefore we are led to wonder whether a law of human nature must not be a law articulating the being of the best man, not the average man. The difficulty is further complicated by the consideration that the law is nevertheless for the sake of the average man, and his being average means precisely that he lacks the capacity to be an excellent man. Does one hold him to a standard he cannot meet, or does one encourage mediocrity by speaking only about the average case? Or does one follow Aristotle's suggestion, which is to speak of excellent men as beings of a superior genus, or as gods? The average man must emulate or at least revere the best man, without the legislator's expecting him to be that godlike man. The law combines the best and the average cases by teaching that something surpasses humanity. But what then does one say if the best case should be actualized and a man surpass humanity?

What Aristotle might say about such a man is what Antisthenes did assert. Antisthenes, a pupil of Socrates, was the first of the Cynics; he was known for his flagrant disregard of conventional mores and for his teaching that virtue, by which he meant intellectual virtue, was strong in itself.[24] Antisthenes asserted something about the lions when the hares made popular speeches and claimed equality for all, but Aristotle does not himself assert the lions' reply to the hares' demands: "Your *logoi* are fine, O hares, but where are your claws and teeth as we have?"[25] The hares had words or arguments, but speech as they used it lacks force. Antisthenes, "force in opposition,"[26] opposes to the strength of the demagogues' speech the strength of speech for the sake of reasoning. To Antisthenes the use of speech to make political speeches is ridiculous in comparison to the leonine strength of the outstanding man who uses speech for more serious purposes.[27] But Aristotle compares the ridiculousness of the hares to the legislator's legislating for (or against) the outstanding. Thus, politics as a whole without philosophy is ridiculous to serious men like Aristotle.

Yet while Antisthenes made assertions and laughed aloud, democratic cities seem to find a weapon befitting hares: ostracism. The claws and teeth of hares are the real claws and teeth of the *dēmos*. Aristotle leads us to wonder whether the opposing strength of the philosopher is ever of a sort that he should not keep his jokes to himself or whisper them to a few friends. In this light the reader might notice that in Books I and II of the *Politics*, where Aristotle seems to defend the dignity of the economic and political life, all the quotations from the poets are used ironically. Aristotle finds ridiculous what all political men and the poets who speak for them take seriously—that is, wealth and honors. One can *say* what Antisthenes meant without *asserting* it. If Aristotle takes the political capacity seriously, he does not thereby take politics seriously, for that capacity has other uses. He takes politics seriously to examine political men and to educate them to take the part of greater lions.

Antisthenes asserts that the speech on behalf of the democratic hares lacks defense. Because of "such a cause," Aristotle says, democratically governed cities use ostracism. What this cause might be is somewhat unclear. Is it Antisthenes' insult against the hares who engage in demagoguery, or is it something in the nature of the average man that makes him resent the best man? Perhaps this is clarified in what follows, for a cause of this sort was also responsible for the Argonauts leaving Heracles behind, "as is said in the myth." According to the myth, as Aristotle reports it, the Argonauts left Heracles behind because the *Argos* did not wish to carry Heracles with the others, for he was too heavy.[28] In order to speculate about what Aristotle wishes us to understand, we should recall his earlier comparison of a regime to a ship's crew (1276b20–27, 1279a2–8). The crew rides the ship, but perhaps not every ship will tolerate every regime. The *dēmos* dictates to its rulers, and not the legislator or the political men, but the many rule.[29] The *dēmos* seeks equality, but it recognizes no equality other than bodily equality, and it therefore rejects the "weighty," just as it ostracizes those who exceed in any manifest superiority, such as wealth, friends, and bodily strength. Heracles, of course, was a demigod; the *dēmos* rejects what it should revere, and the philosopher may never overcome this hostility. As for the cause of the hostility, Aristotle refers to democratic cities (plural): Does the human *dēmos* imitate visible nature in permitting no visible excesses? If nature is body, the cause of ostracism seems to be that it is just by nature. But are the bodies in nature self-ruled, as the human *dēmos* wishes to be?

Indeed, we might wonder how the many would explain the way in which the *Argos* dictated to its crew, making its wishes known. About the Argonauts' leaving Heracles behind, there were two different accounts in the literature that Aristotle might have known. The one to which he seems to refer is the myth that the *Argos* had a talking timber built into her by the goddess Athena. The account not given by him was that some of the crew—and most notably Jason, the man who did not know how not to be tyrant (1277b24–25)—left Heracles behind because they wanted the honor of capturing the golden fleece for themselves.[30] Aristotle surely knew of this version, given by Herodotus, for here in this passage as elsewhere he repeats stories from Herodotus. The second version suggests that the sovereign is free to choose, and that all that must be done to reconcile the city to demigods is to tame the honor lovers. But Aristotle reports the myth that places responsibility on the *Argos*—that is, on the *dēmos* or the god that brought the *dēmos* into being. Even if the men who tell myths or speak for the *dēmos* do so out of a concern for their own honor, one must address oneself to the content of their speeches, which are about the divine things.

According to the myth, the gods have given us a world in which matter, if anything, rules, and nothing can be done to correct the maker. The myth attributes the cause to a defect in matter for which the gods' gift of the capacity for speech is an inadequate compensation. The whole is antithetical to the truly divine. The cause of matter is *the* cause, and man's works cannot overcome his necessities. There is no strength in opposition to the democratic *logos* because speech cannot reach a completion in wisdom, or perhaps because it cannot demonstrate that strength to the many. Aristotle neither denies the fact nor finds the intolerance of the many an unmixed curse, for those who are ostracized are "set free," not exiled. Yet neither does he abide with the myth; perhaps one can compensate for nature's insufficiency by using man's arts to write a new myth. The *dēmos* that rules is ultimately ruled by what it holds true about the god, but someone speaks for the god. Aristotle reports the myth rather than Herodotus's account because the poets who make myths are the ones whose correction is essential, not Jason.

To democratic ostracism and the *Argos*'s rejection of Heracles, Aristotle opposes tyranny and the advice of Periander. The censure of these, he says, must be thought not simply right. Antisthenes attempts to speak of what is according to nature, and so do those who speak on behalf of democrats. The first implies that speech or reason for its own sake is strength according to nature, and therefore that reason rules. The latter imply that matter or its cause is nature. According to what "they assert" about the tyrants, when the herald came to him for counsel, Periander spoke nothing, but stripped away (abstracted from) the outstanding stalks of grain to level the field. The herald reported what had occurred, although he himself was ignorant of the cause. Thrasyboulos, to whom he reported, understood: one must make away with, that is, destroy or capture, the manly.

Most obviously, those who make the assertion are not right because they do not have the facts straight, for the historians report that not Thrasyboulos but Periander asked for advice.[31] Those who censure have neither seen for themselves nor paid much attention to the written word, and they are quick to blame the wrong man, perhaps unjustly. Furthermore, if those who blame tyranny are democrats, their own deeds seem to differ little from those of tyrants. For all their talk, the many are also sovereign by force, and the tyrants even achieve the equality the many desire without all the babbling of the hares and the *Argos*.

The tyrants understand (*synnoeō*) one another without speaking, while the herald who makes reports remains ignorant (*agnoeō*) of the cause. The cause is nature, which the tyrants know by *nous*. They could understand one another presumably because fields of grain are the same in Corinth as in Miletus, and their intellects make reference to this same thing. This is how science must be possible. Speeches without reference to nature are useless, for they leave men in ignorance. But of course we must notice that the tyrants did not understand identically. Periander, whose name means "all-around man," is as courageous as a man and as silent as a woman, thus a good hermaphrodite.[32] He uses his marvelous virtue to philosophize; what he did was to abstract (*aphaireō*) from the tallest stalks in the same way that one would attempt to study the workings of nature by using the average case as a form. But Thrasyboulos had asked about politics, not nature; according to Herodotus, he wanted to know how to manage the affairs of the city most nobly. Thrasyboulos, whose name means "bold in counsel," understood Periander's advice to be applicable to political beings. Living up to his name, he thought that he must make away with (*anaireō*) the manly, that is, destroy or capture the manly. We wonder whether Thrasyboulos's was a misunderstanding or an improved understanding of Periander's advice. If men do not take their bearing from talking timbers, then they seek some guidance for politics from nature. What Thrasyboulos understood was that if the rule of natural philosophy is right, what must be done is to obliterate the manliness that incorrectly manifests itself in noble political deeds, or to teach the manly that the only noble deed is to philosophize.

The "tyranny" of philosophy has the same effect on political nobility as does democracy. Periander and Thrasyboulos are the culmination of humanity if what is right by nature for human beings is wisdom. The tyrants make political nobility immanifest, which is what the *dēmos* or its spokesman wish to do and what Antisthenes would have done. Joking aloud about politics, keeping silent about nobility, allowing the *dēmos* to speak through its demagogues, or the mythmakers to speak, destroys the dignity of politics, though it is obvious that the demagogues and the tyrants do political deeds. It seems that a politic philosopher must speak in the way Aristotle writes this passage: he shares his jokes, his recognition of the superiority of philosophy to politics, and his teaching about nature with the few. Aristotle, no less than Periander, teaches that one must abstract from body to study forms.[33] But he does not want to be misunderstood, and therefore he speaks about politics too. His *logoi*, while being critical of democracy and tyranny, report that it is correct to understand nature as democratic or tyrannical and politics as tyrannical. He, too, uses his manliness in speech, "legislating," or writing and philosophizing. But in speaking well, Aristotle succeeds, as we shall see, in capturing the manliness of noble political men without destroying it, as Antisthenes failed to do. Aristotle, strong only in speech, cannot afford to destroy the manly assertiveness of doers of noble deeds as might a hermaphrodite tyrant. His politic and esoteric speech is a mean between joking aloud and being silent. And perhaps he, too, benefits from speaking well. Periander and Thrasyboulos looked at the same phenomenon but may have had different intentions. Consequently, they failed to understand perfectly. We cannot help but wonder whether, if they had spoken to each other, they would have attached the proper significance to the difference between *aphaireō* and *anaireō*. It may be that if human beings wish to speak about nature as scientists, they must speak to one another to confirm their judgments about what the things they see mean. Philosophers need to speak as much for their own benefit as for that of political men.

Furthermore, even if nature were brought together in the way democrats are led to believe and tyrants think, there would be no similar solution for political men. If human beings wished to live according to this nature, they would have to do what modern political philosophers have told us more clearly, but not more surely, than Aristotle does. After stating the cases for democracy and tyranny, Aristotle immediately switches to a discussion of foreign affairs, and especially of the imperialism of democratic Athens and monarchical Persia. If manliness could be quashed within the democratic city, it would not thereby be obliterated. The city as a whole would use manliness against others. Justice may require equality, but the *dēmos* of equals itself becomes a tyrant or uses its would-be tyrants, and breaks its contracts with those of inferior strength.[34] Aristotle tells us that as soon as they had secured their power, the Athenians broke their contracts with the Samians, Chians, and Lesbians, depriving them of their freedom. The natural tyrannies are duplicated by political tyrannies.

Aristotle himself, who is strong in speech, lords it over his reader and commits an injustice against Athens. Thucydides tells us that Athens conquered her former dependents only after they had broken their contracts by revolting from her.[35] He also tells us that Samos, Chios, and Lesbos were moderate oligarchies, and he especially praises Chios for its moderation. Aristotle's point seems to be that the moderate cannot survive in politics if they do not defend moderation immoderately. Hence Aristotle's manly unjust speech against a perhaps immoderate use of force on the part of the Athenians. But Aristotle also shows us that a man can be a tyrant in speech as well as deed. Indeed, his next example is that of the king of the Persians. The king of the Persians continually felled the Medes, the Babylonians, and others, because they had become proud once they had attained rule. The king of the Persians captured Babylon, Aristotle's example of the city par excellence.[36] These conquests are recorded in Herodotus,[37] where we learn that they were all accomplished with fraud as well as force, and with the assistance of dissatisfied noble men. Babylon, the central example, was conquered when a noble man maimed his body in order to succeed at a beautiful deed—or, as Herodotus has Darius say, in Zopyrus's maiming his body for the sake of the king, he gives the ugliest deed the most beautiful name. "Kings," as distinguished from tyrants, rule when they enlist the aid of those who can distinguish between noble and ignoble uses of force and those who speak well.

Thus it seems that philosophers must not only speak and keep their jokes to themselves, but speak nobly about noble political men. Aristotle writes his own political histories in order to educate the manly doers of noble deeds.[38] If politics is essentially tyrannical, Aristotle nonetheless gives the impression that the Athenian dependents did not deserve what they got, whereas the Persian enemies did. Political philosophy does not quash manliness; it educates it. Discriminating manly men are the only ones who might oppose democracy and tyranny for the sake of making manifest man's nobility. Manly men will emulate the noble men of whom they hear tell; hence the importance of telling it nobly.

Perhaps we should connect our conclusion that politics is essentially ty- rannical to Aristotle's apparent approval of the felling of those who become proud because they have reached the *archē*. We have assumed that freedom and honors are the first principles, that man overcomes his baseness by making something honorable for himself. Aristotle speaks throughout this passage of tyrants' and democracies' and cities' and tribes' "making." But if man's humanity is an assertion of his freedom against nature, then the con- clusion to which we are led is that the "one" according to which the free man judges is the tyrant, the asserter of freedom par excellence. We have reached the astounding conclusion that freedom, the very premise not only of de- mocracy but of virtue, justifies tyranny. Precisely the good man's intention was to protect politics from tyranny. If he and we, Aristotle's readers, are so proud as to think that we have understood that freedom and honor can be the first principles of the politics of free men, then we are indeed in need of a felling. Aristotle will immediately hereafter begin to speak of the household *archē*, which means the soul, private education, and virtue.[39] If politics must be distinguished from natural science and taken seriously, ultimately it can- not be taken seriously for its own sake.[40]

If the assertion of man's freedom from the whole seems to conclude with sanctioning his tyranny, then it seems better to revise one's understanding of what the whole is or intends to be. Nobility should be possible within the whole, because the whole is a whole of qualitatively different parts, not of equal stalks of grain. The whole must be a whole, not an all, and man as political man must have a natural work that contributes to the beauty of the whole. The good manly man must be a citizen. Aristotle speaks of wholes that are paintings of animals, ships, choruses. They are made by the legislator's art as a field of grain would not be, yet they could not be said to be makings against nature. Rather they are imitations, users of nature, or free creations, but none is a stunting of natural growth. Nature must be understood neither as mere bodies nor as an intellect wholly outside it. The legislator must make a whole that respects the nature or natures of man. Although Aristotle seems to say that all of man's arts and sciences, as well as his other assertions, must submit to the requirement of symmetry for the sake of making a beautiful whole, he gives no example of any limitation on science as he does on art, and he immediately says that monarchs can be "in harmony" with cities if the household *archē* is profitable. There is no limit on excellence in speech if that speech remains private, or publicly harmoni- ous. Someone with a voice too loud and beautiful could not join in the city's chorus, although we might infer that he could speak in the partly private and partly harmonious way Aristotle does. Man's beautiful speeches remain outside of the whole dedicated to his doing beautiful deeds, but Aristotle shows that the two can be harmonious.

Similarly, if nature were to be understood as having been legislated as a beautiful whole, it would allow no visible excesses. *Monarchs* are "in harmony" with cities; the unitary first principles by which multitudes are understood as what they are exist in speech, abstracted from matter. Thus it seems that nature need not be democratic just because it appears to be that way. If we never see the best case in nature, we might still make an inference about there being a best case of the "whatness" of a thing. We might posit intelligible forms which are the best, not the average, case, as was done in the natural science of Plato and Aristotle. It would have been better, Aristotle says, if the legislator had put together the regime from the beginning so that this doctoring would not have been necessary. But the "second sailing" is to try to right it with some correction of this sort. The legislator has made the whole with bodies, whose "whats" and their proper order are unintelligible, and therefore we must examine men's speeches about bodies, for they might be intelligible. The monarchs are in speech, and the second sailing means the examination of speech for the sake of making the whole intelligible.[41]

But, thus understood, the argument for ostracism has "some political justice," and we are again confronted with the difficulty that we sought to overcome—namely, the justification of an ignoble combination of democratic politics and philosophy. This kind of politics and this kind of science are suitable for deviant regimes, that is, regimes according to ones (1283a26–29) and therefore not for the politics of mixed beings or for the science of their being. Hence, there is much difficulty in the best regime, Aristotle says. Virtuous men cannot be ostracized from cities if cities need some virtue, nor can one examine moral virtue as if it were separated from body.[42] "What is it necessary to make?" Aristotle asks. Political philosophy must teach about kingships. For "surely they would not assert that it is necessary to expel and make away with one of this sort nor, indeed, to rule over one of this sort. This is about the same as if they were to claim to rule over Zeus's dividing the rules into parts. Therefore, what remains . . . is for all to willingly obey one of this sort, hence for these to be eternally kings in the cities." The kings, which emerge from the best regime, seem to be the combination of reason and body that results in moral virtue. But Aristotle's king is not only a very good man but a spoken form in matter. And both of these are in the parts of Zeus's domain. If it seemed neither politic nor true to assert that the separated forms have prior being, it seems unnecessary to do so if the forms in matter can be studied as if they were separate. What is necessary, however, if no one is to divide up the parts of Zeus's rule, is that man's virtue be understood as the kind that can be in body, and that it be asserted to be according to nature. Obedience to kings must be made to seem as if it has "grown" instead of being made by the legislator's art. But the rest of Zeus's domain, nature, must also resemble man's sphere, for Aristotle's claim is that he presents philosophic *logoi* as ethical *logoi*. Therefore, we must attempt to understand nature as if it were ruled politically. If it cannot be so understood, then it may nonetheless be necessary to give the noblest name to ignoble deeds and call a "democratic" multitude a king.

Yet if we are correct in understanding a king as a speech that connects bodies and intellect and can be shown to be that which makes science possible, then we must recall the man who is an image of a god among men and who is superior even to the law. Is there, then, not a human excellence that transcends moral virtue, an excellence that is speaking the truth about Zeus? And if this speech could attain perfection, would it not *be* that of which it is now only an image? Aristotle's Zeus is a wise man, or a wise man is Zeus. We are led to wonder what the difference is between a tyrant, a philosopher, and a god, and what the relationship is of kings to gods.

When we look at men's cities as if they were like the rest of nature, we can find no place for man's assertiveness and excellence in them. Prosperous democrats and oligarchs and floundering natural philosophers seem right in deeming politics to be nothing. The manly man who asserts his freedom, his concern for the common benefit, and his demand to be honored for his noble deeds seems wrong. Yet a democratic city is not devoid of rule, even if by demagogues. Nevertheless, if we take politics wholly seriously, we conjure up an image of a tyrant who combines in one man all the qualities we attribute to excellent men: the courage the political man values, and the silent wisdom for which the philosopher strives. His is the rule that is right according to political excellence. The man who wishes to be noble is right in wishing to be free from nature, if nature is understood as bodily nature. But perhaps it is incorrect to understand nature to be only bodily nature. Speech for the sake of understanding speech is an image of a god. Is the god not the wisdom reason aims to be? And is not the divinity that has caused and may now rule nature more "natural" than nature itself? Only a teaching about the god and a nature that is a whole of which the excellent political man can be shown to be a part will allow Aristotle to make politics intelligible and to differentiate kings from tyrants. The problem of the many and the few better is not solved by maintaining the distinction between the two; they need to be brought together into one whole.

The myth that supports the democratic understanding of equality is that the god made matter and nothing else. Yet we can examine the forms man posits in speech to consider whether the whole is not brought together in some way other than that of democracy, but also of Periander and modern natural science, which is to reduce being to as much of being as is shared by all beings. Thus understood, democracy is right according to nature; but thus understood, democracy also must be ruled by a tyrant or a god, because human or humanlike excellences exceed the limits of democracy. Yet what all men share in varying degrees with each other and with Aristotle's nature or god is speech or reason. It seems that there is no defense of a democracy of self-governing men without a defense of the man who is *logos*. Aristotle must rewrite the myth, for an examination of bodily nature can support the belief that nature is a democracy ruled by a god or a tyrant who is as foreign to it as *nous* is to body; and thus nature would be a tyranny rather than a democracy. Aristotle must take the *Argos* on a "second sailing," and thus posit forms and examine those forms as if they have being in speech in order to show that speech, which is each man's own, has a divine completion and is the ground of a city in which citizens are both equal and men.

3. Kings (1284b35–1286a9)

We have yet to confirm that a democratic whole in which all rule in turn and live as they wish, or one like the mixed regime in which the assembly is sovereign, but in which the respectable (reasonable) may have special places as deliberators and judges, is both possible and defensible. The primary claim of democracy must be understood to be freedom, not equality, because each is equal in being free; and Aristotle's argument seems to be that the city in which freedom is best realized is a mixed regime. As he has just described it, it is a whole beautiful for its symmetry, that is, its orderly differentiation, rather than for its uniformity or equality. Nevertheless, we have not had a demonstration that a whole of this sort is just, because we have not found a "one" against which political multitudes can be measured. A political "one" should allow us to understand how cities that are wholes of free men must be ordered so that each is free and the whole as a whole is free, because the political "one" should be a measure of the characteristic that makes a multitude of many "ones" one multitude. We should be able to order and rank the parts of the whole according to the degree to which they possess the quality measured.

Thus far we have seen a democracy like the Athenian empire, which uses demagogues to speak on its behalf at home and military men to war on its behalf abroad. But it is unclear that this democracy is ruled by a *dēmos* of free men rather than by its talking timber—that is, its poets or priests. Its customary preference for democracy is unquestioned, and so it lacks a natural standard that justifies a democracy of men each of whom is free in the decisive respect, the capacity for choice that self-rule presupposes. We have also seen a "democracy" like the field of corn overseen by the tyrant, a whole of perfect unfreedom because it is measured by a standard according to two natures, body and intellect, not brought together in politics or law. What seems necessary is a standard for politics that can be shown to be natural and knowable by reason, and therefore a defense of reason, and which at the same time takes into account that the twofold nature of man is connected in spiritedness, which is the raison d'etre of politics. The "one" must emerge from politics, serve as the justification for politics, and therefore be its standard, yet be such that we can demonstrate its correctness according to nature.

Aristotle teaches, we contend, that an examination of kings clarifies these difficulties and at least enables us to see what a full resolution of them might require, even if we cannot yet resolve them. A king, we recall, is the most perfect case of the one characteristic exhibited to some degree by each in a multitude. The king makes it possible to speak of a multitude as one multitude, and as one of the multitudes into which nature can be distinguished. A king as a form is also a *logos*, man's speech about what he distinguishes, and therefore one of the parts that comprise the reason of the scientist himself. More obviously, a king should be said to rule rightly, for we think of kings as serving to benefit the whole, whereas tyrants rule for their private benefit (1279a32–34, 1279b6–7). The king is the standard against which the political multitude might pass judgment on the positive laws of cities that make them wholes. The king personifies the assertiveness of the political man not quashed but made noble. Because he is the epitome of political aspirations, an explanation of kings to the political man who aspires to political honors and wants to deserve them is the best way to educate men who want to take both freedom and virtue seriously. What remains to be seen, however, is whether in examining kings for these various reasons, we examine the same king and can therefore speak of a science of politics that is a science and is politic.

Aristotle "asserts" that kingship is a right regime, and it is the only regime about which he makes such an assertion in his own name. The kings, we repeat, are forms posited in man's reasoning about nature, and they are men of moral virtue. Men of intellectual virtue are images of gods, and whether Zeus is not the greatest king remains unclear for the present. In commencing this fifth examination, Aristotle speaks of a "crossing over" to examine kingship. A crossing over reminds us of the problem posed by Heraclitus in his assertion about the river: If all things are mutable and corruptible bodies in flux, then what necessary and eternal thing remains for science to examine? The crossing over, which is Aristotle's "second sailing," would mean, we suggest, an overcoming of the flux of the visible world to reach a new shore, a new kind of being that is eternally, and that therefore can be known by science.[43] Yet Aristotle asserts, but does not say, that the kings he now examines are a regime, an order of being. The contemplation of forms and of virtues is the *vehicle* of the discovery of a new kind of being, not necessarily the discovery itself.

Aristotle would also want to assert that kingship is a right regime and is perhaps noble, we have contended, because he wishes to demonstrate that the life of virtue, as distinct from and in addition to the economic life, is right for man. Virtue might be the form of law, the standard for justice. To argue that philosophic virtue is right, it might be sufficient to show that science is possible. To argue that moral virtue is right, it might be necessary to explain why form is as much being and as necessary as substance. Nature as described by mathematical physics does not support this argument. Does Aristotle's natural science support it?

The specific question Aristotle raises about kingship is whether it is beneficial or brings things together. Thus, we examine kings to determine whether and in what way bodily nature, politics, and intellect are brought together. Is it possible for political science to demonstrate that there is something just, according to nature, for men? What is necessary to make this demonstration, Aristotle assures us emphatically in contrast to modern science, is not that all things be understood as the same and as ruled in the same way, but that there be one first principle. Kings, Aristotle advises us to learn well, encompass several genera[44] and ways of rule.[45] How the beings subordinate to the rule of kings differ we learn by examining what seem to be five different forms of kings.

The first form is the form that *seems* to be most according to law, and this because it is the form of the law political men take most seriously: the political or moral law. This king in the Laconic regime also seems to be most according to law because it seems necessary that he should follow the city's law. We desire to find a place for manly political virtue that is in practice beneficial to the whole, even if the desire to make political virtue manifest is in theory tyrannical. The first form of king is thus most obviously meant to attract and educate, practically rather than rigorously, the excellent political man who has been weaned on praises of Sparta and accounts of Homer's heroes. As we shall see, in following the discussion of all the forms of kings, we find a more rigorous explanation of what would be necessary to ensure that the kings who are good men are beneficial to the whole in practice, and bring things together in theory.

The king in the Laconic regime must obey the law, and he is sovereign only when he goes out of the country. (Earlier, the wealthy were said to have a just claim to honors in the country.) The country is the realm of the everyday economic matters of the city, and what are out of the country are "foreign" affairs, the affairs of war and of the gods. The country made a whole by its laws must have an eternal general to guard it. But if this guard has something to do with the gods, then being a king of this sort should not mean simply being a good warrior. Why we might nonetheless think that a king is essentially a military man is again linked by Aristotle to what we learn about kings from the poets. The example given of a Laconic king is Agamemnon, who of course was a king not in Sparta, but in Homer's poem. The ancient kings were sovereign "by law of hand," that is, they took the law into their own hands. Agamemnon, we are led to believe, bore hearing ill of himself at home in the assembly, but tolerated no disobedience when away on expeditions, lording it over his troops. Then, Homer tells us, Agamemnon said, "But whomsoever I see aloof from the fight . . . / He shall have no hope to escape the dogs and vultures. / For death is mine." Surely this king impresses us as one who would do tyrannical deeds whenever he had the opportunity and is therefore useful in war and dangerous at home.

In order to better understand the Laconic kings, however, we must consider Aristotle's use of Homer more carefully. That we ought to do so is called to our attention by Aristotle's addition of a line to Homer's text, that is, his correction of the poet.[46] First, what we learn about makers like poets is that they are not true makers, for Aristotle no longer says that Homer "made," but that he "made manifest."[47] He brought to light the anger he discerned in men's souls, though in portraying it so beautifully that others might wish to imitate Agamemnon, he strengthened it and made it even more manifest. If earlier we thought that the poets were so important because they made something honorable for men, we now see that if their making is a making manifest, then it is or can be based on a knowledge of men's natures. For this reason, the poet's making is both truer and less free than it had seemed. Do men have natures that are found, not made?

For the sake of what is the poet's making manifest, we see clearly. Agamemnon lords it over his soldiers for the sake of ensuring that they are courageous fighters; he punishes their cowardice, which is a vice. When we read Homer, we infer that nature punishes the cowardly, and that there is a natural sanction for human vice. When we read Aristotle's correction of Homer, we infer that there is no natural sanction for vice. Agamemnon is a policeman, and he is the only one. Being an eternal general means being the arm of the law. It is according to the moral law that kings who seem to be most according to law are, and Agamemnon is king in the "Shriek-Victory" regime.[48] The moral law must scream and coerce, because nature is silent.

Our difficulty is in determining what the cause of that law is. Aristotle's other correction of Homer is to say that Agamemnon did not mind being reviled in the assembly, though Homer gives us no indication that Agamemnon would have tolerated any opposition in speech, Aristotle leads us to wonder whether he wishes to teach the would-be Agamemnon he addresses to stay out of domestic politics, or at least to listen to some speeches. But to whose speeches ought he listen, and why?

The first form of king is a general, either according to genus or to choice. He is a generic one, the representative of a class, and therefore, in the case of political beings with spiritedness, he is spiritedness personified as courage. He is the courageous guarantor of courage and assertiveness, the minimal political or moral virtue.[49] He is sovereign, lording it over others in the same way that the law coerces. He is the force of the law, but not its reason or substance, so he is not said to rule or to be a first principle. Spiritedness, we have also seen, is expressed in making distinctions and in choosing. Choosing is the political work of man, because no particular morality beyond the minimum is necessary according to nature.[50] But we are led to wonder if there is no first principle according to which the speeches of the law and the things chosen are. If the general ought to listen to speeches, we can surmise their general topic, if not their specific content. What we learn from Aristotle's correction of Homer is that the customary law has no basis in nature, but man has a need to make one that seems to have natural sanctions. Is it for this reason that Aristotle says that kings are not only leaders in war, but "are given" some of the things of the gods? The substance of the speeches to which they must listen are speeches about the nature of the "divine" things.

The second form of monarch is a ruler. He is said to rule as do some kings over barbarians, who are more slavish than Greeks and therefore deficient in spiritedness. If this king were himself a barbarian, it would be difficult to understand how he, lacking in spiritedness, could rule; and perhaps for this reason Aristotle says that he has a guard. But his guard is comprised of citizens who bear arms for him and who consent to his rule. If we wished to interpret slavishness as a deficiency of spiritedness, we would have to understand how a citizen could guard with arms if he lacked courage in the usual sense. In any case, Aristotle's explanation of barbarian citizens is problematic. After having just distinguished between customary law and natural law, he speaks of the barbarians as those who are *by nature* more slavish *in their customary ways*, and who therefore submit to the despotic rule bearing nothing with ill grace. The barbarians are natural beings, but perhaps not exclusively natural beings if they have habits, unless "nature" means the nature to which human excellence points. The barbarian kingships have the same capacity as tyrannies, and they are tyrannical because they are "skilled despotic rules," which we have identified as being in accordance with nature or natural science. Barbarian kingships are kingships not because they are according to law, but because they are inherited from one's ancestors, or are consented to. What distinguishes them from tyrannies is their form, not their substance. And the form depends on those who are ruled: the cause of the distinction is the same as the cause of the difference in the guards of kings and tyrants. The barbarian monarch himself is beyond the formal distinctions that those who are ruled tend to make. Yet in this case, those who do not distinguish between the form of kingship and the substance of tyranny are only the slavish barbarians, who show no ill grace. We wonder whether these barbarian citizens, whose habits accord with nature, are subhuman, philosophic, or both. But they are not free political men, and the one that rules them is not one of them. We also wonder whether and how spirited Greeks might live both as free men and according to nature.

Indeed, Aristotle does tell us of at least one instance in which the Greeks chose to submit to be ruled. Thus we have an example of the combination of form and substance in the submission of ancient Greeks to the third form of monarchy, the *aesymnateia* exemplified by the rule of Pittacus. Whatever Greeks called him, Pittacus was in fact a chosen tyrant, we are told. He ruled according to law and he differed from the barbarian king only in not being ancestral; his rule was new. Aristotle's assessment of this tyrant is as ambivalent as his assessment of the barbarian monarch. He gives the appearance of approving the choice of such tyrants because they do good deeds. Pittacus, for example, helped the Mytilenians to resist the exiled oligarchs. Pittacus was nonetheless reviled by the old poets, who for perhaps unreasonable causes decried the election of a tyrant who was base-born. We, however, might think it beneficial for Greeks to do as they did in the past and choose to be ruled by a virtuous tyrant like Pittacus, whatever his pedigree.

When we examine Aristotle's explanation more carefully, we can see more clearly what the difficulty might be. Pittacus, "Remedy-of-Pitch," resisted the exiled "Steadfast-in-Opposition" and the maker "Prowess." Pittacus, one of the Seven Sages, ruled for the sake of politics, not in the name of philosophy;[51] but he nonetheless, or for that very reason, seemed to rule in opposition to politics as it seems to be, not as its completion. He had to oppose what is political par excellence, assertiveness. Aristotle suggests that Pittacus failed to make clear some connection between his own political skill and his divine wisdom. What the maker "Prowess," the poet Alcaeus, made manifest was that Pittacus was chosen as tyrant, not that politics could do without tyrants or that politics ought to have wise kings as a matter of course. Alcaeus made this choice manifest because of his understanding of the circumstances of Pittacus's rule: The city was oppressed by fate. Pittacus's rule was a new beginning, made in opposition to the old, but its cause seemed to lie not in a nature that welcomed man's manliness, but in man's necessary combatting of nature. Pittacus's rule differed from kingship in not being ancestral; it could not be ancestral because the poets responsible for the ancestral traditions themselves courageously speak out about a whole that defies man's efforts to tame it.

There is an alliance, Aristotle shows us, between the old-style manly men, who are steadfast in their opposition to philosophy, and the poets who assert themselves. The poets continue to teach about a whole that is not well ordered, not about a whole in which man is provided for at least in the sense that his arts and sciences and political capacities might reach fruition. In the poetic version, the whole is unruled, and man is at the mercy of capricious fates. Aristotle says that Pittacus's rule was limited, but the poets made it tyranny. If man had a niche in the whole, he could manage his affairs in accordance with nature, but because he has none, he must first conquer nature in order to make his own modest achievements secure from the fates.[52] Pittacus would have to oppose the poets with some brave assertions of his own about the whole; he would have to speak about his divine wisdom in addition to doing good deeds. Without some politic assertions, Pittacus's rule seems to be man's greatest freedom or tyranny, *hybris* against the fates, but also his greatest estrangement from the whole.

Nonetheless, what makes a king a king and not a tyrant is his subjects' choice or formal consent to be ruled. But form alone seems insufficient, for we see that while some surrender utterly to what they understand to be nature, others understand freedom to require the conquest of nature. Perhaps not all men are suited to live in a certain way, or perhaps the various ancestral traditions are a substantial influence on what men are suited for. In either case, a king must rule with consent, and we are led to wonder what makes men consent. Aristotle has once substituted kingship "consented to" for ancestral kingship (1285a19, 1285a27), and he now speaks of what is consented to and becomes ancestral according to law. The ancestral is only what was originally consented to,[53] and, in turn, what men will now consent to may be influenced by what they have been habituated by custom to consent to. The poets seem to be legislators of custom and therefore to be makers of men, but perhaps they do no more than state clearly what presently is. Aristotle corrects the old poets with an improved account of the ancestral, attempting to change what is consented to, and in so doing he acts as a legislator might. The fourth form of kingly monarchy, "according to heroic times," is the kind of monarchy to which men ought to be habituated to consent.

The rule of men like Pittacus is necessarily understood as tyrannical because it is made to appear to be an overcoming of the hostility of the fates, of chance. We wonder how the kings of Aristotle's poetry differ from Pittacus. Aristotle's kings were heroes who ruled with consent because they did good deeds, and they became the source of a new ancestral order. Heroes, we might remark, were traditionally understood to be heroic by virtue of their divine descent,[54] but Aristotle's heroes are so called for their attempts to overcome, if not the divine, the natural. Their rebellion took the form of "doing good works" in the arts, in war, and in unifying the country. Aristotle says that they sacrificed to the gods, although it appears to us that they took measures to make the favor of the gods unnecessary, and some, we are told, did leave off sacrificing. In any case, they did not make justice depend upon the gods, for they judged, or rather made the just with or without oaths. Furthermore, their very oath was an extension of the scepter. Did they make this gesture to signify that their sovereignty, not that of the gods, encompassed with goodness the whole over which they were sovereign? Now kings properly so called, Aristotle tells us, are leaders in polemics "beyond the boundaries." Perhaps we are to understand that the heroic kings made a whole of the reasonable and regular things by excluding the domain of the fates. Aristotle's hero is thus a king, not a tyrant, because he does not make a determination of the just depend on the conquest of chance. But if these divine difficulties could be ignored, why is the king now busily engaged in polemics, and why in Aristotle's restatement of the forms of kings does he say that these are kings "roughly in heroic times"? Are there noble things, surpassing the just things, which, though not now comprehended by reason and law or subject to chance, would lead to a new principle of justice that would secure kingly rule? Are the new ancestral kings future kings?[55] And are new gods descended from heroes?

Aristotle's heroes are, of course, meant to be a replacement for Homer's heroes, and in the reiteration of the kings the two are interchanged. Homer allows us to see what morality is and, when corrected, he shows us that men make and enforce a virtue that is beyond the everyday necessities of the country, the economic community. But Aristotle's kings make virtue with full responsibility. Homer's king was only a general, but his kings are judges of the just as well, and they display their wisdom about the gods as would a poet. How much of the divine a king must know in order to speak about what is just and good we shall learn in the next sections. But in any case, it seems necessary that kings become legislators, correcting the Spartan morality supported by Homer and by the other poets, who make it seem as if courage were the supreme virtue because we cannot count on natural or divine beneficence.[56]

The list of kings is an explanation of how tyrants might be made kings. The Laconic general's courageous assertiveness is effectively made beneficial if it is used by the city in war, and if the city as a whole asserts the supremacy of domestic over foreign policy.[57] The monarch over the barbarians rules according to the natural law, and he is a king simply by being recognized as one, but he would have to be a being of a superior genus, a wise man or a god. Lacking such beings, this alternative is not available to us; so Aristotle makes barbarian kingship unattractive. What reader of the *Politics* would wish to be ruled as is a slave by a master? Pittacus's rule, never called kingship by Aristotle, remains a tyranny as long as men are led to believe that the whole is oppressed by fates which they must conquer. Pittacus's rule is the extreme of tyranny because it is *hybris* against the gods, or fates. It could be made a kingship only by delimiting the sphere in which the wise man's conquests need be made. The divine order must be regular and intelligible, or so must one assert, with the hope that its being so can eventually be demonstrated.

Nonetheless, monarchs are kings in the country only if their sovereignty is consented to. Aristotle's heroes lost their sovereignty to the mob. We seem to have come to the conclusion that there is no way for kings to remain sovereign over free men, and thus that it is not possible to make a tyrant into a king in any meaningful sense.[58] Then if kingship is impossible, what would seem desirable would be to combine the form of freedom, consent or choice, with the substance of kingly rule, wisdom.

Of what this wisdom is and, therefore, what the first principle of kingly rule is, we do not yet know. The two kings said to *rule* thus far were the barbarian kings who ruled according to natural science and the tyrants who, similarly, would rule if there were some divine science that made man the greatest god. Neither is the first principle of a whole in which human or political beings have a home. Therefore, neither can be the substance of political or moral laws. So Aristotle must add a fifth form of kingship: the king sovereign over all in the way a nation or a city is when it is ordered by the principle of skilled household rule. Household rule, we recall, seemed to be the rule or training of souls, and this with art and care (1278b37–1279a1). Aristotle speaks at first only of the sovereignty of this king. Perhaps a new rule or first principle of a political whole can be inferred from a consideration of the excellent political being. And perhaps we can at the same time speak of how the science of his being replaces or brings together natural and divine science. This would be the political "one" that emerges from politics, serves as the standard for politics, and is perhaps at the same time a natural standard, knowable by reason.[59]

Aristotle now says that the forms, "so to speak," are "almost" two. The forms, he says, reduce almost to two because the others are between them, being sovereign over more than the Laconic and less than the skilled household ruler, or king of all (*pambasileus*). The Laconic general is called by Aristotle the form of law, and he might bring together the cities, either according to genus or according to part. He is a representative of a genus or, in the case of man, he represents the part of him that is *thymos*. He might bring together the city that is nature, if nature could be brought together under someone of one genus, although this is doubtful. Aristotle has insisted that there is more than one genus, and the barbarian king, for example, rules over at least one lesser genus. The general might bring together man's city if one part can rule as the whole. We can resolve neither of these questions by examining the general, because from him we can make no inferences about the relation of the "ones." We need to examine the king of all, who is said to be a form of a regime, and thus of an order.

Aristotle invites us not only to contemplate the king of all, but to "run after substantial difficulties." When we began our discussion of kings, we suggested that a king was, among other things, a form posited in speech by man and therefore a part of science or the scientist, as well as of what is examined by him. The eternal general is *thymos* if understood politically, but he is also a form of law, a measure of each thing about which there can be a law or a rule. In his reiteration of the list of kings, Aristotle ambiguously refers to the Laconic general as eternal according to genus, or as according to an eternal genus, thus of a genus about which there could be a science. The eternal general, as a form of law, connects nature to intellect by being a form in speech or reason. The king of all, who is authoritative and is the king in a household and the form of a regime or soul, we can understand as the human mind that grasps what is intelligible. We shall learn of substance by examining this king of all, the scientist, not by examining the things of which there are sciences. The things of which there are "laws," in the discussion of the best laws and the best man which follows, are represented by the general, and he will help us to determine of what kinds of being there are "laws" or sciences. Is there a science only of political beings, of whom the general is most characteristic, or are all sciences merely modeled on political science? Finally, by considering whether and in what way the two forms of kings become one, we learn how all things might be brought together, or how a science of a whole might be possible.

The forms, "so to speak," are in fact form and substance. They reduce "almost" to two because it is not yet clear how these two are a sufficient replacement for *aesymnateia*, which conquers the fates, or chance. What is by chance is by definition not subject to law, and its cause is not intelligible. How much of "nature" remains after we exclude what is controlled by the fates we shall consider in the next section. In order to know whether Aristotle is justified in neglecting the chosen tyranny of men like Pittacus, we need to know more about the relations of man's makings to nature and chance.

4. The King of Kings (1286a7–1286b40)

Laws, properly speaking, seem not to be the laws of a city, as the political man thinks, but laws of nature. Yet nature may have laws rather than one law if the beings in it have different principles of rule, and it is necessary to respect those differences. Therefore, we may not be able to learn about a law that makes a city a whole by examining the laws of nature. Furthermore, we have been understanding "nature" as natural necessity, which seems not to include human nature, or at least not as much of human nature that exceeds bodily nature and seems to be free. The laws that cities have, which are commands of virtue and injunctions against vice, are not by nature, and we must suppose them to have been made by a legislator. If we wish to speak of good laws, we need to speak of some art or science of legislating. In order that there be a science of legislating, there must be a human nature that the legislator studies and then either reproduces or attempts to correct according to some standard of excellence. The legislator would have to learn about the necessities of human nature, and thus of a "nature" that includes at least as much of the human soul as is affected by its being in bodily nature. But the legislator would also want to know whether the noblest human possibilities are subject to some science, and how he as a legislator might replicate human excellence. If virtue can be codified in laws, perhaps it can be made coextensive with the city's laws. That intellectual virtue could be comprehended by laws that command is of course problematic. If the deeds of moral virtue could be reproduced, we wonder how philosophic virtue or even the prudence of a legislator or a statesman could be taught. Even a nature expanded to include the nobility of political beings within the whole might not include the highest possibility. Hence the beginning of our inquiry: Should the best laws or the best man rule?

This, the fifth examination, corresponds, according to our understanding, to the suggested topic of the being busy that we do not see of the legislator and the statesman.[60] Earlier it seemed that Aristotle acted as a legislator, articulating the law of moral virtue as a standard for a just city governed by a prudent statesman. Now, however, he educates men who must become legislators themselves, for, as we have seen, the deliberations of the statesman, like Agamemnon's, are not governed by law, but are in effect the making of law. The statesman who deliberates in particular cases makes the law, or at the very least amplifies it,[61] and he should be taught to do reflectively what Agamemnon did out of necessity. And Aristotle must do responsibly what Homer did incompletely—that is, to teach others how to correct the poets and, ultimately, to demonstrate that there is a science of human excellence.[62]

The legislator or statesman's being busy is an education in what, given human necessities, the limits of the city and its laws are, and it is thus an education in the relation of art to nature and chance, or an explanation of causation. If this is so, then the legislator's question is virtually the same as the philosopher's question. The philosopher, too, seeks to know whether man's making or legislating, his positing of forms and ordering of them into a whole, is according to something necessary, and not merely his tyrannical imposition of form upon the flux that is by chance. Tyrants, we recall, were necessary to bring the things that seemed to be by chance or the fates into the whole. In order to know what is by chance and whether it can and should be conquered by man, the philosopher needs to know more about the causes of things. Are the intelligible forms in nature and the causes of being? Is there a form of forms, one cause in the light of which all things are brought together and made intelligible? What falls under this cause we would call nature, or being. Perhaps, however, the only kind of being that is fully intelligible and has a cause that is fully intelligible is human excellence. If so, then the philosopher's question is not only virtually the same as the political man's, but it is the political man's question. Both must learn about the relation of man's arts to human necessities and to chance, and about the order of these causes.

Thus the beginning or first principle of the search is whether it is more beneficial or whether more is brought together by the rule of the best laws or the best man. For the legislator: Is reliance on the laws that habituate to moral virtue better than trusting in a coincidence of the appearance of a man with a political art, good intentions, and willingness to rule with the city's consent to his rule and the occasion for it, as in the case of Pittacus?[63] For the philosopher: Is the whole or the first principle that makes all things intelligible as one in nature itself, or in the mind of the man who might come to comprehend all things?

At first it is not clear why the whole must have one ruling principle. It would perhaps not seem unreasonable to us were someone to say that science is the sum of the particular sciences, a knowledge of the several laws. If science were no more than this, however, we could not explain exceptions to general laws or the cause of either regularity or irregularity; hence our attribution of causes to the fates, or to chance. We seem to need a science of the first cause, a divine science. In particular, the political things seem to be more irregular than regular, and there seems to be no political science that provides universally applicable laws. If circumstances differ so much that the prudence of the statesman seems to be always needed, then at the same time it seems that there are no rules of statesmanship for the same reason. How then could the statesman's wisdom be embodied in laws?

Aristotle tells us that those who believe kingship is beneficial are those to whom it seems that the laws speak only about the universal, that is, about things "on the whole," but not to give commands about what befalls one. Therefore, they reason, just as in every art, it is foolish to rule by what is written. The example given in support of their belief is that of Egyptian doctors who, even in the land that epitomizes tradition, are allowed to "move" things. The men who believe in kings are those to whom it appears that the best regime is not according to what is written or laws, "for this cause." They believe there is a political art, and that art is the cause of motion, hence *the* cause.[64] They are not so much contemplative men as political men, or men who think like political men,[65] who wish to do well in everything and are ardent admirers of the arts.[66] They believe in the omnipotence of the makings of reason. Their intentions may be the noblest, but perhaps their ambitions are excessive, not to say tyrannical. They attribute no contribution to nature,[67] but seem to find only a realm of chance that must be conquered by man's arts. Indeed, they are far from the slavish studiers of nature philosophers seem to be. How are these noble souls to be educated?

They need to be taught, if possible, that there is a nature that is regular or "necessary," and therefore Aristotle is quick to point out a consideration that their argument neglects. If the regularity does not lie in the things upon which art works, then perhaps it lies in the intention or end for the sake of which the artisan "moves" things. Even if a doctor treats each case differently, there is little question that he has "some general reasoning" about what human health must be and, therefore, about what he intends to make. Does the reasoning of the artisan not point to the existence of a law, indeed, a best law that might underlie the best regime? The law, or "nature," lies in the intended end of the artisan.

If there were such a law, it would seem to be superior to the artisan who holds it, for if regularity is desired, then what is devoid of passions that might deflect the rules is superior to what has passion. It is, however, a necessity that the human soul have passions, we are told. Therefore, it seems that the best law, not the best man, should rule. That there is such a law superior to the passionate soul in which it is found is, of course, problematic. Even if there were such a law, it would not obviate the original objection: doctors would still be necessary to apply the rules in particular cases, adjusting them to fit the exceptions. If there is no such law, we do at least learn about something necessary for our political science to examine: The human soul necessarily has passions. The artisan who is the cause of motion is characterized by an *eros* toward some end.

Hence the assertion on the part of "someone" that he would deliberate more nobly about the affairs of each and Aristotle's response: Make this same one a legislator and have him lay down laws. If he legislates *and* lays down laws, then legislating and laying down laws are not the same thing. What Aristotle means, we suggest, is that his noble political man, who distinguishes so well and therefore might be taught to deliberate and choose well, must be taught to "legislate," that is, to reason in terms of general principles and to make wholes. His excessive concern with recognizing distinctions among these is corrected precisely in having to formulate general rules and to bring things together into a whole. His oligarchy is tempered with a bit of democracy. Added to his *thymos*, his recognition of distinction, and his assertiveness, must be a bit of philosophic *eros*, a yearning to be one with the whole.[68] But he also lays down laws, or underlies laws. The oligarchic political man with whom Aristotle has conversed is a noble man, a good manly man, and perhaps the best human being to be expected to care about politics. His soul is the one cities ought to strive to make of its citizens; his the regime underlying right laws.[69] Were he not a lover of what is noble and amenable to education, he would be a mere economic man or an intransigent Achilles; were he wholly passionate, he would be a tyrant or a philosopher, not a political man.[70] His exceeding what seems to be politics proper and his tending toward what seems to lie outside of politics are precisely what make him the most excellent political being. His combining *thymos* and *eros* make him the best human being. His legislating for the city is ultimately a generalization from what is his own: a noble human soul.

Thus, it might seem that political science is possible because art can be understood as caused by something necessary, an intention to make one's nobility apparent. Therefore, political science, the science of beings who make themselves, becomes the science of the passions. We might learn of something necessary in the human soul by examining the passions that are ultimately responsible for the substance of man's assertions. Perhaps, however, in attempting to speak of a law of the passions, we would have to speak of the fact of their existence, not their differing ends. In doing so, we might establish a defense of democracy as just according to a nature like human nature, for the capacity of all men to have passions is surely equal.[71] But if we make the law of political beings the passions, not their ends, it seems that all we can do is to justify body, from which the passions originate, and not to establish how what exceeds body might be ruled or rule. This difficulty Aristotle recalls to us by raising the question of whether the one best or all must rule when the law cannot judge.

That accounting for man's rational faculties would be problematic, Aristotle indicates as follows. He speaks of multitudes that now come together to judge the just, to deliberate, and to judge—that is, human multitudes of citizens, free men, and philosophers, all of whom must reason in some way. Earlier,[72] the demotic and the nonhuman bodies in nature were said to provide a better feast than the one or the few, although we could not understand why. Now the reason is clearer: many brought together provide a more beautiful feast. Beauty inheres in body; and each of the many has body, whereas the one against which all things might be judged could not have body. Furthermore, many are more incorruptible, exactly as is more water. Body is more enduring; the many are not more virtuous, only more indestructible. But "there," Aristotle says, it is the work of all to be angered and err, and judgment is necessarily destroyed. The many cannot judge. The *mob* judges better than one *whomsoever*, or a multitude of bodies *perhaps* judges no worse than one of them, arbitrarily chosen, although perhaps it does judge worse. If the one against whom the many compete is merely the best body among them, then the rule of many may be preferable, although for no other reason, it seems, than that they ensure that the visible whole will continue to be and to be beautiful. Still, if by the one best we mean nothing more than the one with the noblest passions, then we can make no argument against democracy in favor of aristocracy, for example. We can make an argument only more or less correct against one "whomsoever," a would-be tyrant.[73] Political science as the science of the passions is incomplete if we find it reasonable to take seriously man's rational capacities.

Thus we cannot make a political whole by reasoning from bodily nature.

We must recall, however, that Aristotle has a hypothesis that men are citizens in a different way from the bodies that grow to be citizens (1278a4–6). If this hypothesis could be substantiated, then we could defend democracy and other political regimes on some firmer ground. Therefore, Aristotle posits a multitude of free men. Free men, we recall, are free in being free from the necessities of the body, or as free as men could be from such necessities. They seem to be especially men of moral virtue, though in principle they are all men. Because it is "not easy" for the many to be good, all are included in principle, and the exceptions are intelligible by the same principle or its deficiency. Free men, we are told, do no deeds against the law, although they omit some.[74] We wonder if, in addition to what they "practice," they substitute theorizing for sacrificing. If so, the multitude of free men, who are "serious" in soul, remind us of philosophers who are virtuous, though not for the sake of morality, and whose virtue includes intellectual virtue.

If we judge against a multitude of free men, we can understand how a multitude can be both many and one.[75] As serious in soul, free men are intelligible as one, although visibly many in body. Multiplicity is caused by body, unity by soul—if we can speak of some soul that is distinct from bodily necessity. The examination of free men and what makes them free, not the examination of necessity, may be the basis of political science,[76] and political science may be the only science. We wonder if this science in turn justifies political freedom.

Because the multitude of free men is intelligible as one, a kingship instead of an aristocracy of this sort is said to be possible but unnecessary. Aristotle speaks of this sort, who are good and men and citizens, and we have contended that the good represent the forms modeled on the virtues. If we are correct in our contention, then Aristotle's argument must also be understood to mean that the forms do not become one in the form of the good, as they did for Plato.[77] For Aristotle, aristocracy is "more choiceworthy" for cities than is kingship. But Plato's form of the good unified beneath it not only all things intelligible, but intelligible with intellect. Aristotle has yet to explain how this is done by his good men and citizens.

Nevertheless, if the Platonic teaching about the form of the good seems unnecessary or incorrect according to Aristotle, then we might expect a corresponding revision in the consequences of that teaching. Plato gave a famous account of the history of regimes,[78] which was meant to be, among other things, an explanation of causes, that is, an explanation of the relation of art, virtue, nature, and chance. The purpose of that account could be said to be a lesson for legislators in training in political moderation. All these themes are appropriate to Aristotle's present concerns. Thus, we are not surprised to find that Aristotle gives a revised history of regimes at this point. The history is an explanation of why it is more choiceworthy to understand the best regime as an aristocracy of good men and the whole as a community of forms instead of a kingship of the form of the good.

Aristotle's history of regimes is as follows:

> Because of this, perhaps, kings ruled earlier: that it was rare to find men much different with respect to virtue, especially as they made their homes in small cities. Still, they established their kings because of good services, the very thing that is the work of good men. When it happened that many similar in virtue came into being, they no longer used to abide, but they used to seek some common thing and to establish a regime. When having become worse, they did business away from the common things, then from that, it is well said, comes oligarchy. For they made wealth honorable. From these they first changed into tyrannies, then from tyrannies into democracy. Always leading few into base greed for gain, they rendered the multitude stronger (in body), so democracies were brought on and came into being. And when cities happen to be even greater, perhaps it is no longer easy for another regime besides democracy to come into being. (1286b8–22)

The political man learns about the causes of regimes. Aristocracy requires as a condition neither a small nor a large city, and the size of the city is by chance. But size is merely a necessary, not a sufficient condition, for many virtuous "happened" to come into being. Their virtue was uncaused. The cause of their constituting a regime was their assertiveness. But their being virtuous or doing good deeds was the essence of their regime. When they lost their virtue through their own baseness and greed, they lost their special regime. They caused oligarchies by becoming oligarchs themselves. Then tyrannies and democracies, which seem to differ from oligarchies only in number, arise. Thus, their own loss of virtue seems to be responsible for the present democracy noble men abhor. Or is it? Cities "happen" to be large now. Even virtue might be insufficient now, although it would only be hard, not impossible, for regimes other than democracies to come into being. Nature or chance sets limits, and one's political aspiration must therefore be moderate, but one must assert oneself and take public virtue seriously. The virtue inspired by noble passions is not omnipotent, however.

If we have been given the impression that vice is responsible for the degeneration of aristocracy, this is correct, though with a qualification. Enterprising oligarchs are not the only men who wish to do business away from the common things. Others are philosophers who do not wish to study politics, because the political things may not be all things. They become tyrants, as was Pittacus, until they might become wise, thus equal and ruling citizens of a democracy. Their democracy is not the city's democracy, but they are responsible for the city's democracy too. They are base lovers of gain, because they care about gaining wealth or wisdom, not honor. By corrupting the few with their bad habits, teaching noble men to prefer philosophy to politics, they effectively encourage democracies by leaving no one but the demotic interested in politics. If aristocracy is preferable to democracy because virtue is necessary and democrats cannot be virtuous, then philosophers must be more politic, leaving a few noble lovers of honor in the city.[79] If political men must be moderate in their acquisitiveness, philosophers must be moderate in their speeches by not publicly distinguishing between moral and philosophic virtue and prudence. But politic philosophy must also be a true substance, whatever its form.

Aristotle tells us what form philosophers who are politic, or good men, must use. It is the work of good men to set down, that is, posit, kings. The king we are examining, the king according to law, is a form of a form. The good men who are similar to kings in being of outstanding virtue are said to constitute a regime, the best regime, or the community of forms. The king that is a form of forms that are good is the form of the good. Good men speak as if there were "ones" in nature that are good and do all the work of the forms and of men. But Aristotle leads us to ask whether it is either necessary or reasonable that this king be.

According to Aristotle's history, the king is earlier or "prior" to the forms. He is logically prior to the forms, but not the cause of their being, for they happen to come into being. Nor do the forms become one; rather, they seek some community. Moreover, although similar as forms, they differ in being ones of different things, and therefore, when they do business away from the common things they are oligarchs, or the different parts of which the whole is composed. Insofar as the whole seems to be not a whole but its parts, making a whole first emerges as a tyrannical act. Tyranny becomes democracy when the few base lovers of gain become equal and ruling citizens, that is, when they become similar in their thoughts, by a procedure of which we shall learn. Is the king that is prior necessary for them to suppose that their potential unity in thought is also a unity with an intelligible nature, and therefore wisdom?

By good men, kings, or aristocrats, the political man seems to mean human beings capable of deliberating and of doing the deeds of moral virtue, that is, prudent men. By good citizens, kings, or aristocrats, we also mean forms. Why aristocracy is more choiceworthy than kingship, and what kind of a king is "prior," need to be made clearer. Therefore, we consider two additional objections made to kingship. If the king is a human being with a body, he is mortal and we must give some thought to his successor. Aristotle assumes that the king will appoint his offspring to succeed him, that his love for his own children could not be overcome, and that we cannot ensure against chance that they will be as good as he was. The king who combines *eros* and *thymos* on the level of humanity is a lover of himself, and the greatest assertion of self-love is the desire for immortality, which human beings seem able to approximate only by the physical generation of offspring. We wonder if this is why man conceives of what is good as eternal. In any case, if the king has being like human, therefore corruptible, being, we must suppose that there will be a genus of similarly good beings to perpetuate the good throughout eternity. Furthermore, the generation of the genus would have to be of a king that would not be subject to the vagaries of chance. Even Plato's regime of philosophers failed for this inability to conquer chance.[80] Finally, the king would have to be beyond the love of oneself exhibited by even the best of human nature; he would have to be godlike, or perhaps monstrous, in being devoid of passions. It seems that we could not conceive of a human king who would be good enough to rule men, and if we talk about the rule of the one best, we believe in a kind of being that is eternal, the master of chance, and either selfless or superior to selfish passions.

We seem to be thinking of a being who might rule over the whole in the way we would think of a god's being responsible for the whole. But how does a god rule? He rules over the natural bodies when they work according to the laws of nature. Aristotle says that he would need bodily strength to force his subjects to obey the laws, unless he managed the office like a household. He would need guards. We wonder if these strong bodies, that guard him with a strength greater than that of each and one and all, are not simply the whole of nature itself. Why a king would be necessary to rule over an orderly nature is unclear; his rule would be active only in combatting the fates. Unless nature needs to be ruled as is a body by a soul, his being would be virtually superfluous. Furthermore, were he to rule over the "multitude," that is, free men, then they would no longer be free, or self-ruling. The god cannot be said to rule over men, so Aristotle says he must have less strength than the multitude. But we then fail to learn how political excellence might be said to be according to some nature.

In speaking of the guards of this king, Aristotle says that he must have strength exactly as the ancients gave guards when they set down an *aesymnetēs*, or tyrant, in the city and, as someone advised Dionysius, tyrant of Syracuse, when he asked for guards, that the Syracusans also have guards.[81] Pittacus ruled as a tyrant; and by definition, his guards were "foreigners" (1285a26–27). Pittacus was a wise man who tried to combat the fates, and who made it seem as if he also had to oppose politics to do so. And so the "ancients," previous philosophers, understood that wisdom was not by nature but by art, and they denigrated politics as inferior to philosophy. Aristotle, however, teaches that wisdom is according to nature because something given is intelligible, and that politics and philosophy need not be in opposition. The guard of Pittacus is the same as the guard of the citizens of Syracuse. But "someone" gives advice to tyrants like Dionysius. Do philosophers teach men how to rule as tyrants yet for the benefit of citizens? The guard of Pittacus and of Syracusans is, we suggest, in the speech that follows. This, by the way, is how barbarian kings could have guards from among barbarians of the more slavish sort, who bear all things gracefully.[82] Aristotle is about to explain how the one that rules nature as a whole is spread throughout the political multitude, as if each were a whole and a one, thus justifying both philosophy and a democracy of free men.

Bodies are not brought together into a one, nor should they be, for their multiplicity can be beautiful and it is necessary since they are corruptible. They are brought together into a whole if they are under one law. Kings, instead of laws, are necessary to bring natural beings together only if we suppose that nature had a beginning and now has a ruler who overcomes chance. Aristotle, however, teaches that visible nature is eternal, and that attribution of some things to chance is not incompatible with the understanding that nature itself is regular and reveals an intention.[83] If there were a king in nature, a form of forms, he would have a substance other than body, but Aristotle does not demonstrate the existence of this kind of being in nature. "Aristocracy is more *choiceworthy* for cities than kingship" (emphasis added). Is this why Aristotle's assertions about nature assume the form they do?

In any case, even if there were such a being, it would not be the kind that the political man needs to know about. The kind of man who believes it beneficial to be ruled by a king believes that someone has an art of doing well in each thing he does. He thinks, correctly, that even good laws fail to do this; but the problem is to determine who or what might do better. The only cause of good laws seems to be a good man. Yet goodness for men means having noble passions. Good laws originate in an assertion of one's own good nature, and in the creation of a whole city in one's own image. The noble passions of the noblest human being remain passions because he is a human being with a body, who becomes angry and errs and has a preference for his own good. Neither the law that emanates from him nor any of his deliberations will be any less partial than their source. Either we must learn to trust him in his imperfection or imagine that the cause of law was a more perfect being, or we must determine to judge for ourselves. If we were to imagine a more perfect cause of law, we would do so by making inferences about what would be necessary to meet Aristotle's objections to kingship. In doing so, however, we posit the existence not of a moral being but of a rational being: a perfect artisan, a soul superior to human soul in lacking all passions, a perfect judge, incorruptible. This is the god of which the philosopher is an image (1284a10–11), but he is very different from the free man who is moved by the desire to be good. Therefore, Aristotle would give this king less strength than the "multitude." We still need to know about the souls of men since they rule themselves.

Yet we also need to know about human souls because it seems that all we have learned about this king is inferred from comparing and contrasting it to human soul. This king is similar to human soul if we say that human soul is not body, but it is dissimilar to human soul in being wholly free from the attributes consequent to being in body. Only with reference to human soul, it seems, can we make inferences about how nature might be ruled. The being of nature is its bodies and their law, but from this nature we learn nothing about causes or first principles.

If, as we have suggested, the political man has become a bit of a "democrat," formulating general laws in order to become a legislator, it seems that the philosopher has become a bit of an "oligarch," making distinctions and forming some opinions about what kings, first and ruling principles, are. And this he does with reference to political science. The political man began to consider whether the rule of an excellent man was more beneficial than the rule of good laws, and what he has learned is that the rule of good men is most choiceworthy. The best laws, emanating from the best man, are originally biased; perhaps the rule of the best men means that the laws will be corrected by a succession of good men in the future. Indeed, we wonder to whom Aristotle spoke when he said, "It is necessity that this same one be a legislator" (1286a21–22). Perhaps all the legislator can do is to make his intention known to future legislators by attempting to speak clearly about what moves him.[84] Others will perfect his work in accordance with his intention. The philosopher begins to examine whether the best laws or the best men bring together more in order to determine whether his making of a whole can be said to be a finding, or science, rather than a making, art. He learns that as much as is brought together under one first principle is brought together in the mind of the man who judges, not in nature, except in the case of the good men who are "serious" in soul. Therefore he, too, needs to know more about the passions of men who legislate and judge, for the serious soul and the judge might be the same and therefore one. Thus, perhaps ultimately the only verifiable science is political science. The philosopher, too, must reason about the ruler's intention, the cause of there being a whole. The sixth and final examination is of the king who does everything according to his own intention.

5. The King of the Beasts (1287a1–1288b6)

We first undertook an examination of political beings on behalf of democrats in order to ascertain whether the presumption in favor of democracy can in fact be justified. By democracy we mean the rule of all, not of the poor, and therefore, the fundamentally democratic mixed regime outlined by Aristotle in the middle of Book III.[85] In order to ascertain the justness of democracy or any other regime, we have contended that we need a measure of equality and inequality that measures the "what" of human beings, which we have found to be their virtue, their resistance to enslavement to bodily nature. This means, for one thing, that their "what" cannot be their economic being, for economics is intelligible as provision for necessity, not freedom from it. Thus, the choice is not between democracy and oligarchy, but rather between the rule of all free-born citizens and the rule of those who are essentially characterized by moral and intellectual virtue, even if the latter are accidentally wealthy.

The democratic citizen initially attempted to argue that judging and ruling were somehow connected with manifesting human being in completion, and also that every man born a citizen, and only the citizen, was capable of judging and ruling, as if being a man meant being political.[86] We found his argument inadequate because he had no reasonable explanation for his assumption that doing the work of a citizen made one fully a man, or that only citizens were able to do the work of a man well. Moreover, he seemed to forget about man's rational capacities, exemplified by speaking well, having arts, and even deliberating and judging with skill. Intellectual virtue was not a part of his city. When the democrat nonetheless wanted to establish the justice of democracy by invoking arguments from natural science that seemed to prove that democracy is just because it imitates a nature composed of bodies, each of which is a one and an equal, then the democrat forgot about his humanity altogether. Man resembles bodily nature only when one abstracts from what distinguished man from other beings, and this is man's freedom, his capacity to be the cause of his own being insofar as he can choose his own end. Perhaps even a devotion to economics could be understood as befitting men, if it were understood as chosen.[87] Yet the reliance on natural science seemed to distract the spokesman for democracy from making the relevant argument: How can it be said that citizenship contributes to one's ability to choose well, and that only the knowledge a citizen has is necessary to this end, so that all citizens are equal as free men? The relevant argument will be made by Aristotle on the citizen's behalf in the context of his explanation of the nature of a political "one."

We also undertook an examination of political beings for the sake of educating men who did take both politics and their own excellence seriously. The existence of these, the manly men, first became apparent to us when the democratic definition of citizenship was corrected more or less satisfactorily: A citizen is one who has the power or ability (*exousia*) to judge and deliberate with skill.[88] The manly man senses his superiority, perhaps not incorrectly, and therefore asserts a claim to a disproportionate share in rule. But power and ability do not always coincide, although they might do so. Aristotle writes in a democracy, but democracy is not inevitable. Aristotle demonstrates the good citizenship of the political philosopher by attempting to reconcile the capable to their powerlessness while attempting to make the powerful more capable, and to defend their power only insofar as it is defensible.[89] In other words, he provides both the manly man and the democrat with a demonstration that democracy is just, a public demonstration that Socrates might have made and profited from.

But if our interpretation of Aristotle's intention is correct, we must also understand the demonstration to further the education of the capable, albeit powerless, man. He must know whether to continue devoting himself to politics, however minimal his influence will be; whether he ought to attempt a revolution; or whether he ought to retire from politics to his country estate.[90] At the same time as an allegiance to democracy is defended, the free man must be presented with all the alternatives, for otherwise his choice cannot properly be said to be wholly reasoned or free. He must be shown how to examine himself to understand what he does and should intend. He must be shown what the truest freedom or the greatest tyranny is; he receives the advice Dionysius was given. Yet the free man is meant by Aristotle to personify all political men, and surely all democrats assert that they are free. If we conclude that full awareness of the alternatives is not available to democratic citizens, as it is to political scientists, then we can bring together politics and philosophy, measuring both by the same "one": the man who chooses freely because he knows his own intention.

In suggesting, as we now do, that Aristotle can defend both the nobility of democracy and the correctness of noble choices, we must address ourselves to some difficulties raised earlier. The first is that the habits of mind exhibited by Aristotle's democratic citizen were such that it seemed that no democrat could learn to choose well.[91] The premise of democracy is that men are fundamentally similar and equal, and democrats are too quick to recognize similarities and to overlook differences readily apparent to others. Choosing requires making distinctions. We have suggested that in the examination preceding this one, Aristotle advised that "oligarchs" be made to legislate, because legislating requires formulating general laws; so the legislator must think more of similarities than differences, and of the whole as a whole as well as the sum of its parts. In other words, legislating tempers the oligarchic habit of mind.[92] Similarly, in the present examination, Aristotle speaks again and again of judging, although the democratic citizen originally identified himself as an assembly member as well as a dicast and, in fact, equated ruling with legislating. In legislating the democratic proclivities are strengthened, whereas in judging they are necessarily corrected. In judging, one is confronted with a contradiction, either between the law and one who has broken it for some reason, as for example, Socrates, or between citizens who have some claims of right against each other.[93] The law is tested by objections to it, or one is forced to make new law by applying it to a case it does not presently cover. In legislating by judging a lawsuit, one can better disregard oneself and the many like oneself, either because the interest opposed to the law is given equal weight in court or because the judgment is between the interests of others.

Not only is the democratic defect compensated for, but such testing of the law in the face of exceptions or omissions is not unlike the procedure of a scientist who examines his own working hypothesis. Nor is it unlike the statesman's use of prudence when he must act for himself, yet presumably in accordance with the law's intention. Thus the citizen, the philosopher, and the statesman are similar with respect to soul or habit of mind, and one can suppose that even if the citizen and the philosopher judge according to different laws, the education of a citizen can be justified as a contribution to his humanity. This is not the defense the democratic citizen had in mind, but it is, we suggest, the defense that Aristotle believes he should have had in mind. We have spoken of the desirability of combining the form of freedom with the substance of kingship, which we identified as wisdom. Perhaps it is appropriate to remind ourselves at this point that the wisdom of the philosopher may be no more than knowledge of his ignorance, and therefore of the benefit of philosophizing. The democrat who judges as a juror and the philosopher who makes judgments are similar in judging according to their "most just opinion."

Aristotle's present speech is meant to replace the ancient defense of *ae-symnateia*, the tyranny of wise men like Pittacus, as well as to be a guard of citizens against tyrants. Indeed, its theme is explicitly said to be an examination of the king who does everything according to his own intention, yet the argument appears to be a justification of democracy, not of kingship, much less tyranny. Earlier we raised a question about how it could be said that the manifestation of man's specific excellences, called forth by his efforts to resist nature, were anything other than an attempt to tyrannize over nature. If we grant that neither democracy nor any other regime can be justified according to nature as natural science understands it, we are still left with the difficulty of explaining how politics is not essentially tyrannical.

That man's excellences were to be understood as tyrannical because they were contrary to nature's intention is, we have contended, the teaching of the poets, especially Euripides and Alcaeus. The democrat, we recall, quotes Euripides on his behalf, as if Euripides had some political wisdom. Euripides' poetry, we argued, was meant to be philosophic; and whatever else it might be, was in truth impolitic. Euripides made manifest the necessity of the wise man's tyranny against nature, and at the same time he failed to take seriously the assertiveness or anger of political men, even as he himself exhibited the same anger. Euripides did not understand *thymos*. The cause of both of Euripides' errors was that he looked at politics in the light of natural science, rather than attempting to understand politics as sui generis.[94] Perhaps we can also criticize him for failing to look at nature in the light of politics.

Yet when we take man's virtues wholly seriously, we are led to imagine the existence of a suprahuman being, a wise and willful tyrant.[95] This kind of being enables us to understand how nature can be ruled, as distinguished from how it can *be*. Thus understood, however, man's virtues, his reason and assertiveness, are in accordance with natural rule; man's tyranny imitates divine tyranny. It seems that what is needed in order to give a politic defense of man's politics is to give a plausible account of a natural rule by which *thymos*, which is necessary for the rule of bodies, is exercised in a nontyrannical way. God's *thymos* or will must be shown to be unnecessary, not to say impossible. Thus, Aristotle has argued that nature is eternal and that it is ruled by laws of which its parts are the cause. God was neither creator nor legislator. According to this nature, the manliness of citizens would be justified, but that of tyrants outside of the whole would be unnecessary.

Several times we have referred to Aristotle as a poet, contrasting him with other poets. The poets make or make manifest men, as do Euripides and Homer, and they tell tales about the gods, as does Alcaeus.[96] They make men by portraying some men or deeds as honorable and therefore worthy of imitation; they are teachers of virtue. They make men manifest because their teachings about the noble are necessarily limited by the natures of the beings about whom and for whom they write. Man's capacities are given, even if the ends are chosen by him, and it is from among these capacities that the poet makes manifest. He must know souls, both the range of capacities and the tastes of those to whom he must appeal in order to make one or another capacity more or less manifest than it already is. Then the poet par excellence is the legislator, who uses his art to make capacities manifest in such a way that they form a political whole, a city or a whole human being. The legislator's making is most fully a making when he legislates for himself, for then the only previously formed tastes to which he must defer are his own. Then the poet or legislator par excellence is the reflective political man or political philosopher who examines his own intention and, in deliberating about his passions, necessarily asserts the authority of his own reason, or combines reason and desire, thereby making himself in accordance with a nature he can choose.[97] The sixth examination is one that "must be made" (*poieteon*). The limit of man's making is the contemplation of his own intention. The philosophic poet's *nomos* is the same as his *physis*, and Aristotle's poetry is not merely poetry because it makes honorable what is necessarily chosen in the light of a knowledge of man's possible choices. In the sixth examination Aristotle refers to Homer's two most prudent deliberators and speakers, remaining silent about Homer, the poet. The political is natural; it need not be made, and the poet who makes in accordance with it disappears. What the philosophic poet must do, however, is to demonstrate that this indeed *is* nature, or that it is one explanation of nature as satisfactory as any other. Poetry proper would remain necessary if knowledge of the gods were necessary and incomplete, for what is said about them is our creation of them. Aristotle's *Metaphysics* may well be poetry,[98] but his *Politics*, rhetoric and noble speech notwithstanding, is political science.

According to Aristotle's political science, the manly or political man is a citizen by hypothesis (1278a4–5). The hypothesis is that the city that exists for the satisfaction of men's needs and his desire to live with others also has as its end living nobly (1278b15–23, 1281a1–4), and that the city is ruled by one or more artisans who care (1278b1–5, 1278b37–39, 1279a8–20). What confirms this hypothesis is a demonstration that man's noble assertiveness, his politics and his arts, must have been intended by nature. It seemed important to confirm this hypothesis in order to argue that moral virtue, especially moderation, and therefore a politics whose end is virtue, could be justified in the light of what we can know about man's capacities and possible ends. The raison d'etre of politics, as distinguished from economics, is the definition of virtue and vice.[99] But man's natural ends seem to be the economic and the philosophic life; virtue or nobility appears as an end only to Aristotle's political friend. His opinion that virtue is an end can be said to be an opinion that willing adherence to certain forms or laws is the work of a free man. In order to defend his opinion as right opinion, it is necessary to defend his sense as common sense. The kind of reasoning of the political man who begins from what he sees and hears in political life must be shown to be theoretically sound, and this means that philosophic judgments must be shown to be similar to political judgments, even if philosophers reason about different things. The common sense of the political man begins with the observation that the things he sees differ more in form than they are similar in matter, or that form is an essential part of being (1275a34–38). A theoretical defense of this common sense is an account of the whole that makes intelligible the opinion that forms are causes of being.

Nevertheless, there is agreement *up to some point* with the philosophic speeches in which the ethical things are distinguished. Aristotle may agree with political men as to the necessity of virtue, and he may profit from an examination of the virtues, but he has led us to doubt that he is of the opinion that forms are sufficient to explain being. The forms, we have learned, are not wholly responsible for being, and those who make a whole of forms neglect substance.[100] The final step in the education of the noble political man is an explanation of the cause of forms.

The philosopher has nevertheless learned from the political man the importance of taking forms seriously, and of making distinctions among the parts of the whole. But the philosopher, we must not forget, seeks the cause of there being a whole, the first or governing principle which is responsible for the whole. At first it seemed that substance was body and that the authoritative science could be mathematics, by which we distinguish and compare bodies. But mathematics could not make "whats" commensurable—not even mathematical "whats," the numbers.[101] There was no "one" that was a measure of both substance, or body, and form, or quality. Yet counting presupposes the recognition of the similarity in form of a particular multitude of things and its differentiation from other multitudes, and mathematics brings things together at the expense of denying what it must presuppose. If there is a science of the whole that can give an account of the cause of there being a whole and of itself as science, then the first cause or substance must be shown to be grasped through forms.

From the political man the philosopher has also learned the importance of taking political man seriously as one of the beings in nature to be accounted for. Political men are self-ruled, and the way they seem to rule is by imposing forms upon themselves. The forms are the virtues chosen or commanded by law. Citizens who do not rule are formed by the law; but those who do rule, kings or legislators who make the law, are both form and substance and cause. The man who can be held fully responsible for his making of forms and who can give an account of his intention has an explanation of causes that is more reasonable than the one provided by natural science insofar as it does not deny what it must presuppose. Political science will thus be the model for natural science.

Thus we must make an examination of the king who does everything according to his own intention in order to understand how a first cause rules. This king is not like the king we have previously imagined that might rule over nature, for Aristotle distinguishes this king from "the king according to law spoken about." We should have learned, as is now made clear, that that king is unnecessary to nature because each regime has its own "eternal general" that makes each class obey its own laws. As the legislator of human cities and the ruler at "Subdued" and at "Wherever" in a smaller part, he is like Agamemnon, the *thymos* and *logos* that law and virtue embody. As an annunciator of a moral law, however, he is not a justification for any particular law. Indeed, since he is found in each of the regimes, which presumably have different laws, he does not teach us how the regimes are related to one another. He especially does not teach us how men's laws and virtues are related, if at all, to something that can be said to be nature. Presumably the "so-called king of all" does precisely that, since he rules all. More precisely, the king of all is the same as "that according to which the king who does everything according to his own intention rules." The king is nature, or that which is the same as nature, and therefore the standard against which human kings or legislators who have intentions can be said to rule when their rule is according to nature.

The king of all, when introduced, was said to be authoritative, though not to rule over the common things of a city ordered by the principles of skilled household rule (1285b29–31). Skilled household rule is exemplified by the artisan who serves, albeit like a father, and therefore because he cares. He is a statesman, which means above all an educator of souls.[102] In order that this king be said to rule, to be a cause and a first principle as well as to be authoritative, it would be necessary to show not only that man's soul can rule his body or that there is an art of ruling bodies in a city, but that such intended rule is unhindered by any cause greater than man. In particular, this requires the demonstration Aristotle has just given that an active god cannot rule nature. Rule requires *thymos*, and purposeful rule, *thymos* and *eros*, but assertiveness and desire are attributes of beings with bodies—beasts—not gods.[103] The god said to rule the bodies in nature by being responsible for the intelligibility of their order *does* nothing like beings with bodies and passion, and he can at least be said not to be hostile to man. There must be no fates to be overcome;[104] it would be better to know that the god does not care about men than to suspect his intentions. Political science requires at least this much of a consideration of natural and divine science. If the goodness of the god cannot be demonstrated, his existence as a willful being must be disproved. If the god had will, he would need a body. If he has a body, why can we not see him? The king we now examine cannot be a god.

The examination of the king of all is presented in the form of opinions about what is just or according to some law; it is thus an attempt to determine whether there is not some law according to which the king can be said to rule. An agreement that there is none is apparently reached. Indeed, the intention of the argument seems to be to reach agreement; it proceeds dialectically until there is nothing to be said in opposition and things can be shown to be similar, though not the same. The conclusion is admittedly aporetic. Thus the argument is more or less philosophic in form. It seems that as the political man learns how the substance of philosophic disputes differs from the ethical things he knows, he learns how to "do" philosophy himself, thus learning about the difference between political and kingly doing.

The first opinion of which we are told is that it seems to some that the sovereignty of one is not according to nature. The nature according to which it seems not to be is a nature understood with reference to the human bodies one sees in a city, for those to whom this seems speak of a city put together of similars by nature. These similars must have the same just and the same worth (weight), just as it would be harmful for bodies, if unequal, to have equal nourishment and clothing. If nature is bodies like human bodies, then all men, being roughly equal in body, have the same just or equality and must also have the same honors.[105] Honors, like clothing, are an adornment of the body,[106] but men differ not so much in the bodies they have by nature as in the other capacities they actualize. Unless one contends that nature and human nature are something other than body, then there is no argument against equal honors. If nature were soul, however, it might be hoped that precisely the man who properly understood what care for his soul was would not care for honors.[107]

The argument that nature seems to be bodies is first addressed to the honor-loving man who reasons from inequality. Just as it is harmful for unequals to have the equal, it is harmful for equals to have the unequal. Similarly, it is not more just to rule than to be ruled. As we have learned from

Hobbes, an argument that there are only bodies, among which human bodies are more or less equal, might be a sufficient argument against tyranny.[108] The man who wishes to be a tyrant for love of nourishment of his body or love of honor must either resign himself to democracy or learn that there are souls to be nourished, and that these do not visibly rule the bodies of others.

Aristotle tells us that the description of bodily nature as ruled by law rather than by one citizen is "more choiceworthy."[109] The argument is that visible nature is a whole in its being ordered; its order brings together each of the many of its parts into what is perceived as a whole. The parts are responsible for a law that allows them to be what they are, and to be parts of a whole. Visible nature as a whole is this order or law, a form.[110] Insofar as there need be rule in nature, the law's being enforced means the citizens' keeping their place; there is no cause of the law beyond this.

A whole composed of human bodies would similarly be bound to respect the fundamental law that reflects the equality of human bodies, and which is otherwise uncaused. There could be an orderly democratic whole on this basis. However many rulers there need be would be guards of the law. A democracy so put together would be according to nature, and there could be no appeal from the law to nature by outstanding citizens wishing to justify tyranny. It would then be the task of the politic philosopher or scientist to demonstrate that no part of nature is dissimilar to body as soul would be.[111]

A further demonstration that this is a democracy of political beings or free men would be required, however. Modern political science provides this demonstration by arguing that the law that orders bodies must be made by consent. The law is presumably in accordance with nature, but not made by nature. More precisely, however, it would seem necessary to argue that there is no nature found by science, since we must suppose that those who must consent can decline to consent, remaining in disorder. For modern political science, if political freedom is to mean the consent of all, there can be no law other than that made by the sovereign, authorized by consent to represent each. Law is altogether made and known as made. Yet it is still argued that that this law embodies a law of nature, although its origin is an overcoming of natural disorder made necessary by nature. Then for modern natural science it would seem that laws of nature similarly must be hypotheses about the natural order which must be understood not merely as hypotheses, but as purely artificial constructs, because nature must be said to be in truth unordered. For the sake of politics it seems that modern science must deny the possibility of science or philosophy as it has previously been understood.

Even this demonstration might be deemed inadequate, for it is not clear that living as one wishes, being a free man, means living according to a law that one has presumably consented to have made for oneself. In fact, liberty, according to the proponents of early modern political science, lay in what the law did not command. The law was to be limited to a preservation of the order of equal bodies. Modern political science attempts to make men free by making it seem as if they could be free from politics once politics has been established.[112] But, as Rousseau has reminded us, even if living as one wishes means living lawfully, not licentiously, one's wish or choice cannot be represented.[113] The citizen's freedom ought to be his moral or political freedom, the freedom of a man. Thus it seems necessary to defend the nobility of the legislative sovereignty of the *dēmos*, or of as many as are to be called free.

Aristotle's reservation against democracy can be understood in terms of his previous consideration that it is not easy for the many to do all that a law that commands the virtues requires (1286b36–37). The law that is made as an expression of man's freedom must reflect the content as well as the form of freedom, an opinion about what is good and choiceworthy. Choosing well requires both moral and intellectual virtue. Modern political science attempts to derive a universal rule of justice from natural equality, and to establish as a natural law the law that preserves this order of equality. It relegates considerations of choosing the end, and therefore of happiness, to a private sphere. The end of government and political virtue is to guarantee to each the equal right to choose his private happiness.[114] Modern political science does not wish to make a political whole; the political purports to be all form and no substance. For this reason, modern political science equates a just law with a law that is purely formal.

Modern political science defends democracy by explicitly denying that true science is possible, that natural equality requires the rule of the *dēmos*, and that anyone need rule in the decisive respect. It apparently overcomes political objections to democracy by denying that that for which kingship or aristocracy was deemed necessary by Aristotle, its wisdom or prudence, is the proper concern of politics. Perhaps, however, it is more correct to say that modern political science overcomes democratic objections to tyranny by obscuring the extent to which consent is the product of the manipulations of political science and is compatible with the imposition of the wisdom of tyrants.[115] It pretends to rest its defense of democracy on the law of nature that Aristotle also recognizes, but which he deems an insufficient ground for political justice. He deems it insufficient for reasons that early modern political philosophers would have granted: If this is the only law, then there is no defense of either science or political prudence. Our contention, however, is that the deepest justification for political freedom would be a demonstration that it is necessary for intellectual and moral freedom. Aristotle's defense of democracy is both more hesitant and more earnest because he squarely faces the objection that, although political freedom is demanded by all men, and perhaps justifiably so, it is not easy for the many to be good. Indeed, his apparent defense of democracy is explicitly an explanation of kingship.

We do find in Aristotle an explicit objection to the definition of law as order: "As many things as the law does not seem capable of distinguishing, neither would a man be capable of gaining knowledge of." The response offered is: "But, educating them for the purpose, the law sets up rulers to judge and manage the rest by their most just opinion. Still, it gives to those making attempts to set up what seems better than what is laid down." The law that articulates the visible order tells us nothing about "whats," and therefore nothing about the things we want to judge or have sciences of, and nothing about how to "manage (households)" or care for our souls. The law tells us nothing about the most important things. Presumably what it does do is to teach us how to begin to learn by making distinctions.[116] Our "most just opinion," which may be wholly inadequate insofar as it leads us to apply the measure of bodies to all other things, is nonetheless all we begin with. In speaking of our "most just opinion," Aristotle uses the oath of the Athenian dicast, who so swore in judging. We, as did he, begin with a law insufficient for our purposes. Our judgments are similar to the juror's in having to correct an inadequate law, on the basis of either sense perception or ancestral tradition, in the light of some standard for which we can give no other account than that it "seems."

Man apparently has no knowledge of the first principles of nature or politics, yet he presupposes their existence by his very attempts at judging and correcting the law. Hence, the argument continues: If there is intellect, it is possessed by the god and the laws only or, as it is reformulated, by the law. There is a law of perfect intellect to which human reason points, but which it does not attain. This law presumably differs from the law that articulates the visible order; it is the law the existence of which modern political philosophy wishes to deny, but the existence of which is a necessary presupposition for a defense of wisdom about the whole and of political wisdom, or prudence.[117] The god is omitted in Aristotle's restatement, either because a god who is the same as the law of intellect is superfluous, or because the god has desires insofar as he himself has not yet attained perfect intellect and remains in motion thinking about his thoughts.[118] The latter would be the case if the god were similar to the best man. The best man has desires because he lacks wisdom; he is only a philosopher. It is said that even the rule of the best man would be distorted by *thymos*. What this means, we suggest, is that man's intellect is dependent upon the forms he posits his speeches about what he sees, and the "one" by which he must judge may not be the "one" that measures all beings. The following apology of Tocqueville perhaps conveys the thought:

> When the world was full of men of great importance and extreme insignificance, very wealthy and very poor, very learned and very ignorant, I turned my attention from the latter to concentrate on the pleasure of contemplating the former. But I see that this pleasure arose from my weakness. It is because I am unable to see at once all that surrounds me that I am allowed thus to select and separate the objects of my choice from among so many others which it pleases me to contemplate. It is not so with the almighty and eternal being, whose gaze of necessity includes the whole of created things and who surveys distinctly and simultaneously all mankind and each single man.[119]

The law is the necessary working of perfect intellect, which the philosopher must presuppose, but which he cannot employ.

Thus it seems that there are two meanings of nature or of necessity: the order of the visible whole and the regularity of intellect. Although one of these might be that according to which the king who does everything according to his own intention rules, neither can be that king himself, for necessity does not allow for intention. Neither is a law of a nature that cares about men or serves the needs of human beings, but this is what allows man his freedom. It then also follows that neither law is a suitable standard against which to judge free men. The first law, which seems just to some, takes into account only the body; the second, which is not said to be just but which is divine, neglects man's body and therefore his bestiality or passions. Is there not some standard to determine the just for man in the light of his capacities?

In what follows, Aristotle does propose a just that is a measure of man's capacities for politics and philosophy. We are now told that the paradigm of the arts seems false, that it may not be more choiceworthy to use artisans rather than the general and necessarily imperfect rules that we find in their books. The objection made to reliance on artisans is that they, as human beings with passions, cannot be trusted to do things only according to reason instead of out of friendship. Men in political offices act out of spite or grace, and those who prefer to be ruled by written laws do so because they

suspect the doctors who would treat them of being in the pay of their enemies. It cannot be denied that political philosophers and other men who
speak of a political art often treat their patient in a way that the patient cannot understand to be for his health. At the least, Plato and Aristotle express
a preference for the rule of one or a few,[120] Socrates befriended would-be
tyrants,[121] and rhetoricians teach the art of being unjust.[122] On the whole,
the many's distrust of those who claim to have a political art is not unsound,
for an art does not supply a guarantee of its good use. And one need not
be so optimistic as to think that ruling makes invalids healthy; it suffices to
realize that in almost all cases the rule of many, even according to the most
defective laws, is more beneficial to those who rule and are ruled than is the
lawless rule of a tyrant.[123] Unfortunately, the many are unable to distinguish
what might be rare exceptions to this rule. Some men rule not out of spite,
but out of *grace*. Those who acknowledge this possibility acknowledge the
superiority of the artisan to his textbook; they call in doctors when they are
sick. They, however, are doctors themselves. Granted, when sick, doctors do
not treat themselves; but they do call in other doctors instead of relying on
what is written.

Rule by law or rule according to what Aristotle has written, not what he
has left us to infer, is suitable for cities. The paradigm of the arts seems false,
however, not because there is no political art, but because art is insufficient.
Grace or care is required in addition to art. If human beings were to allow
themselves to be ruled, it would be only by someone in whom they had
trust. There is no trust between the many and the political scientist, perhaps
because the political scientist neither defends democracy nor has the force
to replace it. Perhaps the political scientist could befriend the democrat sufficiently to treat him. But art and friendship are more easily combined in
political rule if one of the political rules mentioned means rule in speech
over souls.[124] When the ailing doctor calls in another because he has to
judge about "the household things" and because he himself has passions,
he looks for another soul against which to measure his own. One graceful
soul requests the grace of another, and the two engage in dialectic. They go
beyond the written things[125] by speaking to one another or by reading the
kinds of books that provide answers to the questions they pose.[126] If man
acquires wisdom, it must be acquired through speech.

In considering the political *archai* we are led to formulate another meaning of the just. The just is the mean, and the law is the mean. What the
mean is a mean of is not immediately clear. Is the law a mean between the
first two laws, the law that orders bodies and the law that is intellect, and
thus the imperfect meeting of the two in human judges? A mean between

what is just for bodies and what is divine? A mean between written law and political wisdom? A mean between the benefit of art and the need to secure friendship? A mean between two philosophic judgments about how a healthy soul is acquired? If any or all of these formulations are correct, then the law can be said to be an opinion about political things that is neither the minimal ability to distinguish or count nor the ability to bring all things together into a whole by grasping the first principle. It is an opinion that attempts to transcend the city's just law in the direction of a standard of justice and goodness, if there should be one. The standard of justice or goodness seems to be the needs of the healthy soul.[127] These needs are manifested in examining with others what the health of the soul is. The best answer we have to this is the mean that emerges from two souls philosophizing about political beings. The human soul at work examining soul is the law and it is the "just," the measure of what a political "one" is. The highest art is dialectic, and it is the use of the political capacity. Dialectic is just because it is a form in which one's own good and the benefit to what is common are the same, and this is the requirement for the assertion that the political good is the greatest good for man.[128] The standard for political justice is known only with reference to man's necessity to reason about political or human excellence. Political philosophy is that measure, and it is derivative not from either natural science or theology, but from a consideration of what man reasonably cares to reason about. What a human being intends is his own health or good; substance or the first cause is this *eros*. What remains to be seen is whether political philosophy, an intention to know soul, is the same as the cause of the law of nature, and whether it is at all reasonable to speak of cities dialoguing.

An answer to the second question is sketched as follows: If political philosophy is the simultaneous or successive dialogue between souls,[129] it is approximated in cities by a custom or habit superior to the individuals who are said to be more sovereign than the written laws. Each man who philosophizes necessarily exceeds the bounds of the written law's content. What "laws" he lives by are those necessitated by the habit of philosophizing. Dialectic, for example, proceeds according to certain rules. Philosophy as substance is more a way of life than a corpus of dogma, and is both more open to new opinion than is written law, and more regulated than the opinion of one man. Similarly, in cities there are men who have habits that embody virtues superior to what the law commands and which, as habits, are not erratic. In particular, we have in mind the reasonable or equitable men who make prudent judgments, adjusting the rule to circumstances as a statesman would.[130] It is not inconceivable that their particular judgments would come to be embodied in an unwritten law: We have only to think of the common law and its use in courts of equity. The existence of this unwritten law might cause a regime to be more just than its written laws would reveal.[131]

Aristotle's point, we suggest, is again clarified by Tocqueville in his chapter "What Tempers the Tyranny of the Majority." What does this is the predominance of lawyers in politics, the intervention of the judiciary in politics, and the jury system.[132] Lawyers, Tocqueville explains, are the democratic aristocracy; their instinctive preference for order and their natural love of formalities are the tastes of an aristocracy. They share a knowledge of the law. "Add that they naturally form *a body*. It is not that they have come to an understanding among themselves and direct their combined energies toward one object, but common studies and like methods link their intellects, as common interest may link their desires." The lawyers are nonetheless committed to democracy, for it is favorable to their political power and they are not distrusted by democrats. "In actual fact the lawyers do not want to overthrow democracy's chosen government, but they constantly try to guide it along lines to which it is not inclined by methods foreign to it." The method of the lawyer is that he "values laws not because they are good but because they are old; and if he is reduced to modifying them in some respect to adapt them to the changes which time brings to any society, he has recourse to the most incredible subtleties in order to persuade himself that in adding to the work of his fathers he has only developed their thought and completed their work." Tocqueville advises princes facing democracies encroaching on their power to bring lawyers into the government; lawyers "are less afraid of tyranny than of arbitrariness." A judge is but a lawyer in office; specifically, Supreme Court justices are referred to by Tocqueville as statesmen.[133] Lawyers and judges constitute a power "constantly working in secret upon its unconscious patient, till in the end it has molded it to its desire." Tocqueville's lawyer or judge is Aristotle's legislator or statesman, who, in a continuum of statesmen, insinuates his wisdom into law. His work is virtually the same as that of the political philosopher who cares for the city, but the statesman is not conscious of his making by reasoning.

If the striking similarities in the language as well as the content of Tocqueville's argument allow us to surmise that it is a restatement of Aristotle's argument, then we can consider the remainder of Aristotle's argument in the light of Tocqueville's explanation of how the jury system tempers majority tyranny or the rule of the *dēmos*. We must suppose Aristotle's argument to require some such self-limitation if we are to understand how he can appear to argue that the many, in doing for themselves, become friends of and similars to the monarch. Tocqueville's prince ought to enlist lawyers or judges in his government to preserve the substance of his authority. But in a democracy not judges alone, but juries necessarily judge cases. Tocqueville describes democracy as if it were similar to ancient democracy with its dicasts. The jury is said by Tocqueville to be responsible for the execution of the laws; the jurors are sovereign rulers. The advantages of the jury system lie not in the excellence with which it administers justice, but in the political effect of juries on jurors. "Juries, especially civil juries, instill some of the habits of the judicial mind into every citizen, and just those habits are the very best way of preparing people to be free."[134] Juries teach men equity in practice; they teach men responsibility; they make them think of their duties to society. But, most important, the nation's judgment is shaped and its "natural lights" are increased. While the juror is acquiring the habit of judging, the substance of his judgment is necessarily guided by the judge, who explains the laws and restates the lawyers' arguments. "The jurors pronounce the decisions made by the judge. They give that judgment the authority of the society they represent, as he gives it that of reason and law." Furthermore, the good will created by the jury system enables the judges to decide the most important cases on their own authority. "The jury is both the most effective way of establishing the people's rule and the most efficient way of teaching them how to rule." Wisdom is willed by all, and thus the one rules as many. If not philosophy, statesmanship or political activity is imitated, and because it is partly or apparently dispersed, it is respected rather than envied. Above all, formal respect for forms is maintained by all. With the assistance of such statesmanship we come as close as possible to justifying democracy as the rule of men who are neither lawless nor pious, but free as men through law, or form.

Thus Aristotle can say first that the serious man rules justly because he rules better; and second, that if this is so, two or ten good men could rule. Earlier it seemed that philosophy could not be just, because philosophy necessarily calls into question the opinions about the good and the god by which men live.[135] Serious men are, above all, impious. The identification of seriousness with goodness and justice requires a replacement of the city's belief in Homer's gods with the belief that the greatest gift the god, who is wise, might bestow is a prudent advisor. The replacement of the just rule of one serious man by that of two good men is said to be the meaning of Agamemnon's prayer that he have ten such fellow counselors.[136] The reference is to silver-tongued and prudent Nestor, who advised Agamemnon how to muster his troops. Agamemnon's preparation for battle was undertaken at the suggestion of a false dream sent by Zeus. Presumably the Zeus to whom Aristotle's Agamemnon prays is not spiteful. More to the point, if Nestor's prudence is humanly acquired, a prayer to Aristotle's Zeus is superfluous. The rule of two good men and of Agamemnon and ten counselors is further equated with "the two going together."[137] This is a reference to Homer's most courageous citizen, Diomedes, choosing Odysseus, for his prudence, to lead on a spying mission in the night. Aristotle uses the same quote in the *Ethics* as his example of friendship for the sake of noble deeds. A spying mission in the night reminds us of philosophizing about things difficult to see: souls and gods. The serious man is a man who examines souls, but in politics he is a courageous and prudent speaker. The good men who do noble deeds with courage and prudence are capable of acting prudently even if they cannot see for themselves the end of their doing.[138] What is essential in order to argue that the end of philosophy is similar is that there be gods who, rather than intervening in men's affairs, permit them to make themselves prudent and wise.

Agamemnon was sovereign as a policeman but not as a deliberator; he made laws with the advice of others. The "divine" speeches to which he must listen are speeches about how to secure human virtue.[139] Agamemnon, in needing such speeches, is only part of a political "one" or whole. In understanding what a serious man is, we can determine what constitutes a political whole. The "what" of a serious man is philosophic *eros* and *thymos* or, in politics, prudent speech and courage. What Aristotle's references to the prayer of Agamemnon and the friendship of Odysseus and Diomedes show is that in knowing the "what" of a man who is serious about being a man, we can measure and compare political "ones" and "manys," parts and wholes, factions and cities. Each is potentially a one that is a whole, but insofar as he does not fully actualize his capacity for virtue, he is a part of a whole. We need to add an Odysseus to a Diomedes to make a whole noble man, and apparently Nestor is one-twentieth of a man, or rather one-tenth of a woman and one-twentieth of a human being, because Agamemnon needs ten of him. The mean, or measure, is doing or making nobly. Making now includes making speeches and making examinations, but political making is for the sake of practice, not theory.[140] However many are needed and are able to make the city act (*prattō*) like a noble human being constitute the part that does the deeds of the whole. The city might be a kingship, an aristocracy, or a democracy.

The king who rules doing everything according to his own intention could rule an actual city only by making a *nomos* that educates citizens nobly to do for themselves what he would do politically. What this amounts to, we suggest, is to be understood with reference to Aristotle's remark about the sovereignty of custom and his use of Homer here. In this passage Aristotle makes no reference to Homer at all; the poet is completely hidden while his characters live, as if there were no maker of custom. Nevertheless, there are interpreters of custom. Aristotle gives a meaning to Homer that makes the most authoritative educator of Greeks seem to confirm the recommendations of Aristotle's political science. The ruler is the political man who judges. But there is another judge who speaks or writes descriptions of politics as does a statesmanlike political scientist. This judge rules readers who contemplate politics. Aristotle says that the judgments of those who judge are informed by the law that has educated them; and among those who judge seeing with eyes and ears and doing with feet and hands, many judge as well as one. These many are allowed to do [so] because they would otherwise not be friends of the ruler. These correspond to Tocqueville's jurors, who have been guided by the judge but who do the actual judgment. But is it not strange that men use ears for seeing, not hearing, that is, for listening to speeches or taking reading seriously?[141] When Tocqueville discusses the forms of American government and the federal Constitution, at each level the judge exceeds the forms, and among federal officials only Supreme Court justices need be statesmen.[142] Their judgment would seem to be more or less limited by the Constitution, to which they claim to reconcile laws. Tocqueville concludes his discussion of the forms by providing an example of how the written rules of the Constitution, which makes the nation a whole, contradict the factual distribution of power among the states, a power supported by legal sophistries; and the reader is asked to *judge*. The many are made one only in speech, hence by the law, but only in reading is this speech truly omnipotent. The whole made in theory is made by resolving contradictions in speech; the whole made in practice is made insofar as deeds are governed by one speech. Friends who read and understand are ones equal to the ruler or judge who writes; friends who make with eyes and closed ears, hands and feet, are ones that are "similar." These similar ones rule in cities, and the speeches of statesmen and political scientists perhaps educate them to rule well.

The rule of these similars cannot be presumed to be a wholly adequate replacement for the rule of a prudent statesman. But to make this argument was not Aristotle's intention. His political intention seems to have been to make politics friendly to philosophy by demonstrating the friendship of philosophy to politics. The philosopher wins the trust necessary to treat his patient by giving the best possible defense of democracy, which is at the same time a proposal for its improvement.[143] The argument is meant above all to be a defense of politics against tyranny and unfreedom. The intention of some would-be tyrants is to do good for the city, and they are shown that the most effective tyranny requires trust, or friendship, and its exercise consists of dominion in speech, primarily over those who have ears for listening, or who read books. But this tyranny, when fully effective, necessarily becomes a democracy of equals, a friendship.[144] The intention of democratic citizens to be free from tyranny is achieved by putting trust in themselves, insofar as they are worthy of trust and in the law which is articulated by prudent statesmen. The ultimate justification of both philosophy and politics must be their benefit to man, properly understood; and the measure, the "monarch," is deliberate choice, the quality of a free and virtuous man. On this basis, philosophers and political men can be friends.

It is of course necessary to demonstrate that what is beneficial to man is the health of the soul acquired in politics and in philosophy. Philosophy must be both possible and necessary. As for its necessity, it is perhaps sufficient to recall that Aristotle speaks of two different laws of nature: a law articulating an order of bodies and a law that is intellect. Although politics cannot be understood in terms of either, it is a mean, which therefore presupposes that both of the extremes are. If the second extreme does not exist, politics can be reduced to the first justice or to economics, not choice. Therefore, whether nature is body, intellect, or both is a matter of concern to politics. Political philosophy is necessary because only by examining man and men in cities can we hope to judge by our reason the relation between body and intellect. Philosophy and political philosophy can be shown to be possible only if we suppose that intellect, not body, rules. Philosophy must presuppose that the first principle of nature is intelligible like a human soul. Whether the philosopher comes to recognize this necessity only from an examination of politics is unclear, but the reasoning could not be expressed more clearly than it has been by a political man:

> Judicial power presupposes an established government capable of enacting laws and enforcing their execution, and of appointing judges to expound and administer them. The acceptance of the judicial office is a recognition of the authority of the government from which it is derived.[145]

The philosopher judges like a judge. On the one hand, in order that wisdom be possible, it seems necessary to argue that man's intellect finds laws as much as does a judge; the judge does not make them arbitrarily. On the other hand, it is not inconsistent with this to argue that laws need execution to be proper laws; if the lawmaker is sovereign in theory, the judge is sovereign in practice. If there is a first cause, its being is articulated only by the judge who pronounces his judgment; only man has speech or reason.

Political philosophy can demonstrate that philosophy is reasonable if the whole is ruled politically. Philosophy learns this defense from philosophizing about politics. But politics ultimately requires the defense given it in demonstrating the reasonableness of philosophy. Both politics and philosophy are beneficial and brought together.

That Aristotle does intend his argument to be a model for the understanding of wholes simply is suggested by his reference to the just rule of the serious man who is good. Forms *are* because the whole is composed of parts that might be ordered, and because there is a man who wishes to perceive the order and therefore posits the forms for the sake of grasping the order with his intellect. The efficient cause of forms is philosophic *eros* and *thymos*, and the final cause is *nous*. There are forms because there are bodies, and we are able to posit forms through the passions, which we owe to our having bodies. Just as man uses his "bestial" qualities to transcend his bestiality, we use our visible perception of variety and multiplicity to awaken our intellects, bringing intellect into being. The whole is its parts, yet the whole as a whole, and the cause of its being a whole are known only by the man who, by using the parts of the whole, has come to be outside of it as its first cause.[146] What would be the same as the form reached through an examination of forms is in fact the first cause. Each of the forms can be retained without having to become one form, because the "one" by which all things are judged to be one is a qualitatively different "one." Thus in politics, the equivalents of philosophic *eros* and *thymos*, prudent speech and courage, are, as parts, moral or political virtues, and are understood as parts of the whole of virtue by intellectual virtue. The whole of virtue is in the law, but the law is the statesman, who is also beyond the law. When Aristotle says that one serious man rules justly because he is good, and that this is the same as the rule of two or ten good men, he mentions the numbers that suggest to us the range of integers: 1, 2, 10. Unity is in the measure of the "what" of the things we count,[147] for example the goodness of serious men and good men, not in the multitudes of "ones" we call both one and many. All the parts of the whole, in being comprehended as parts of a whole, contribute the unity that is the cause of the whole. There is no necessity for showing that the whole itself is anything other than beautifully ordered multiplicity and variety. Form and beauty are rightly conjoined in body by intellect. Seeing through forms is right, and political science, in showing how the parts of the whole are related to the first cause, is a model of what a science of the whole might be.

Thus understood, political science cannot be subordinate to mathematical physics or to theology, for it achieves what they fail to do: it accounts for both quantity or body and the qualities exhibited by human beings. Mathematical physics abstracts from quality, and it cannot account for intellect. Theology abstracts from quantity and body, and fails to account for the existence of the visible world and the moral virtues befitting divine beasts. To attribute body and passions to the god is unreasonable; it is necessary to suppose the purity of his intellect and to suppose that he cannot rule as men do. It is this apparent conclusion in Aristotle's argument to which there can be no argument or speech in opposition (1287b23–25).

If political science is rightly the authoritative science, political science is not thereby authoritative over politics. Aristotle speaks of citizens who become friends of the choice of the monarch and of the *archē*. Political science cannot simply be authoritative over politics, we suggest, for two reasons. First, political science articulates a measure for politics: Philosophizing constitutes the human health or good, but cities make philosophy possible without doing philosophy, and philosophy lays down no laws. What is choiceworthy in politics in the light of this standard will depend on circumstances, and must be left to the deliberations of political men (1287b19–23). Second, political philosophy accepts the hypothesis of the political man, that man is free, without proving it deductively. The first principle of political philosophy is derived from politics. Aristotle's political philosophy is an attempt at a theoretical defense of the correctness of that derivation, but it remains tentative (1287b36–37). The political beginning is the only beginning a man can make, and the political beginning is prior to science itself. Justice Taney, in his capacity as a political man, knew what political philosophy must suppose. What political philosophy attempts to do is to show that the political beginning is the same as what a "natural" beginning would be. This it does by attempting to demonstrate that it is unreasonable to oppose this beginning; there is no reasonable objection to the political man's hypothesis.

Aristotle does not prove beyond a reasonable doubt that even if nature is not ruled by a tyrant it is ruled politically, and therefore that political philosophy is sufficient. Nor does he show that the philosopher and man as political are more than similar. He has shown that politics is sui generis and that tyranny cannot be justified, but he has not shown that all the natural beings are ruled politically (1287b36–39). Nor has he shown that all of the political multitude can be ruled by speeches about virtue (1288a6–15). But these demonstrations need not be made in order to establish the intelligibility and independence of politics as a whole, and to defend the lives according to moral and intellectual virtue as choiceworthy. How the political multitudes here distinguished are in fact to be ruled in the light of these choices is the concern of the last five books of the *Politics*. That politics and philosophy are reasonably concerned with the best regime, understood as the best order in the soul, has been demonstrated in Book III.

In the first *logoi*, Aristotle asked whether the virtue of the citizen of a good city was not the same as the virtue of the good man, as if to ask whether the city could not be a whole that made manifest whole men (1288a37–39). The city that is a whole is a city put together in speeches about virtue, and a whole man is a prudent political man or a political philosopher. When the law supplies the force needed to compel the acts of moral virtue that its speeches command, then the city in deed can also be said to be a whole. That democracy be such a whole is not in principle impossible, but it is doubtful, for it is not easy for the many to be good. The city is nonetheless a whole, complete in itself, although only philosophy provides the defense of politics and freedom as distinguished from economics and necessity. Similarly, political or moral virtue and practical wisdom are complete, but only theoretical wisdom supplies the theoretical defense of the premise on the basis of which political or moral virtue is intelligible.

In Book III of the *Ethics* Aristotle raises the ultimate question that the man concerned about virtue and the legislator must raise: When can a deed be said to be done voluntarily and therefore merit praise and honor or blame and punishment?[148] The premise of moral praise and blame and of laws that establish regimes is that men are the causes of their deeds, or that they are absolutely responsible for themselves. It seems that in order that the deeds of virtue be voluntary, they must be deliberately chosen. Yet what a man chooses to do, if he chooses freely, ultimately depends on the end he intends, and thus on his vision of the good.[149]

How can men be said to be responsible for this vision? Any particular moral or legal code must suppose that it knows the end for the sake of which actions are chosen; it does not admit that all visions of the good are equally correct, for then it has no claim to authority. But if men always act responsibly on their visions of the good, and their actions and therefore their visions differ, it seems that we can call one vision superior only by attributing to the man who we say judges nobly and chooses the true good a superior nature that enables him to grasp the end.[150] Yet it is a contradiction to hold men responsible for their natures, and the hypothesis of praise and reward for virtue is then unreasonable. Aristotle saves the hypothesis with the following assertion: "Either it is not by nature that the end appears to each man such as it does appear, but something also depends on him, or the end is natural but because the serious man does (*prattō*) the rest voluntarily, virtue is voluntary."[151] Either man is held responsible for his deeds, as are citizens, or he is responsible for the end in the way Aristotle's political philosopher is. The law that educates nobly is sufficient to make a whole of noble deeds, for the law can supply the end as surely as can right opinion about moral virtue. The end, however, must be made by man in accordance with nature. To the extent that Aristotelian metaphysics is a revision of Platonic philosophy as to the manner of being of the "one," it seems to be for the sake of making moral praise and blame universally reasonable. There is a whole, but no first cause without the philosopher. The philosopher makes himself the part within the whole that comes to surpass the whole, the one of very great age that happens to come to be (1288a24–28).

That the good intended as an end is intellect is, we have argued, the necessary first principle of man's attempts to transcend his bestiality. It is therefore what ultimately makes politics or morality, the living by forms which is the only means by which most men can transcend their bestiality, intelligible even if the end is not seen by the political man. This end Aristotle sometimes calls "the god." Despite the fact that the end is human perfection, Aristotle acknowledges that most men need to conceive of a human excellence they will never experience as suprahuman or divine. In particular, the demotic need to believe that this "being" sanctions the punishments that rulers devise and inflict on men who do not obey the laws that command a modicum of virtue.[152] Aristotle can consistently speak of such a god without depriving man of his freedom and his responsibility for his virtue, insofar as he can demonstrate that it is unreasonable to suppose that man is not the chief executive.

Hobbes tells us of Aristotle's teaching about "entities and essences" that he may have known it "to be false Philosophy; but writ it as a thing consonant to, and corroborative of their Religion; and fearing the fate of Socrates."[153] This is said in the context of his criticism of the use of Aristotle made by the Church. When many people came to believe the speeches of those who claimed to have seen a man who was God, thus a being with a body and capable of ruling, it no longer seemed possible to assert that man's freedom was in accordance with a nature that was divine. There could be no nature according to which man's makings, including his political makings, were free, and by which he was befriended. The modern defense of politics is necessarily either tyrannical or democratic in form. If man is free, he must rebel against God's rule, proving himself a greater tyrant or prince. Or, if there is to be justice and rule by law instead of tyranny, politics is no longer assimilated to the measure of divine beasts, the mean between two laws of nature. Instead, the existence of the second kind of being is denied, and the measure is made the law for bodily nature. Aristotle's mixed regime is reconstituted on a democratic foundation, and the consequent changes in the explicit accounts of political prudence and wisdom are made. Political science becomes the science of managing the passions, and natural science becomes mathematics.

Originally, the modern defense of the sovereignty of the *dēmos* was no less qualified than Aristotle's. But it was thought that the qualification could not be made explicit because the standard in light of which the qualification was intelligible had come to be confused with the Christian God. The qualification and the standard that could not be publicly defended have come to be publicly forgotten. So has the best answer to the question "Why democracy?"

A Note on the Translation

For the convenience and occasional frustration of the reader and, ultimately, for the defense of this writer, my own translation of Book III of Aristotle's *Politics* is included in this volume. In translating, I have abandoned any attempts at gracefulness because of my greater concern with literalness. It is my opinion that most of the English translations are deficient in the latter respect. Of those translations the best, to my knowledge, is the one done by Thomas Taylor[1] at the beginning of the nineteenth century. I became aware of its existence only as I was completing my own translation. I have drawn from it to some extent, as well as from the English translation of H. Rackham[2] and the French of J. Aubonnet.[3] E. Barker's translation[4] was consulted but not used. The notes and commentaries in editions of the Greek by W. L. Newman[5] and by F. Susemihl and R. D. Hicks[6] often proved helpful. The text used was that of the Oxford Classical edition.[7]

The premise guiding my procedure in translating is a conclusion painfully arrived at, not a presupposition. The contention of this book is that the *Politics* can and should be read literally in order to be understood fully. Once it was thought that the *Politics* might only be a set of lecture notes. That this is in any case Aristotle's own work is no longer seriously contested, and that the *Politics* might indeed be a book is conceded as a possibility.[8] The manuscripts of the *Politics* are late, and are often asserted not to be good; that some passages are exceedingly difficult to read with confidence remains a problem. Nevertheless, that the book may have been written with as much care as, for example, a Platonic dialogue;[9] that the manuscripts are not hopelessly corrupt merely for being late; and that there are not arguably better guesses at difficult passages are possibilities that the translator should not foreclose to the reader's own consideration without serious reflection. My attempts at serious reflection, not any alleged superior knowledge of Greek, have led me to take issue with previous translators. Most authorities are not on my side; my argument must be judged on its merits. The argument, stated briefly, is that the *Politics* is intentionally written in an ambiguous manner with the understanding that, while philosophers do not tell untruths, not all philosophic truths—or, rather, philosophic speculations—can be baldly announced. The argument is, further, that the explanation of this necessary circumstance of philosophy and a suggestion about what must be done to face it are presented in Book III of the *Politics*. Thus, an explication of the meaning of the text is a justification of this awkward but literal translation.

The translation presented here will perplex some readers in one respect. In the case of words or constructions that are ambiguous in the Greek and could not be rendered sufficiently so in English, I have often deliberately rendered them in a way that brings out the less obvious meaning. For example, the word *oikeios* has the primary meaning of "pertaining to the household" and the secondary meaning of "proper, suitable" as well as "akin to." Because Aristotle seems to use the household to stand for the human things as distinguished from the rest of nature, and for the training of souls for politics and philosophy under the guidance of philosophy rather than convention, I have retained the primary sense of the word whenever it occurs, however awkward it may seem. What I have translated as "management" is also, in its primary meaning, "household management." A crucial word with several meanings is *archē*: "beginning," "first principle," "rule," "office," "magistrate." I have rendered it consistently as "rule," even when "office" or "magistrate" may be the intended meaning, or as "beginning" when necessary. *Genos* is "genus," the technical term for a class of things, but also "race" or "family"; both translations have been given. *Sympherō* means "to benefit" or "to bring together"; I have rendered it as "to benefit."

The reading of the text is facilitated by recalling several reasonable procedures that are useful for reading any book unless one simply assumes that it need not be read with special care. First, an example, especially when said to be an example, is to be understood as being no more than one example. Merely because a statement is illustrated with a political example, one should not infer that the principle stated has only political application. Also, two nouns or verbs connected by "and" are not necessarily identical to one another, no matter how similar they may appear. For example, Aristotle once speaks of political rules over citizens put together according to equality and according to similarity. Reasonably, equality should apply to quantities and similarity to qualities. If things equal in mass can still differ from each other as might a big baboon from a small philosopher, then the "citizens" referred to are not necessarily the same. Furthermore, there is no reason to suppose that repetitions with the phrase "exactly as was said before" should not be exactly, not almost, as they were said before. Differences should, therefore, be noted. Finally, conclusions that are "apparent" should perhaps be distinguished from those that are not so qualified. Other suggestions will be offered as necessary in the body of the commentary.

Translation of Aristotle's *Politics*, Book III

1274b32–1275a2

For one inspecting the regime [regimes],[1] what each is and of what sort it is, almost the first examination is to behold the city, what the city is. For now they dispute, some asserting the city to have done a deed, some not the city but the oligarch or the tyrant. And we see all the business of the statesman and legislator to be with the city. And the regime is some ordering of those who make their homes in the city. Since the city is of composed things, like some other whole organized from many parts, it is manifest that first the citizen must be sought. The city is some multitude of citizens, hence, who must be called a citizen and who is a citizen must be examined.

1274b41–1275b21

The city is some multitude of citizens, hence who must be called a citizen and who is a citizen must be examined. The citizen is often disputed, for not all agree that the same one is a citizen. He who is a citizen in a democracy is often not a citizen in an oligarchy. We omit those who have chanced upon the title in some other way, for example a made citizen. A citizen is not a citizen in making his home someplace, for even resident aliens and slaves share in domicile. Nor are they (citizens) who have a part in the just things, in such a way as to submit to right and to try [or be tried]. For this also belongs to those who share in contracts and they have these things, while resident aliens everywhere partake in these things, though not completely; but they must have a patron because they partake somehow incompletely in this sort of community. But, like children who because they are not yet of the age to have been enrolled, and like the old who because they have been discharged, they must be asserted to be citizens; not quite absolutely, but adding, on the one hand, incompletely, and on the other, passed the prime or some such thing. It makes no difference, as is manifest from what has been said. We seek the citizen simply, one who has no such accusation needing to be straightened out, since the same difficulties are raised and solved concerning the dishonored and exiled. The citizen simply is defined by nothing so much as by partaking in judgment [*krinō*] and in rule [*archē*, also office, the first principle or cause, the beginning]. Of rules, some are limited in time, so in some for the same one to rule wholly twice is not possible, or (he rules) only through some defined time. But another is unlimited, for example, the juror and assembly member. Perhaps someone would assert that these are not rules, nor does one partake in rule through these things. Yet it would be ridiculous to defraud the most sovereign ones of rule. But let it make no difference, for the argument [logos, argument, reason, or reasonable speech] is about a name. What is common to a juryman and assembly member is nameless; that is, what ought to be called the matters of both. For the sake of definition, let it be unlimited rule. We set down as citizens those who partake in this manner.

A definition almost like this would best fit all the citizens spoken of. But it is necessary not to forget that among things in which what underlies them differs in form and among which one is first, another second, another next, and being such as they are, either there is nothing of what is common in them or a niggardly amount. But we see regimes differing in form from each other, some being later, others prior. The erring and divergent necessarily are later than the unerring. What we mean by divergent will be apparent later. Thus, a citizen is necessarily other according to each regime. Because of this, the one spoken of is a citizen especially in a democracy, while in the others it is a possibility, but not necessary. For in some there is no people [*dēmos*], nor do they customarily believe in an assembly, but rather in specially summoned councils. And they try lawsuits according to parts. For example, in Sparta those about contracts are tried by different ephors in different cases, and the elders try murders, and perhaps some other rule others. And it is the same way in Carthage, where some rules judge all lawsuits. But the definition of a citizen admits of correction. In the other regimes, the assembly member and juryman is not an unlimited ruler, but is defined according to the rule. It is given either to all or some of these to deliberate and judge about either all or some things. Therefore, what a citizen is is apparent from these things. He who has the possibility [or right] of sharing in the rule of deliberating with skill and judging with skill we say is already a citizen of this city, the city being a multitude of such men sufficient for self-sufficiency of life, to speak loosely.

1275b22–1276b15

For use, a citizen is defined as one from citizens on both sides, not one or the other only, for example, father or mother. But some seek further, for example, for two or three or more ancestors. Given this political [or statesman-like] and brief definition, some raise a difficulty about that third or fourth man. How will he be a citizen? Thus Gorgias of Leontini ["Little Lion"], perhaps at a loss about some things and being ironic about others, asserted that exactly as mortars are the things made by mortar makers, so the Larissaeans are those who have been made by the demiurges, for some of them are Larissa makers. [The name given Larissaean magistrates was demiourgos; demiourgos also means craftsman, and the city of Larissa was famous for its kettles, called Larissas.] But this is simple: if they had a part in the regime according to the mentioned definition, they were citizens. It is not possible to fit the qualification of being from a citizen father and a citizen mother to the first who made their homes or were founders.

But perhaps, rather, those who came to partake after a change in the regime have a difficulty; for example, in Athens those made by Cleisthenes ["Lock, of Key, or Strength"] after the expulsion of the tyrants. For many foreign and slavish resident aliens were enrolled in tribes. The dispute about these is not who is a citizen, but whether one is so unjustly or justly. And even about this someone might raise a further difficulty: whether if one is not justly a citizen, is he then not a citizen, as if the capacity of the unjust and the false were the same. Since we see some ruling unjustly, we shall assert that they rule, but not justly. But the citizen is defined by some rule, for a citizen is one sharing in some such rule, as we asserted. It is manifest that even these must be asserted to be citizens, but whether in justice or not is bound to the dispute previously mentioned.

Some raise the difficulty, when did the city do something and when did the city not do it, for example, whenever a democracy comes into being from an oligarchy or tyranny. Then some choose neither to discharge their contracts, alleging them not to have been undertaken by the city but by the tyrant, nor many other such things, alleging that some regimes *are* because they are strong, not because they are for the benefit in common. Therefore, if some democracies are ruled in the same way, one must assert that the deeds of this regime are of the city in the same way as are the deeds of the oligarchy and the tyranny.

The argument seems to be of the household of this difficulty, somehow: When should one say that the city is the same or not the same, but other? The most superficial search of the difficulty is concerning the place and the human beings. It is possible that the humans have been unharnessed from the place and have come to make their homes some in one and some in another place. In this way the difficulty must be set down as tamer, for in the city being spoken of, such a search as this is often somehow more at ease. Similarly, of humans settling down in the same place, when must one believe the city to be a one? Surely not with respect to walls, for it would be possible to throw one wall around the Peloponnesus ["Dark-colored Toil"]. Perhaps even Babylon is a case of this sort, and all cities that have the outline more of a nation than a city. They assert of it that three days after having been conquered, some part of the city did not sense it. But the examination of this difficulty will be useful for another occasion. The statesman must not forget about the extent of the city and how many and whether one or several nations are beneficial [or brought together]. But of these settling down in the same place, must the city be asserted to be the same as long as the race [*genos*, also family or genus] of settlers is the same, even though some are always perishing and some coming into being, exactly as we are in the habit of saying that rivers are the same and springs are the same even though some running water is always being added and some gradually disappearing? Or must it be asserted that while the human beings are the same, through such a cause the city is another? If the city is some community, it is a community of citizens in a regime. The regime becoming another in form and differing in regime, it would seem necessary that the city be not the same, exactly as we assert that a chorus that is sometimes comic and sometimes tragic is another chorus, even though it is often of the same human beings. And, similarly with every other community and other compound, should the form of the compound be other. For example, we say that a harmony of the same sounds is other if it is sometimes Dorian and sometimes Phrygian. Therefore, if this is the same, it is apparent that the city must be said to be the same mostly with a regard for its regime. It is possible to call it by the same or another name both when its settlers are the same and when they are entirely other human beings. Whether it is just for the city to dissolve or not dissolve (its contracts) when the regime changes into another is another argument.

1276b16–1277b32

What follows from the things now mentioned is to inspect whether the virtue of the good man and the serious citizen must be set down as the same or not the same. But surely if it is necessary to chance upon this search, the (virtue) of the citizen in some impress must first be taken hold of. Therefore, exactly as the seaman is some one among those who share, thus we assert the citizen to be also. And even as seamen are dissimilar in capacity, for one is a rower, another a pilot, another a helmsman, another having some other name of this sort, it is manifest that the most accurate argument about the virtue of each will be peculiar [private]. But similarly, some common one will fit all. The saving of the voyage is the work of all of these, for each of the seamen reaches for this. Similarly now, also for citizens, although they are dissimilar, the saving of the community is the work. The regime is the community. Because of this, the virtue of the citizen necessarily must be according to the regime. Therefore, if indeed there are several forms of regime, it is manifest that it is not possible for the virtue of the serious citizen to be one and complete. But we assert that a man is good according to a virtue one and complete. Therefore, it is apparent that it is possible for a citizen who is serious not to possess the virtue according to which a man is serious.

But now, by raising great difficulties it is possible to go through the same argument in another way, with reference to the best regime. If it is impossible for the city to be composed of all serious ones, but each must do well a work that is his own [according to the same], this is by virtue. Since it is impossible that all the citizens be similar, then the virtue of the citizen and the good man would not be one. All must have the (virtue) of the serious citizen, for this is necessary for the city to be the best, but it is impossible that (all have the virtue) of the good man, if it is not necessary that all the citizens in the serious city be good. Still, the city is from dissimilars, as a creature is immediately of soul and body, and soul of reason [*logos*] and desire, and a household of man and woman, and property of master and slave. In the same way, the city is formed together from all these, and besides these other dissimilar forms. Then it is necessary that the virtue of all the citizens not be one, exactly as it is not of dancers, the head dancer and the one who stands beside him. Wherefore that it is not simply the same is apparent from these things.

But then will the virtue of some serious citizen and some serious man be the same? We assert that the serious ruler is good and prudent, while the statesman is necessarily prudent.[2] And some say that the education of the ruler is immediately other, exactly as the sons of kings are seen to have been educated in horsemanship and warlike skills, as indeed Euripides asserts. "Not for me the sophisticated things, but what the city needs,"[3] implying that there is some education of the ruler.

If the virtue of the good ruler and the good man is the same, but he who is ruled is a citizen also, the virtue of a citizen and a man would not be simply the same, although of some citizen (it would be). For that of the ruler and the citizen is not the same, and because of this, perhaps, Jason asserted that he was hungry whenever not tyrant, meaning that he did not have the science of being a private man. But the capacity to rule and be ruled is surely praised, and the virtue of the esteemed citizen is to have the capacity to rule and be ruled nobly. Therefore, if we set down the virtue of the good man as skill in ruling and the citizen's as both, both would not be praised similarly. Therefore, since sometimes it seems that the ruler and ruled need learn other, not the same, things, but that the citizen must know both and partake of both, from there someone could look down.

There is the skilled master's rule. This rule, we say, concerns the necessary things, concerning which the ruler need not necessarily have the science of doing [making], but rather of using. The other is slavish. I mean by the other the capacity to be an underseaman in the serviceable practices. We say that there are several forms of slave, for the works are several. The handworkers fill one part. These are, exactly as the name itself signifies, those living by their hands, among whom is the banaustic artisan. [The handworker is *chernēs*; hand is *cheir*.] Hence, in some places the craftsmen did not partake in the rules in ancient times until the extreme people [*dēmos*, also democracy] came into being. Therefore, neither the good one nor the statesman nor the good citizen need learn the work of being ruled in this way, unless sometimes for the sake of use by himself for himself. The coming into being of master and slave does not yet follow from this.

But there is some rule according to which one rules over similars in genus and over free men. This, we say, is the political rule, which the ruler must learn by having been ruled. An example is to command the cavalry by having been under a cavalry commander, to be a general by having been under a general, and a squadron commander, and a company commander. Because of this, even this is nobly said: that it is not good to rule without having been ruled.

While the virtue of these is other, the good citizen must know and be able to be ruled and rule, and the same virtue belongs to the citizen, to know the rule of free men from both sides. And that of the good man is surely both. If the form of moderation and justice of one skilled in ruling is other than that of one who is ruled, but free, it is manifest that the virtue of the good would not be one. For example, justice has forms according to which one rules and is ruled, exactly as the moderation and courage of a man and a woman are other. A man would be opined to be a coward if he were as courageous as a courageous woman, and a woman a babbler if she were as discreet as a good man. The household management of man and woman are other, the work of the former being to acquire, of the latter to guard. Prudence is the only virtue peculiar [private] to the ruler, for the others seem necessarily to be common to ruled and ruling. But prudence is surely not the virtue of the ruled, but true opinion. Exactly as the ruled is a flute maker, the ruler is the flute player who uses them.

Whether the virtue of the good man and the serious citizen is the same or other, and how they are the same and how other, is apparent from these things.

1277b33–1278b5

Concerning the citizen, some one of the difficulties still remains. Is it truly that the citizen is one for whom it is possible to share in rule, or must even the banaustics be set down as citizens? If even these in whom there is no part of ruling must be set down, then it is not the case that such virtue belongs to every citizen. Such is a citizen. If none of this sort is a citizen, in what part must each be set down? For he is neither resident alien nor foreigner. Or shall we assert that even from this argument, nothing out of place follows? For neither are slaves anything of the mentioned, nor are freed men. This is true, that not all must be set down as citizens without whom there would be no city, since not even children are citizens in the same way as men, but the ones are simply so and the others are so based upon an hypothesis. They are citizens, but incomplete ones.

In ancient times in some places the banaustic was a slave or a foreigner, and for this reason many are of this sort even now. The best city will not make a banaustic a citizen. If even this one is a citizen, the citizen's virtue of which we spoke must be said not to belong to all, nor only to the free man, but to those who are released from necessary works. Those performing such service in necessary (works) for one are slaves; those in common are banaustics and hired agricultural laborers. How it is about these is apparent to those who, starting from this point, inspect it themselves a bit further. For what has been said, having been made apparent, makes itself manifest.

Since the regimes are several, even the forms of citizen necessarily must be several, and especially of ruled citizens. Thus, in some regime it is necessary that the banaustic and the hired agricultural laborer be citizens, but in others there is no capacity. For example, there is some one that they call aristocratic and in which honors are given according to virtue and worth [axia, also claim and weight]. In oligarchies it is not possible for a hired agricultural laborer to be a citizen, for participations in rules are from large (property) estimates, but it is possible for a banaustic. For many of the artisans are wealthy. In Thebes there was a law [nomos, law or convention, also song] that one who did not stay away from the marketplace for ten years could not partake of rule. In many regimes the law even attracts some strangers. He from a citizen mother is a citizen in some democracies in the same way as in many (regimes) things are with illegitimate children [the spurious]. Nonetheless, when because lacking in lawfully begotten citizens they make for themselves these sorts of citizens, for through scantiness of human beings they use such laws [or are used by the laws], when they gain an abundant mob little by little they detach first the (children) of male slave or female slave and then of women. Finally they make only those of both townsmen citizens.

Therefore, that there are several forms of citizen is apparent from this. He most truly said to be a citizen is he who partakes in honors, exactly as Homer created [*poieō*, to create in poetry, and more generally, to make, to do]: "Like some wanderer without honor,"[4] exactly as a resident alien is one who does not partake in honors. But where this sort of thing is cloaked, it is for the sake of deceiving those who make their homes together.

Whether that according to which a man is good and a citizen serious must be set down as other or the same is manifest from the things mentioned. In some city it is the same and in another, other, and even in the former case not for everyone, but only for the statesman who is sovereign or has the capacity to be sovereign, either by himself or with others, over the care of the common things.

1278b6–1279a21

Since these things have been distinguished, what must be examined after them is whether it must be set down that there is one regime or several, and if several, what they are and how many they are, and what the differences between them are. The regime is an order of the city with respect to the other rules and especially the one sovereign over all. While the ruling body of the city is sovereign everywhere, the regime is the ruling body. I mean, for example, while in those (regimes) favoring democracies the people is sovereign, in those favoring oligarchies the few in opposition is (sovereign). We even assert that the regime of these is other. And in the same argument we shall speak about the others.

Surely one must hypothesize about for the sake of what the city was put together, and how many forms of rule there are with respect to the human being and the life of the community.

Surely it was mentioned in the first arguments, in which household management and mastery were distinguished, that by nature the human being is a political animal. Because of this, even should no one need the help of each other, they no less desire to live together. But then even, the benefit in common brings them together, so far as to each falls his lot of living nobly. Therefore, this most of all is the end, both for all in common and separately. They come together even for the sake of life itself and maintain the political community. Perhaps there is some portion of the noble even in life itself alone. Should there not be too great an excess of the hardships of life, it is manifest that the many of human beings strive for life, bearing patiently much suffering, as if there existed some good time and natural sweetness in (life) itself.

But now it is easy to go through the mentioned ways of rule also. Even in the exoteric arguments we distinguish them often. One is despotism. Although, in truth, the same thing is beneficial to the slave by nature and the master by nature, nevertheless it is no less rule for the benefit of the master and incidentally for the slave. For it is not possible for the despotism to be saved while the slave is corrupted. The rule of children and woman and of all the household, which we surely call skilled household management, is either for the sake of the ruled or something common to both. But in itself it is for the ruled, exactly as we see in the other arts, for example, medicine and gymnastics, and incidentally for themselves. Nothing stops the gymnastic trainer from sometimes being among those exercising himself, exactly as the pilot is always one of the seamen. Therefore, the trainer or the pilot looks to the good of the ruled, but whenever he himself becomes one of these he incidentally partakes of assistance. For the one is a seaman and the other comes to be one of those exercising, though he is a trainer. Hence, even with regard to political rules, whenever the citizens have been arranged according to equality and similarity, these claim to rule according to part [in turn], which is prior, and in the natural way, claiming to do service by part, and, again [on the contrary], to look after some good of the same, exactly as it is prior that the same, ruling, had looked to the benefit of that one. But now, because of the assistances away from the common things and those from rule, they wish to rule continuously [*sunēxōs*, primary meaning "by constraint"]. For example, if it followed to those ruling, being sick, to be healthy always, thus perhaps they would seek the rules.

It is apparent, therefore, that as many regimes as look out for the benefit in common chance to be right according to the just simply, but as many as (look out) for only that (benefit) of those who rule are all erring and deviate from the right regimes. They are skilled despotisms, but the city is a community of the free.

1279a22–1280a6

These things having been distinguished, what follows next is to inspect the regimes, how many in number and what they are, and first the right ones among them. The deviations will be apparent once these have been distinguished. Since the regime and the ruling body signify the same things and the sovereign in the cities is the ruling body, it is necessary that the sovereign be one, few, or many. Whenever the one, the few, or the many rule for the common benefit, it is necessary that these be right regimes, while those for the private (benefit) of the one, the few, or the multitude are deviations. For either it must be asserted that those who partake are not citizens or one should share in the beneficial. We are in the habit of calling kingships those monarchies that look out for the common benefit and aristocracies (rule by) the few, but more than one, either because the best rule or because it is for the best of the city and those who share in the same. Whenever the multitude takes part in politics for the common benefit, it is called by the name common to all regimes, polity [*politeia*, regime]. This happens reasonably: it is possible for one or a few to differ in virtue, but already for more it is hard to have become perfect with respect to all virtue, but especially with respect to skill in war, for this arises in a multitude. Because of this very thing, according to this regime war making is most sovereign, and those who possess arms partake of the same. Deviations from what was mentioned are tyranny from kingship, oligarchy from aristocracy, democracy from polity. Tyranny is monarchy for the benefit of the monarch, oligarchy for those with resources, and democracy for the benefit of those at a loss. None of these is for the profit of what is common.

One must speak at a little greater length about what each of these regimes is. For there are some difficulties, and it is characteristic of one philosophizing in each pursuit to regard not only the household of practice and not to overlook or leave out anything, but to make manifest the truth about each. Tyranny, exactly as was mentioned before, is a skilled despotism over the political community; oligarchy is whenever those who have substance [*ousia*, also being] are sovereign in the regime; and democracy, in opposition, is whenever those who do not possess a multitude of substance, but are at a loss (are sovereign).

The first difficulty is with regard to the division. If it should be that more who have resources are sovereign in the city, but it is a democracy whenever the multitude is sovereign, and similarly, again [on the contrary] if somehow it should happen that the few at a loss, being superior to those with resources, are sovereign in the regime, but where the few in multitude are sovereign they assert that it is an oligarchy, it would seem that the division of regimes has not been noble. But now even if there should be some addition of fewness to having resources and multitude to being at a loss, one would call the regimes oligarchy, in which those who have resources, being few in multitude, have the rules, and democracy, in which those at a loss, being many in multitude, (have the rules). There is another difficulty. What will we say about the regimes mentioned just now, the one in which those who have resources are more and those at a loss are few, each sovereign in the regimes, if indeed there is no other regime besides the ones mentioned?

The argument seems to make manifest that whether few or many are sovereign is incidental, the former in oligarchies and the latter in democracies, because those who have resources are few and those at a loss are many everywhere. Because of this, the differences do not happen to come into being from the causes mentioned, but that by which democracy and oligarchy differ from each other is poverty and wealth. And necessarily, wherever they rule because of wealth, whether fewer or more, this is an oligarchy; where at a loss, democracy. But it happens, exactly as we mentioned, that they are few, on the one hand, and many, on the other. For few are wealthy, but all partake of freedom, through which causes both dispute about the regime.

1280a7–1280a25

First one must grasp what they say are the boundaries of oligarchy and democracy and what the just favorable to oligarchy and democracy is. All cleave to some justice, but advance until some point and do not speak about all of the sovereign just. For example, the just seems to be the equal, and it is, but not for all, but for equals. And the unequal seems to be the just, and it is, but for unequals. But they strip this away [abstract], the "for whom," and judge badly. The cause is that the judgment is about themselves, and most are bad judges about their own [household] affairs. Thus, since the just is for someone and it is divided in the same way with respect to the things and the "for whom," exactly as has been mentioned in the *Ethics*, they agree about the equality of the thing, but about the "for whom" they dispute. (This is so) especially because of what has recently been said; because they judge badly in their own affairs, and then also because each, speaking the just up to some point, believes what he is speaking is the just simply. Some, should they be unequal with respect to something, for example, in useful things, think themselves wholly unequal, and others, equal with respect to something, for example freedom, (think themselves) wholly equal. But the most sovereign thing they do not speak.

1280a25–1281a10

But the most sovereign thing they do not speak. If they associated and came together for the sake of acquisition, they would partake of the city as much as in acquisition. Thus, the argument of those favoring oligarchy would seem to have bodily strength. For it would not be just for someone bringing in one mina to partake equally of one hundred minae with someone giving all the rest, whether of the things from the beginning [*archē*] or those coming after. But if (they associated and came together) neither for the sake of life only, but more for the good life—otherwise the city would be even from slaves and other animals, but now it is not, because they do not partake of happiness or of the life according to choice—nor for the sake of an alliance in order that they not be done an injustice by anyone, nor for the sake of exchanges and the use of one another. . . . Even the Etruscans and Carthaginians and all who have contracts with one another would virtually be citizens of one city. For surely among them would be conventions about what can be imported, guarantees concerning not being unjust, and statutes about alliances. But neither have common rules been set over all these, but different ones for each, nor must each think about making something of the other or (think about) how no one under the conventions will be unjust or have any other wretchedness, but only how no one will commit an injustice against one another. But as many as think about good law look at political virtue and vice in different ways. And it is apparent that in the city truly so named, not for the sake of argument, it is necessary to be careful about virtue. For the community becomes an alliance, differing only in place from allies from afar. And the law is a covenant and, exactly as Lycophron ["Wolf-Minded"] the sophist asserted, a guarantee to each other of the just things, but not of the sort to make the citizens good and just.

That it is this way is apparent. Even if someone should bring together the sites into one, so that the city should touch the walls of the Megarians and Corinthians, even so, it would not be one city. Nor (would it be) if they should intermarry with one another, although this is among the private intercourses in cities. Similarly, (it would not be) if some should make their homes separated; not, however, so far that they do not share, but so that they have laws in order that they not wrong them about giving them their shares. For example, if one were a carpenter, another a farmer, another a shoemaker, another some other such thing, and the multitude were ten thousand, but they did not share anything else but such things, for example, exchanges and alliances, it would not be a city. What, indeed, is the cause? Certainly it is not because the community is not near. Even if those who associate should thus come together, each using his own household like a city, only as being an alliance helping themselves against those who do injustices, not even this would seem to those who observe carefully to be a city, if they consort similarly having come together and separately.

It is apparent, therefore, that the city is not a community in place and in not being unjust to one another and for the sake of giving a share. But while these things are necessary if there is to be city, if all these things are present, there will not yet be a city, but a community of households and families [genē] in the good life for the sake of the complete and self-sufficient life. Nevertheless, this will not be without dwelling in the same and one place and without making use of intermarriage. Because of this, marriage relations have come into being down in the cities, and brotherhoods, and sacred rites, and the pastimes of living together. This sort of thing is the work of friendship, for friendship is a choosing to live together. Therefore, the good life is the end of the city, and these things are for the sake of the end. The city is a community of families and villages in the complete and self-sufficient life. This is, we assert, the happy and noble life. Therefore, the political community must be set down to exist for the sake of noble deeds, not for living together. Because of this very thing, to as many as contribute most to this sort of community belongs a greater share in the city than to those who are equal or greater in freedom and family but unequal in political virtue, or to those who exceed in wealth but are exceeded in virtue.

Therefore, that all disputing about regimes say some part of the just is apparent from what has been mentioned.

1281a11–1281a39

But who [what] ought to be sovereign in the city raises a difficulty. It is either the multitude, or the wealthy, or the reasonable, or the one best of all, or the tyrant. But all of these appear to involve discontent. Why? If the poor, because they are a majority, should distribute among themselves the things of the wealthy, is this not unjust? "No, by Zeus, it seemed just to the sovereign!" What, then, must one say is the extreme of injustice? Again, all being taken into account, if the majority should distribute among themselves the things of the few, it is apparent that they will destroy the city. But surely virtue does not destroy its possessor, nor is the just destructive of the city. So it is manifest that this law is not of the sort to be just. Still, even the deeds the tyrant has done necessarily are all just, for he, being superior, uses force, exactly as the multitude does with respect to the wealthy. But then is the rule of the few and the wealthy just? Therefore, if they should do these things and plunder and strip away [abstract from] the possessions of the multitude, is this just? Then so is the other. Indeed, it is apparent that all these things are base and not just. But must the reasonable rule and be sovereign over all? Is it then not necessity that all others be dishonored by not being honored in political rules? For we say that the rules are honors, and these ruling always, the others are necessarily dishonored. But is the rule of the one most serious best? But this is still more oligarchic, for there will be more dishonored. But perhaps someone should assert that for the sovereign to be wholly a human, not law, is base, (a human) surely having the passions found in the soul. But should it be law, either oligarchic or democratic, what difference will it make as regards the difficulties raised? Similarly, the things that have been mentioned would follow. Therefore, concerning these other things let there be some other argument.

1281a40–1282b1

That the multitude, rather than the best, but few, ought to be sovereign seems to have been said and to have some difficulty, but probably also truth. For the many, of whom each is not a serious man, it is nevertheless possible, having come together, to be better than those, not as each but as all. For example, common meals (are better) than those provided by one expenditure. For each, being of many, has a portion of virtue and prudence, and, having come together, the multitude is exactly like one man, multifooted and multi-handed and with all the perceptions and, even in this way, the customary things and intelligence. Because of this, the many judge better the works of music and those of the poets. Some judge some part and all, all. But in this way the serious of men differ from each of the many, exactly as they assert that the noble [beautiful] do from the not noble [beautiful], and the painted by art from the true things, and the scattered separate having been brought together into one, although surely among separated things, this eye has more beauty than the painted one and another part more than some other.

If it is possible for every people and every multitude to differ in this way from the many as compared to the few serious, it is not manifest. "Perhaps, by Zeus, it is manifest that it is impossible for some." For then the same argument would even fit beasts, and yet how do some differ from beasts, so to speak? But with respect to some multitude nothing stops what has been said from being true. Therefore, someone might solve the previously mentioned difficulty by means of these things, as well as that following upon it: Over what must the free and the multitude of citizens be sovereign? These are of the sort who neither are wealthy nor are reputed for virtue nor are a one. On the one hand, for them to partake of the greatest rules is not safe. Through injustice and through imprudence, they are necessarily unjust in some things and erring in some. On the other hand, for them not to be given a share or not to partake is fearful. Whenever there are many dishonored and poor, this city is necessarily full of enemies. Surely it remains for them to partake of deliberating and judging. Because of this, Solon and some other legislators appointed them to choose the magistrates and to make corrections of the rulers, but did not allow them to rule according to ones. All, having come together, have sufficient perception; and having been mixed with the better, they aid the cities, exactly as impure food with pure makes all of it more useful than a little amount. And each separated is incomplete with respect to judging.

But this order of the regime has a first difficulty. It would seem to belong to the same one to judge whether someone treats rightly as it belongs to treat and to make the one suffering under the present disease healthy. But this is the physician. And similarly in the other experiences and arts. Exactly as a physician must be corrected by physicians, so in the others it should be done by similars. But a physician is a craftsman, a master builder, and third, one who has been educated about the art. These sorts are found in all the arts, so to speak. And we permit to judge no less those who have been trained than the knowers. Further, it would seem to be the same way with respect to choosing. To choose rightly is the work of knowers, for example, geometers by those skilled in geometry, and pilots by those skilled in piloting. If even in some works and arts some private men partake, they do not do so more than the knowers. Thus, according to this argument, the multitude should not be made sovereign in either the choosing of magistrates or the making of corrections.

But perhaps not all these things are nobly said because of the argument made before; that is, if the multitude should not be too reduced to slavery. Each will be a worse judge than the knowers, but all, having come together, will be either better or not worse. Also, concerning some things the maker is not the only or the best judge, but those who, without having the art, do learn to know the works of them (are the best judges). For example, the household is known not only to the maker, but the user of it will judge even better, the user being the household manager; and the pilot (judges better) the rudder than the carpenter (does); and the diner, not the cook, the feast.

This difficulty probably seems to be sufficiently solved in this way. But another follows it; it seems out of place that the base should be sovereign over more important things than the reasonable. Making corrections and choosing of rules are the greatest. These, in some regimes, exactly as was mentioned, are given to the peoples, for the assembly is sovereign over all such things. Yet those who partake in the assembly and deliberate and judge [*dikazō*] are of small property estimates and of any age, while those who rule in treasurerships and generalships and the greatest rules are from greater. Someone might solve this difficulty similarly. Perhaps even these things are right, for neither the juryman nor the deliberator nor the assembly member is a ruler, but the court and the council and the people. Each of those mentioned is a part of these. By a part I mean the deliberator, the assembly member, and the juryman. Thus, justly the multitude is sovereign over greater things. For the people and the council and the courts are from the many, and the property estimate of all these is more than that of those who rule according to one and according to a few great rules. Let these things be distinguished in this way.

1282b1-13

Let these things be distinguished in this way. But the first difficulty mentioned makes nothing so apparent as that rightly laid down laws must be sovereign. But the ruler, whether one or more, should be sovereign over as many things as the laws are unable to speak about accurately, because it is not easy to make manifest a general rule about all things. Nevertheless, of what sort the rightly laid laws ought to be is not yet manifest, for the previous difficulty still remains. The laws are necessarily base or serious and just or unjust at the same time, and similarly with the regimes. Then surely this is apparent, that the laws ought to be laid down with a regard for the regime. But if this is so, it is manifest that those that correspond to right regimes are necessarily just and those to the ones that have deviated, not just.

1282b14–1284a3

Since in all the sciences and arts the end is good, and the greatest and most final is (the end) of the most sovereign of all, the political capacity is this same thing and the just is the political good, and this is the benefit in common. But the just seems to all to be some equality, and surely up to some point they agree with the arguments according to philosophy in which the ethical things are defined. The just is something for someone, and they assert that it must be the equal to equals. But equality in what sort of things and inequality in what sort surely should not be neglected. This involves a difficulty and political philosophy. Perhaps someone should assert that the rules should be held unequally according to superiority in every good, even if in all the rest they should differ not at all, but should chance to be similar. To those who differ, the just and the according to worth are other. But if this is true, there will be some grasping for more from political justices by the superior with respect to color and to magnitude and to any good whatsoever. Or is the falseness of this on the surface? It is apparent in the other sciences and capacities. Among flute players similar with respect to art, a greater share of flutes must not be given to the better-born, for they will play no better, but the superior instruments should be given to someone superior with respect to the work. If what has been said is not yet manifest, it will be apparent to those who have brought the thing itself forward still further. If someone should exceed with respect to skill in flute playing, but be greatly lacking with respect to good birth or nobility, and if each of these, I mean good birth and nobility, is a greater good than skill in flute playing, and they exceed skill in flute playing proportionately more than that one (exceeds) according to skill in flute playing, nevertheless to him must be given the superior flutes. For superiority in both wealth and good birth must contribute to the work, but they contribute nothing.

Yet surely according to this argument every good would be commensurable with every other. If some magnitude were more,[5] then wholly magnitude would be an equal match for wealth and freedom. Thus, if this one differed more in magnitude than this one in virtue, and if magnitude wholly exceeded virtue,[6] then all things would be commensurable. For if so much magnitude is superior to so much, it is manifest that some so-much must be equal. Since this is impossible, it is manifest that also even of political things it is well said that they do not dispute about rules with respect to every inequality. If some are slow and others are fast, the former should not have more because of this and the latter less, but the difference between these takes the honor in gymnastic contests. But the dispute is necessarily made about the things out of which the city has been put together. Because of this very thing, the well-born and free and wealthy are well said to contend for honors. There should be those who are free and those who bear estimates, for the city could not be from all at a loss, exactly as not from slaves. But if there must be these, it is manifest that there must be justice and political virtue. Without these, it is impossible for the city to be managed. Without the former it is impossible for the city to be; without these, for it to be nobly managed.

Therefore, for the city to be, all or surely some of these would seem to dispute rightly. Nevertheless, for the good life education and virtue would most justly dispute, exactly as was mentioned before. But since equals in some one thing only should not have equality in all things, nor should unequals according to a *one*, it is necessity that regimes of this sort are all deviations. Therefore, it was mentioned even before that all dispute utterly in some way justly, but not all simply justly. The wealthy (dispute) that theirs is a greater share in the country, but the country is common, and still that they are more trustworthy in contracts, for the most part. The free and well-born, being near, (dispute) with each other, for the better-born are more fully citizens than the base-born and good birth is honored in each household, and still because the better look like they come from the better, for good birth is virtue of family [*genos*]. Similarly, indeed, we shall assert virtue to dispute justly, for we assert that justice is virtue in associating, from which all the other (virtues) necessarily follow. But also the majority (dispute) against the fewer, for they are superior (stronger) and wealthier and better, the more being taken in comparison with the fewer.

Therefore, if all should be in one city, I mean, for example, the good, the wealthy and well-born, and still some other political multitude, will there be a dispute about who should rule, or will there not be? With respect to each of the regimes mentioned, the judgment about who should rule is undisputed. They differ from each other in their sovereigns, for example, in the one it is the wealthy, in the other the serious men, and it is this way in each of the others. But nevertheless, we are beholding when they might exist in the same one at the same time: How are they to be distinguished?

If, indeed, those who have virtue should be quite few in number, in what way should one thrust through? The fewness should be examined with respect to the work: either they have the capacity to manage the city or are so many in multitude that the city can be (made) out of them. But there is some difficulty with regard to all disputing utterly about political honors. Those who claim to rule because of wealth would seem to say nothing just, similarly those according to family. It is manifest that if, again [or, on the contrary], some one were wealthier than all, according to the same, just this one should rule all. It is similar with those who differ in good birth and dispute because of freedom. Perhaps this same thing will happen even about virtue in aristocracies. If some one man should be better than the other serious ones in the ruling body, then he should be sovereign according to the same just. Then surely if the multitude must be sovereign because they are superior (stronger) than the few, if one or more than one, but less than the many, should be superior (stronger) than the others, these must be more sovereign than the multitude. Surely all these things seem to make it apparent that none of the boundaries (principles) according to which they claim themselves to rule and others to be ruled by them is right. For surely against those in the ruling body who claim to be sovereign according to virtue, and similarly those according to wealth, the multitudes would have some just argument. For nothing stops some multitude from being better and wealthier than the few, not as each, but as a crowd.

Hence, the difficulty some seek and put forward can be met in this way. Some raise the difficulty whether the legislator, intending to establish the rightest laws, should legislate for the benefit of the better or of the majority whenever what has been mentioned should occur. The equally right must be undertaken, the equally right being for the benefit of the whole city and what is common to the citizens. But a citizen in common is one who partakes of ruling and being ruled, and he is different according to each regime. In relation to the best he is one who has the capacity and chooses to be ruled and rule with a view to the life according to virtue.

1284a3–1284b34

If there is some one or more than one who do not have the capacity to produce a full city for themselves, but who differ so much with respect to an excess of virtue, since neither the virtue of all others nor the political capacity (of others) is commensurable with that of these if many, or of his only if one, they must no longer be set down as part of the city. Being deemed worthy of equal things they will be done an injustice, being so unequal with respect to virtue and political capacity. This sort is exactly like an image of a god among human beings. From this it is manifest that even legislating must be for equals in genus and capacity, but for this sort there is no law. They themselves are law. It would be ridiculous if someone were to try to legislate for them. Perhaps they would speak the very thing Antisthenes ["Opposing Strength"] asserted about the lions when the hares made popular speeches and claimed that all have the equal. Because of such a cause, democratically governed cities set down for themselves ostracism. These surely seem to seek equality most of all, so they ostracize and remove (set free) from the city for a limited time those who seem to exceed in capacity because of wealth or many friends or some other political strength. There was even a myth told that the Argonauts left Heracles behind because of such a cause. The *Argos* did not wish to bear him with the others, alleging that he so outweighed the other sailors. And because of this, those who blame tyranny and the counsel of Periander ["All-Around Man"] to Thrasyboulos ["Bold-in-Counsel"] must not be thought simply right in their censure. They assert that Periander said nothing to the herald sent for advice, instead stripping away [abstracting from] the outstanding ears of corn to level the field. From this, the herald, being ignorant of the cause, reported what had happened, and Thrasyboulos understood that one must make away with outstanding men. This is beneficial not only to tyrants, and not only do tyrants do it, but it is similar with respect to oligarchies and democracies. For ostracism has in some way the same capacity as cutting short and exiling the outstanding. The sovereigns in capacity in the cities and the tribes do the same things, for example, the Athenians with respect to the Samians and Chians and Lesbians. No sooner did they have the rule by force than they humbled them in violation of their contracts. And the king of the Persians often felled the Medes and the Babylonians and the others because they had become presumptuous when in rule.

The problem is, on the whole, with respect to all regimes, even the right ones. While some that have deviated do this looking toward the private (good), it is not that those that examine the common good do not have the same way. This is manifest even in the other arts and sciences. The painter would not let an animal have a foot exceeding symmetry, even if it differed in beauty, nor the shipwright the stern or some other part of the ship, nor yet surely does the chorus trainer allow the one uttering greater and more beautiful sounds than all the chorus to join in the dance. Thus, because of this nothing stops monarchs from being in harmony with cities if, the household rule being profitable to cities, they do this. Hence the argument about ostracism has something of the political just with regard to agreed-upon superiorities. Therefore, it is better for the legislator to have arranged the regime from the beginning [archē, rule] so that it does not need treatment of this sort. But the second sailing, should it occur, is to try to make it straight with some such correction. This very thing did not happen with respect to cities, but they used ostracism to be factious. Therefore, in the regimes that have deviated it is apparent that this is beneficial to the private and just, but perhaps that it is not just simply is also apparent. But in the best regime there is much difficulty, not with superiority in other goods, for example, strength and wealth and having many friends. But if someone should become different with respect to virtue, what must be done [made]? Surely they would not assert that it is necessary to expel and make away with one of this sort, nor indeed to rule over one of this sort. This is about the same as if they were to claim to rule over Zeus, dividing the rules into parts. Therefore, what remains, the very thing that seems like what has naturally come into being, is for all to willingly obey one of this sort, hence for these to be eternally kings in the cities.

1284b35–1286a9

Perhaps it is noble, after the mentioned arguments, to change over and to examine kingship carefully. We assert that this same one is one of the right regimes. It must be examined whether it is beneficial for a city to be nobly managed and a country to be ruled by a king or not, or rather by some other regime, and to whom it is beneficial and to whom not. Surely it should first be thrust through whether there is some one genus [*genos*] of it or several with differences. Surely this is easy to learn well: it encompasses several genera, and the manner of rule over all is not one.

In the Laconic ["Shriek Victory"] regime the kingship seems to be one of those most according to law, for it is not sovereign over all. But whenever he should go out of the country, he is leader in the things regarding war. Besides, the things regarding the gods are given to those who rule as kings. This same kingship, therefore, is, as it were, some generalship, absolute and eternal. He is not sovereign to kill except for the sake of cowardice, exactly as in ancient times on military expeditions by law of hand. Homer makes this manifest. Agamemnon bore being spoken ill of in the assemblies, but going out he was sovereign to kill. Therefore, he surely says,

> But whomsoever I see aloof from the fight . . .
> He shall have no hope to escape the dogs and vultures.
> For death is mine.[7]

Therefore, this is one form of kingship, a generalship throughout life. Some of these are according to family [*genos*] and some by choice.

Besides this is another form of monarchy, examples of which are the kingships among some barbarians. These all have a capacity almost like tyrannies, but are according to law and derived from one's fathers. Because the barbarians are by nature more slavish in their customary ways than the Greeks and the Asians, more so than the Europeans, they submit to skilled despotic rule, bearing nothing with ill grace. Therefore, because of such a thing they are tyrannical, but they are safe because they are according to law and derived from the father's side. And the guard is kingly, not tyrannical, for the same cause. For citizens with arms guard the kings, but that of tyrants is foreign. The former rule according to law and over the willing, the latter the unwilling, so the former have a guard from the citizens, the latter against the citizens. These, then, are two forms of monarchy.

Another is the very one that there was among the ancient Greeks, those whom they called *aesymnētes*. This is, to speak simply, chosen tyranny, differing from the barbarian not in being not according to law, but only in being not from one's father. Some ruled for life in this rule, others for some limited times or deeds. For example, the Mitylenians chose for themselves Pittacus ["Remedy-of-Pitch"] to oppose the exiles who were championed by Antimenides ["Steadfast-in-Opposition"] and the poet Alcaeus ["Prowess"]. Alcaeus made manifest in some drinking songs that Pittacus was chosen tyrant. He censured,

> The base-born Pittacus they did set up
> As tyrant over the gall-less city oppressed by fate
> Greatly applauding as a throng.[8]

These, therefore, are and were tyrannical because skilled despotisms, and skilled kingships because chosen and over the willing.

A fourth form of kingly monarchy are those in heroic times, willing and inherited from one's fathers, having come into being according to law. Through the first of the multitude's becoming well-doers in the arts or war, or through bringing them together or providing the country, they became kings over the willing and were hereditary to those receiving them. They were sovereign in leadership with regard to war and over sacrifices, as many as were not priestly; and besides these, they used to judge [krinō] the justs. Doing this, some did not swear with oaths, and some did. The oath was an extension of the scepter. Some, therefore, in ancient times used to rule continuously [or, by constraint] in matters with respect to the city and those of the people dwelling there and those beyond the boundaries. Later, some of these being omitted by the kings and some being taken away by the mob, in some other cities only the sacrifices were left to the kings; but where it is worthwhile to speak of kingship, they had only the leadership in the skills of war beyond the boundaries.

These, therefore, are the forms of kingship, four in number. One was that roughly in heroic times. This was over the willing but within some limits, for the king was a general and a juryman and was sovereign over the things concerning the gods. Second is that of the barbarians. This is skilled despotic rule out of the family (genus) and according to law. Third is what they call *aesymnateia*. This is chosen tyranny. Fourth of these is the Laconic. This is, so to speak, an eternal generalship according to family (genus). Therefore, these differ from each other in this way. The fifth form of kingship is whenever one should be sovereign over all, exactly as each nation and each city is over the common things, being ordered according to skilled household management. Exactly as skilled household management is some kingship over the household; thus, kingship is household management of the city and the nation, whether one or several.

Surely the forms, so to speak, of kingship that must be examined are almost two: this one and the Laconic. The many of the others are between these two, for they are sovereign over fewer than absolute kingship but more than the Laconic. Thus, the subject for consideration is almost twofold. One is whether an eternal generalship, according to family (genus) or according to choice, is beneficial for cities or not beneficial. Another is whether for one to be sovereign over all is beneficial or not beneficial. Therefore, concerning this sort of generalship it is more a close inspection of the form of law than of the regime. It is possible for this to come into being in all the regimes, so let us neglect it at first. But the remaining manner of kingship is a form of a regime, so about this one must theorize and run after the substantial difficulties. The beginning [archē] of the search is whether it is more beneficial to be ruled by the best man or by the best laws.

1286a7–1286b40

The beginning [archē] of the search is whether it is more beneficial to be ruled by the best man or by the best laws. To those who believe it beneficial to be governed by a king, the laws surely seem to speak only about the universal, but not to give commands about what befalls one. As in any such art, to rule according to what is written is foolish. Somehow even in Egypt after the third [fourth]⁹ day it is possible for doctors to set things in motion, and, if earlier, at their own risk. Therefore, it is apparent that the best regime is not according to what is written and laws through the same cause. But now that universal argument must also belong to the rulers. And that in which the passionate is wholly not there is superior (stronger) to that in which it is congenital. Therefore, while this does not belong to law, it is necessary that every human soul have it. But perhaps someone would assert in opposition to this that he would deliberate more nobly about each of the things. Therefore, it is manifest that it is necessary for this one to be a legislator and to lay down laws which, though not sovereign when they deviate, ought to be sovereign concerning all other things.

But concerning the things the law has no capacity to judge [krinō] wholly or well, should the one best or all rule? Now, coming together, they judge the just [dikazō], deliberate, and judge, and these judgments are all about the each. Therefore, as a one, whoever contributes is perhaps worse. But the city is from many, exactly as a collective banquet is nobler than a single simple one. Because of this also a mob judges many things better than one whosoever. Still, the much is more incorruptible, exactly as is more water, and so is the multitude more incorruptible than the few. Some one, being overpowered by anger or some other such passion, it is necessary that judgment be destroyed, but there [in the other world], it is work that all at the same time be angered and err. Then let the multitude be of free men, doing nothing against the law except concerning the things it itself leaves out. But indeed this is not easy for many. But if a majority should be good [and] men and citizens, is the one a more incorruptible ruler or rather the several in number, but all good? Is it manifestly the more? But they will be factious, while the one will not. But perhaps it must be opposed to this that they are serious in soul, exactly as the one is. If indeed the rule by a majority of good, but all men, should be set down as aristocracy, and kingship by the one, aristocracy would be more choiceworthy than kingship for cities, the rule being both with capacity and separate from capacity, given many similars.

Because of this, perhaps, kings ruled earlier: that it was rare to find men much different with respect to virtue, especially as they then made their homes in small cities. Still, they established their kings because of good services, the very thing that is the work of good men. When it happened that many similar in virtue came into being, they no longer used to abide, but they used to seek some common thing and to establish a regime. When, having become worse, they did business away from the common things, then from that, it is well said, comes oligarchy. For they made wealth honorable. From these they first changed into tyrannies, then from tyrannies into democracy. Always leading few into base greed for gain, they rendered the multitude stronger (in body), so democracies were brought on and came into being. And when cities happen to be even greater, perhaps it is no longer easy for another regime besides democracy to come into being.

If, indeed, someone should set down being governed by a king as best for cities, how will things concerning the offspring be? Must even the family (genus) rule as a king? But becoming the sort that some have chanced to be, this is harmful. But being sovereign, he would not hand it over to his offspring. But this is not easy to believe. It is hard and of more virtue than that in accordance with human nature. But there is even a difficulty about capacity, whether he who is going to be king should have some bodily strength about him, with which he would be able to force those who do not wish to obey. Or is it possible to manage rule like a household? Even if he should be sovereign according to law, doing nothing according to his intention against the law, it is nevertheless necessary that there be present to him a capacity with which to guard the laws. Probably, therefore, it is not hard to distinguish the things concerning a king of this sort. This one must have bodily strength, but such bodily strength that he is superior (stronger) to each and one and several together, but inferior to the multitude. This is exactly as the ancients gave guards whenever they set down in the city someone they called an *aesymnētēs*, or tyrant, and as someone to Dionysius, when he begged for guards, advised that as many guards be given to the Syracusans.

1287a1–1287b36

Of the king who does all things according to his own intention, whom the argument has now stood up, the examination must be made. The king according to law spoken of is not a form of kingship,[10] exactly as we said. In all it is possible for there to be an eternal general, for example, in democracy and aristocracy, and many make one sovereign in management. There is even some rule of this sort at Epidamnus ["Subdued"] and at Opus ["Wherever"] in some smaller part. But concerning what is called absolute kingship, which is the same as that according to which the king rules all according to his own intention, it seems to some that it is not at all according to nature for one to be sovereign over all citizens where the city has been put together from similars. For similars by nature it is necessary that there be the same just and the same worth according to nature, exactly as if for unequals to have the equal in nourishment or clothing is harmful to the body, it is the same in the things concerning honors. Similarly, therefore, the unequal to equals. Because of this very thing, it is not more just to rule than to be ruled, and in the same way, as a part. But this is already law, for order is law. Therefore it is more choiceworthy for the law to rule than some one of the citizens. But, according to the same argument, if some were to rule better, these must be established as guards and underseamen to the laws. Necessarily there are some rules, but they assert that it is just that this not be one, all being indeed similar.

But now surely, as many things as the law does not seem capable of distinguishing, neither would a man be capable of gaining knowledge of. But, educating them for the purpose, the law sets up the rulers to judge [*krinō*] and manage the rest by their most just opinion. Still, it gives to those making attempts to set up what seems better than what is laid down.

Therefore, he who urges that intellect rule seems to be urging the rule of the god and the laws only, and he who urges man also imposes the beast. Appetite is of this sort, and spiritedness distorts even the best men when they rule. Because of this very thing, law is intellect without desire. The paradigm of the arts seems false, that to treat according to the written things is base and that it is more choiceworthy to use those who have the arts. For the former do nothing against reason out of friendship, but earn their fee upon their patients' becoming healthy. But those in political rules are in the habit of doing many things for the sake of spite and grace, since whenever they suspect doctors of having been persuaded by their enemies to corrupt them for the sake of gain, then they would rather seek treatment in the written things. But surely the doctors, being patients, bring in for themselves other doctors, and exercise masters, training, exercise masters, as if not being able to judge the true because judging about the household things and having passions. Thus, it is manifest that those who seek the just seek the mean. The law is the mean. Still, the things according to customary ways are more sovereign, and are about more sovereign things, than the laws according to the written things, so if a human ruler is safer than the things according to the written things, (he is not safer than) the things according to customary ways.

But indeed it is not easy for the one to oversee many. Therefore, if those who rule, set down by him, should be numerous, what difference is there if this happens immediately from the beginning [archē] or if the one sets it down in this way? Still, as was mentioned even before, if indeed there is a serious man and, because better, it is just for him to rule, surely two good are better than the one. This is the "two going together,"[11] and the prayer of Agamemnon, "May ten such fellow counselors be mine."[12]

But even now about some things the sovereign rules judge exactly as the juryman (does), things which the law is not capable of distinguishing, since surely about the things of which it is capable nobody disputes, alleging that about these things the law would not rule and judge best. But since it is possible for some things to be included in the laws and others have no capacity, these are the things that make for raising difficulties and for seeking whether the rule of the best law is more choiceworthy than the rule of the best man. For to legislate about things deliberated about is among impossible things. Therefore, surely they do not speak against this, as if saying that it is not necessary that a human being be the judge about these things, but (they say) that it should not be one only, but many. For each ruler, having been educated by the law, judges nobly. And perhaps it would seem out of place if someone should see better, judging with two eyes and organs of hearing and doing with two feet and hands, than many with many. Even now the monarchs make their own eyes and ears and hands and feet. Their friends in rule are made co-rulers. Therefore, not being friends, they will not do according to the choice of the monarch. But if (they are) friends of that one and of the rule, surely a friend is an equal and similar, so if he thinks that these should rule, similarly he thinks equals and similars should rule. Therefore, those disputing utterly with respect to kingship say almost these things.

1287b36–1288a32

But perhaps these things are this way in the case of some, and in the case of others it is not this way. There is by nature something despotic, another suited to skilled kingship, and another to the political and just and beneficial. But tyrannical rule is not according to nature, nor are as many of the other regimes as are deviations. These come to be outside of nature. But it is certainly apparent from the things mentioned that among the similar and equal it is neither beneficial nor just that one be sovereign over all, neither without law, but himself being as law, nor with law, neither good over good ones nor not good over not good, nor if he should be better with respect to virtue, unless in a certain way. What this way is must be said. But somehow it has already been mentioned earlier.

First it must be distinguished what is that which is suited for kingly rule, what for aristocratic, and what for political. Suited for kingly is a multitude of the sort that naturally bears a family (genus) exceeding in virtue for political leadership. Aristocratic is a multitude that naturally bears a multitude capable of being ruled according to the rule of free men by the skilled leaders with virtue according to the political rule. Political is a multitude in which there naturally has come to be a political multitude able to be ruled and rule in accordance with a law distributing the rules, in accordance with worth, to those who have resources. Therefore, whenever either a whole family (genus) or even some one of the others should happen to become so different in virtue that the (virtue) of this one exceeds that of all others, then it is just for this family to be kingly and sovereign over all and for this one to be king. Exactly as was mentioned before, not only is it thus in accordance with the justice usually brought forward by those establishing the regimes, those (establishing) aristocracies and those oligarchies, and again [on the contrary], democracies, for all claim some preeminence, but not the same preeminence, but even according to what was mentioned before. For it is fitting neither to put an end to nor to exile nor indeed somehow to ostracize this sort nor to deem him worthy of being ruled according to part. It has not naturally come to be for a part to exceed all, but this has happened in the case of one having such extreme age. Thus, it only remains that one of this sort be obeyed and be sovereign, not according to this part, but simply. Therefore, concerning kingship, what its kinds are, whether it is not beneficial to cities or beneficial, to whom, and how, let it be distinguished in this way.

1288a32–1288b6

Since we assert that the right regimes are three, it is necessary that the one managed by the best be the best of these. This sort is one in which it has happened that either some one or a whole family (genus) or a multitude exceeding all in virtue is capable, on the one hand, of being ruled and, on the other hand, of ruling with a view to the most choiceworthy life. But in the first arguments, it was brought to light that it is necessary that the virtue of a man and of a citizen of the best city be the same. It is apparent that in the same way and through the same things a man becomes serious, and someone might put together a city governed aristocratically or by a king. Thus, the education and habits that make a man serious and those that make a statesman and a king are almost the same.

These things concerning the regimes having been distinguished, already it must be attempted to speak about the best: in what way it naturally comes to be and how to establish it. Surely for he who intends it, it is necessity that the examination belonging to it be made.

NOTES

FOREWORD

1. Thanks to Kathryn Hansen for the help of her researches in this regard, and to Jeffrey Tulis for persistently urging this publication.

2. Other improbable debts she acknowledges are to Sir Robert Filmer (p. 79n10) and Roger Taney (p 164n145).

3. For Strauss's explanation of esotericism, see his *Persecution and the Art of Writing* (Glencoe, IL: The Free Press, 1952). For a recent helpful study of the evidence for it, see Arthur Melzer, *Philosophy between the Lines: The Lost History of Esoteric Writing* (Chicago: University of Chicago Press, 2014).

4. See Michael Davis, *The Politics of Philosophy: A Commentary on Aristotle's Politics* (Lanham, MD: Rowman & Littlefield, 2013).

5. Delba Winthrop's four published articles on Aristotle are "Aristotle and Political Responsibility," *Political Theory* (1975) 3:4, 406–422; "Aristotle on Participatory Democracy," *Polity* (1978) 11:2, 151–171; "Aristotle and Theories of Justice," *American Political Science Review* (1978) 72:4, 1201–1216; and "Aristotle's *Politics*, Book I: A Reconsideration," *Perspectives on Political Science* (2010), 37:4, 189–199. Her bibliography is available at delbawinthrop.org.

INTRODUCTION

1. *Politics* V, 1310a32–34.

2. *Nicomachean Ethics* VIII, 1155b1–4.

3. *Politics* V, 1311b30–34.

4. I, 1252a1–7.

5. I, 1252a7–9.

6. I, 1260b8–26.

7. I, 1260b27–32; II, 1274b25–28.

8. The theme of Book II, to be precise, is the political community; i.e., what is common to political beings, which is no more simply identical with the city than is a collection of households. Most obviously, not everything is common in any city of men with bodies.

CHAPTER 1

1. *Politics* III, 1288a37–38.
2. III, 1288a39–1288b2.
3. III, 1278b6, 1279a22, 1282a41, 1288a31–32, 1288b2–3.
4. III, 1283b8–9, 1288a6.
5. III, 1275a1–2, 1276b16, 1278b6, 1279a22–23, 1285a35–36, 1287a1–3.
6. III, 1282b22–23, 1283b8–9, 1283b40–41.
7. III, 1288a26–29.
8. At II, 1273a19–20, the Carthaginian procedure is said to differ from the Spartan in having the same rulers judge all lawsuits rather than some judging some suits and others judging others.
9. Aristotle, *Generation of Animals*, 732a1–9.
10. At III, 1284a15, Aristotle, in reporting an assertion of Antisthenes, tacitly compares philosophers to lions. The leonine quality is the use of speech or reason to understand speech in contrast to the use of speech for political ends, as Gorgias may use it.
11. Plato, *Republic* VI, 507b; VII, 517b–e; IX, 592a–b.
12. III, 1275a1.
13. III, 1274b34–36.
14. Cf. Heraclitus, fr. 12 (Diels): "Upon those who step into the same rivers different and again different waters flow." Socrates' paraphrase is "Heraclitus . . . likens the beings to a river, saying that you cannot step into the same river twice" (Plato, *Cratylus* 402a). *Metaphysics* 1078b12–17: The teaching about forms is said by Aristotle to be directed against Heraclitus: If all being is in flux, science is impossible.
15. At I, 1253a16, *logos* is said to be one's own. The reader should also note that Aristotle's apparent clarifications prefaced by "I say" or "I mean" (*legō*) are, while not untrue, rarely indications of his full thought.
16. If our interpretation of the "democratic" and "oligarchic" arguments is correct, perhaps this will contribute to an explanation of the distinction made by medieval Arabic and Christian Aristotelians in their political writings between the active and passive intellects. The distinction is usually taken to be imported from Aristotle's *De anima* III 5.
17. Consider the introduction to Hobbes's *Leviathan*: Nature *is* an art. The art is said to be God's, but the model of a being with arts is surely man. The Leviathan is, in any case, wholly of man's making, and in his own image. We shall consider later how this point is connected to Hobbes's teaching. Hobbes, *Leviathan*, 1 (original pagination).
18. The inquiry seems to be reopened by Antisthenes ("Strength in Opposition") at III, 1284a15.
19. Cf. Plato, *Republic* I, 331c, the first definition of justice; in Hobbes' *Leviathan*, ch. 15:71, the definition of justice is the performance of covenants.
20. Aristotle, *Metaphysics* X, 1054b20–30. "Not the same" can be an attribute of nonbeing, whereas "other" cannot be.
21. *Politics* II, 1262a21–24. Cf. Plato, *Phaedo*, 88b, a reference to the soul's becoming unharnessed in death. In Plato's *Apology*, 30e, the city is a horse.
22. In Herodotus, *Histories* VIII 73, the Peloponnesus had seven different nations dwelling in it.
23. Aristotle later speaks of Pittacus ("Remedy of Pitch"), the sage who ruled in Mytilene. Consider also the *Nocturnal* Council of Plato's *Laws*.
24. Herodotus, *Histories* I, 191. Aristotle adds the specification of *three* days, for reasons that we shall attempt to ascertain later.

25. Aristotle, *Physics* II, 194b12, and elsewhere.
26. Plato, *Republic* III, 399a–c. In the *Phaedo* the soul is compared to a harmony at 85e and thereafter, although Socrates disagrees.
27. *Politics* IV, 1290a20–29.
28. Aristotle, *Metaphysics* XII, 1075a11–16. Consider Plato, *Apology* 37e–38a: Socrates' wisdom consists in knowing that the greatest human good is in examining speeches about virtue, and this is said to constitute his obedience to the god.
29. *Nicomachean Ethics* I, 1103a4–6; VI, 1144a6–9, 1144b18f.
30. "Serious" (*spoudaios*) also means busy, eager, at work.
31. Euripides, *Aeolus*, Fr. 16 (Hauck). It reads in full: "Brilliant in Ares' battles and in assemblies (*syllogoi*) / Not for me the sophisticated things, lest I become changeful [also, subtle] / But in the things the city needs, should they wish to be great always."
32. Consider *Nicomachean Ethics* VI, 1142a2–6, where Euripides is quoted in support of the opinion that prudence is private and statesmen are busybodies. There Aristotle omits lines from the fragment quoted that would have Euripides say that the greater wisdom is with private men and foolishness with public men. Does Aristotle deny Euripides these lines for the sake of the reader of the *Ethics*, who is a political man? Or does he do so because Euripides, as a poet, did not lead a private life, and therefore could not have thought it the wisest life?
33. Euripides, *Medea*, (551–565). Virtually all of the editors and commentators–Barker, Rackham, Newman, Susemihl, and Aubonnet–make this a reference to Jason, tyrant of Pherae in the fourth century. They do so for no more reason than that he is mentioned in Aristotle's *Rhetoric* (I, 1373b25). There, however, it is apparently deemed necessary to clarify his identity as Jason the Thessalian, whereas the Jason here is not further identified. Furthermore, as Newman notes, the reference does not fit Jason of Pherae insofar as it suggests that there was a time when he was not tyrant. This was precisely the situation of Jason the Argonaut, however.
34. III, 1281b2–3, 1286b29–30; IV, 1290b39–40; I, 1256a19–b2, etc.
35. *Chernetes*, according to Liddell and Scott, stems not from *cheir* (hand), but from *cherna* (poverty).
36. *Politics* I, 1253b33–1254a1. Man lacks tools that do their work without command and with foresight, although the gods may have them.
37. Consider the democratic hypothesis, quoted on p. 1: "One is to live as someone wishes. They assert that this is the work of freedom, if, indeed, the life of being a slave is not as one might wish."
38. In *Politics* VIII, 1342b12–14, the Dorian mode is said to be sedate as well as manly—an apparent correction of Plato's *Republic*.
39. Consider Aristotle's criticism of the *Republic* at II, 1261a13–14: "Still, the end which he asserts that the city must have . . . is impossible, but how it is necessary to thrust through, he in no way distinguishes." In other words, if communism of women and unity are impossible, what does one do instead?
40. *Nicomachean Ethics* VI, 1144b28–30: The virtues are not reason (*logos*), but are with reason—a correction of Socrates.
41. *Nicomachean Ethics* VIII, 1155b1–4.
42. *Politics* V, 1311b30–34.
43. In listing the necessary parts of the city at IV, 1291a1–4, Aristotle says: "Second is the so-called banaustic. This is the one concerned with the arts without which the city cannot be managed. Of the arts, some are necessary and some for luxury or the noble life."

44. The word for poet is *poiētēs*, and the common word for "to make" is *poieō*. In this passage Aristotle calls Homer a "maker" of men.
45. *Politics* I, 1259b21–1260a20. Aristotle asks whether a slave must have moral virtue and, if so, how the free man is superior and his ruler.
46. Aristotle's example of the political art will later be the medical art. The doctor who treats himself is his own artifact.
47. The text can be construed in either of two ways here. We give the one more normal grammatically, but less obviously sensible.
48. Compare Marsilius's use of the similarly ambiguous Latin *valentior pars*. *The Defender of Peace* 1.12.6.
49. For the possible significance of Thebes, consider Plato's *Crito*, 52b. Had Socrates escaped, he would have gone to well-governed Thebes or Megara. At V, 1306a36-b2, Aristotle speaks of the just punishment at Thebes of a man named "Of the *Archē*." Citizens who judge the just do so according to their particular laws, not a universal first principle.
50. Cf. Plato, *Republic* VIII, 561d. For the meaning of "stranger," consider Plato's Athenian stranger in the *Laws*. In Book II, Aristotle consistently and apparently incorrectly speaks as if he were Socrates, not an unnamed stranger. Thus, a stranger is a philosopher.
51. Homer, *Iliad*, 9.648 and 16.59.
52. Consider Hobbes, who does teach that nature is as here described, and who must rest his political science on another ground. *Leviathan*, introduction, 2; the Table of Science, 9:40.

CHAPTER 2

1. The speculations of the commentators as to which of Aristotle's writings are the "exoteric speeches" are, I believe, without firm foundation. The fact that Aristotle acknowledges the distinction is sufficient for our argument.
2. See especially *Politics* I, 1252a7–9, 1252a26–27, 1253a7–18, and 1252b27–1253a1.
3. For the emphasis on noble friendship see, for example, *Politics* II, 1263a29–37; IV, 1295b23–25; and VII, 1323a27–32. See also *Nicomachean Ethics* VIII, 1159a25–27. Passages in Book III will be considered in their place.
4. I, 1252a31–34, 1254a34–35.
5. Cf. Hobbes, *Leviathan*, 13:60–61. To show that men are as equal in prudence as in bodily strength requires a bit of sophistry.
6. *Politics* V, 1313b32–35.
7. Aristotle, *Metaphysics* XII, 1075b10. Aristotle's god is, coincidentally, thought thinking itself.
8. *Politics*, III, 1275bl–2. Aristotle promised an explanation of what is meant by "later."
9. The antecedent of the "these" that are despotic is unspecified.
10. I am indebted to Sir Robert Filmer for this observation. As I understand him, however, he does not supply an adequate explanation for the inconsistencies. See "Observations on Aristotle's *Politiques*," in *Patriarcha and Other Political Works*, 193–200.
11. Without explaining why, Aubonnet notes the comments of one Barthélemy-Saint-Hilaire about Hobbes's opinion of the old classification of regimes. "There be other names of Government, in the Histories, and books of Policy; . . . But they are not names of other Formes of Government, but of the same Formes misliked." (*Leviathan*, 19:95.) We remark that Aristotle agrees with both Hobbes and M. Barthélemy-Saint-Hilaire [1805–95; French statesman and philosopher, translator of Aristotle's *Politics*—ed.]

12. Plato, *Republic* II, 368d–369a.
13. Cf. Plato, *Apology*, 21b and 38a. Despite his ignorance, Socrates knows that philosophizing is the greatest good for man.
14. The beginning of Book VII, whose theme is the best regime, is generally recognized to use arguments taken from Plato's *Apology*. Notice, however, the substitution of friendship for justice, and the reference to flies that bother people, not *horseflies* like Socrates (1323a27–34). Appearances notwithstanding, aristocracy will more likely be a private regime than a public order.
15. My interpretation of the mathematical and ontological problems presented is based on Jacob Klein's *Greek Mathematical Thought and the Origin of Algebra*. He, however, does not attribute Aristotle's arguments to the *Politics* as I do.
16. *Nicomachean Ethics* V, 1131b5.
17. Ibid., 1130a14–15. "We seek the justice that is a part of virtue. For *we assert* that there is such a thing . . . A sign is. . . ."
18. Ibid., 1130b22–24.
19. Ibid., 1130b30–1131a9.
20. Ibid., 1130b31–32.
21. Ibid., 1131a10–14.
22. Consider that two whole books of the *Ethics* are devoted to friendship. The study of legislation proposed in X, 1181b12 at the conclusion suggests an enterprise rather more ambitious than a summer seminar for statesmen.
23. For the suggestion that it is primarily the democrat who *believes* (*nomizō*) in what he says, see *Politics* V, 1301a28–33. The democrat believes and the oligarch seizes an opinion about justice. Recall also III, 1275b7–8, where the oligarch says that all need not rule where they do not *believe* in assemblies.
24. The word used for "to be strong" is *ischuein*, which has the primary meaning of "strong in body." Aristotle more frequently used *kreitton*, which means stronger *or* better. Obviously the latter is the only way in which a *logos* could be strong.
25. Consider Glaucon's speech at the beginning of Book II of Plato's *Republic*. He presents the argument of someone else on behalf of perfect injustice, challenging Socrates to prove that perfect justice is good for its own sake.
26. *Nicomachean Ethics* V, 1130a3–4.
27. Compare Socrates' "just" speech in Plato's *Apology*, which is in fact a praise of nobility in response to what is shown to be the city's understanding of itself as existing for mere life. *Apology*, 28b–30c.
28. Cf. John Locke, *Two Treatises of Government*, II:32, 34, etc.
29. *Nicomachean Ethics* I, 1094a1–3: "Every art and every inquiry, and similarly, every practice and every choice, seem to aim at some good. Because of this they have nobly declared the good to be that at which all aim." *Politics* I, 1252a1–6: "Since we see that every city is some community and every community has been put together for the sake of some good (for all do all things for the sake of something that seems good), it is manifest that all aim at some good, and the most sovereign and inclusive of all others is the greatest and most sovereign (good) of all."
30. *Nicomachean Ethics* VI, 1139b4–5, 1144a6–9.
31. Supra, 2.1, "What he means . . . redirecting, their ambitions." [In *supra* citations, the numbers indicate chapter and section, and the quoted phrases are from the beginning and the end of a paragraph.—Ed.]
32. The official indictment against Socrates, correctly reported in Diogenes Laertius, *Lives of the Philosophers* II, 40, read: "Socrates commits an unjust act by not believing in the

gods in whom the city believes, but leading in (*eisagōn*) other, novel divine things; he also commits an unjust act by corrupting the young."

33. Praised at *Politics* IV, 1296b18–21; *Nicomachean Ethics* VI, 1140b7–11; and V, 1134b23–24.

34. *Politics* III, 1280b19–21. The City of Pigs, with the same parts as are listed here by Aristotle, is spoken of in Plato's *Republic* at 369c–d.

35. At 1280b21–22 a multitude of ten thousand is referred to, which is the number of citizens in Hippodamus's city (II, 1267b30–31). Hippodamus, son of Euryphon ("voice found"; 1267b22), who wanted to be wise about the whole of nature (1267b28), constructed a city in which those who "found" things of benefit to the city were to be rewarded (1268a7). Notice that one of Aristotle's objections is that it will be unsafe because of malicious prosecutions (1268b22–25).

36. *Politics* I, 1252b15–16. The village is a community of households.

37. Homer's account of their noble spying enterprise is referred to at the beginning of Aristotle's discussion of friendship in the *Nicomachean Ethics* (VIII, 1155a14–15), and at the end of Book III of the *Politics* (1287b12–14).

38. Cf. Plato, *Apology*, 28b–30b. Supra, note 27.

39. 1287b32–35, 1295b23–24.

40. Aristotle, *Metaphysics* I, 991b21–23.

41. Klein, *Greek Mathematical Thought*, 101.

42. Ibid., 105–106.

43. Compare the procedure of modern natural right theorists—Hobbes, Locke, Rousseau—who speak about man's nature by describing a pre-political state of nature that reveals why politics is necessary.

44. The word used is *epieikeis*. In the *Nicomachean Ethics* (V, 1137a31–1138a3), *epieikeia*, equity, is said to be the just that is superior to the legal just because it fulfills the legislator's intention in exceptional cases. The respectable or reasonable man can judge the spirit, not merely the letter, of the law. He himself often does not claim all of his just share.

45. See, for example, *Politics* III, 1279a8–13, 1279b20–26, and 1283b14–20.

46. Men make the gods in their own image (*Politics* I, 1252b24–27), but Aristotle's usual procedure is to speak of the gods as examples to be imitated. See especially VIII, 1339b6–10, 1341b2–8.

47. Aristotle's principal criticism of Hippodamus's plan of honoring those who find beneficial things is that law, as distinguished from the arts, has no strength other than its being habitually obeyed (II, 1268b22–1269a28).

48. Consider Plato's *Apology* 18a–c. Socrates understands the most serious accusation against him to be that he was a natural philosopher who taught that the cosmic gods were not. See *Phaedo* 97c–99d for his criticism of the attempt to demonstrate through the study of nature that *nous* governs.

49. For a strikingly similar, but clearer, example of this procedure, see Tocqueville, *Democracy in America*, 2.3.18, 616–17 (Lawrence trans.). Honor seems to point to "some more general, ancient, and holy law," but the law of right and wrong is based on the universal and permanent needs of mankind. The example of honor given is dueling; the example of the universal need is not killing one another. One is led to wonder whether the law to which honor points is the same as this universal law, or a different law. Cf. *Nicomachean Ethics* V, 1135a3–5.

50. Tocqueville, *Democracy in America*, 1.2.6, 245.

51. Hobbes, *Leviathan*, 46:371.
52. Ibid., 46:367.
53. Ibid., 8:39.
54. Klein, *Greek Mathematical Thought*, 49, 64–69, 70–71.
55. Men like Anaxagoras and Thales were commonly deemed imprudent because they did not seem to know how to secure their own benefit. *Nicomachean Ethics* VI, 1141b3–6; *Politics* I, 1259a9–11.
56. Supra, 1.4, "This is why . . . said to correspond."
57. *Metaphysics* XIII, 1078b12–18.
58. *Republic* V, 476a-d.
59. For an understanding of how this might be said to have been the intention of early modern liberal theorists, consider Tocqueville's characterization of the American "aristocracy," both generally and in *Democracy in America*, 2.3.18. Commercial skill is made to replace military prowess as the meaning of courage in the regime consciously formed on the principles of modern political science.
60. Although the grammatical construction of the clause (*peri panta dēmon kai peri pan plēthos*) supports our interpretation that *dēmos* and multitude must be distinguished, both Newman and Aubonnet argue that they are the same, with "multitude" being added for emphasis. We disagree.
61. Contrast the beginning of Descartes and virtually all of modern political philosophy. Their beginning is a radical doubt of sense perception and a separation of common sense, or prudence, from political theory, or science. Cf. Hobbes, *Leviathan*, 5:21, for the distinction between prudence, based on experience and sense, and science.
62. Reading *mede hen* at 1281b25. The text may be corrupt, and we do not mean to accuse Aristotle of directing future corruptions of the manuscripts.
63. Cf. Marsilius, *The Defender of Peace*, 1.13. 4.
64. *Politics* III, 1273b40–1274a3; *Athenian Constitution*, 8. 4.
65. Plato, *Laws* XII, 945b–e, 947a, 951d.
66. Cf. Marsilius, *The Defender of Peace*, 1.1.4–6.
67. At the beginning of Book I, the city is shown to have grown from subordinate associations, and yet is said to be natural.
68. Recall the addition of a part that did not sense until the third day at 1276a29–30. Is the third part, which does not sense, the spiritedness represented by the free man?
69. *Nicomachean Ethics* VII, 1145a4–5.
70. The use of the plural is grammatically unnecessary and unusual for Aristotle. Contrast 1275a7.
71. In Book IV the magistrates are said to deliberate (1299a25–27), and the *boulē* is classed as a magistracy (1299b30–32).
72. *Nicomachean Ethics* III, 1113a2–12.
73. Recall the distinction made in the third examination in the ways of rule. See Part I of this chapter, especially pp. 155–156.
74. Marsilius's interpretation of this passage is that the judiciary spoken of consists of "advocates or lawyers and notaries" (*The Defender of Peace*, 1.13.4). These judges are not the demotic many.
75. Consider the similar equivocation in Hobbes. See *Leviathan*, especially the beginning of 13:60–61, and 5:19: it is unreasonable to play trump all the time.
76. Recall the two principles of democracy. Supra, intro., "Were someone to . . . serious in itself."

CHAPTER 3

1. *Politics* III, 1275a28–29, 1284a14–15. Consider *Nicomachean Ethics* IV, 1127b33–1128b4, on the importance of proper jesting, a distinct virtue.

2. *Nicomachean Ethics* I, 1103a3–4.

3. Klein, *Greek Mathematical Thought*, 105.

4. Consider the praise of legislators given throughout the *Politics*. In Book IV in particular, Aristotle's harsh criticism of a democracy led by demagogues (1292a4–38) and of tyranny (1295a1–24) should be contrasted with his praise of legislators (1296a18–21), including one "Far-Famed," who instituted moderate democratic procedures (1298a10–13).

5. *Politics* IV, 1291b2–13; V, 1301a25–b4; VI, 1318a3–b5.

6. *Politics* IV, 1293b33–34.

7. *Politics* IV, 1295a25–1296a21.

8. Hobbes, *Leviathan*, intro.:2; 11:47.

9. *Nicomachean Ethics* V, 1131a13–14. Compare *Politics* III, 1280a11–13.

10. *Politics* VIII, 1341a18–b8.

11. *Nicomachean Ethics* VI, 1141a20–21.

12. *Politics* VII, 1327b23–1328a7, 1333a16–26; *Nicomachean Ethics* I, 1102a23–1103a10.

13. In Books VIII and IX of the *Ethics*, the friendship of noble or good men is shown to be superior to all other friendships, but it is never explicitly stated that this friendship is most fully realized in philosophizing.

14. *Nicomachean Ethics* II, 1104b3–11.

15. *Politics* IV, 1296b13–24.

16. *Politics* I, 1253a9–10.

17. Supra, 2.2, "That men are . . . speak about politics"; 2.6, "Our criticism of . . . or visible, things."

18. Herodotus, *Histories*, 3:20.

19. *Politics* III, 1275a34–36; supra, 2.2, "That men are . . . good manly man."

20. Aristotle, *Metaphysics* XIII, 1080b19ff. See Klein, *Greek Mathematical Thought*, 67–68.

21. Plato, *Republic* V, 473d. Consider also the Nocturnal Council in the *Laws*.

22. Plato, *Laws* VII, 822a–c.

23. Plato, *Protagoras*, 335a–336a.

24. Diogenes Laertius, *Lives of the Eminent Philosophers*, 6:11–13.

25. The anecdote attributed to Antisthenes by Aristotle is not found in Antisthenes' extant fragments. Susemihl, Newman, and Aubonnet all make reference to Aesop's fable #241 (Halm), which I have quoted. Aubonnet also makes reference to two compilations of fragments in which the saying is attributed to Antisthenes; but there, unfortunately, the only authority given is this very passage in the *Politics*.

26. Recall Cleisthenes, "locking up strength," who enrolled foreign and slavish metics, philosophers, as Athenian citizens (1275b35–37).

27. Recall Gorgias "of the little lions," a rhetorician (1275b26–27).

28. Apollodorus, *The Library*, 1.9.19. Apollonius Rhodius, 1270–1295.

29. Cf. Plato, *Republic* VI, 488a–489a.

30. Herodotus, *Histories*, 7:193.

31. Herodotus, *Histories*, 5:92. There are no other versions of the account prior to Aristotle. Virtually all the commentators give Herodotus as the source, while noting Aristotle's switching of the names.

32. Supra, 2.2, "The virtue of . . . with true opinion."

33. Klein, *Greek Mathematical Thought*, 103–104.

34. Machiavelli, *The Prince*, 18 (end); *Discourses on Livy*, 1:54, 59, 60; Locke, *Two Treatises*, 2:145–148. Tocqueville, *Democracy in America*, 2.3.22–26. Ambition seems to be the one thing democracy cannot equalize, and its last outlet in a democracy is the army.
35. Thucydides, *The Peloponnesian War*, 1:115; 3:2, 10; 8:5.
36. *Politics*, II, 1265a13–15; III, 1276a28–29.
37. Herodotus, *Histories*, I:189–191, III:153–159.
38. Aristotle's historical inaccuracies in the *Politics*, especially in Book V, and in *The Athenian Constitution* might be considered in this light.
39. Supra, 2.1, "The list is . . . knowing man's good."
40. Cf. *Politics* VII, 1325a16–1325b32.
41. Cf. Plato, *Phaedo*, 99d.
42. *Nicomachean Ethics* X, 1178a9–16.
43. Cf. Plato, *Laws* X, 892d–893a. The Athenian Stranger's helping his legislator-friends ford a river is compared to demonstrating the priority of soul to body.
44. Recall the criticism of Plato, who said that the ground of unity was generic unity. Supra, 2.4, "When Aristotle began . . . whole, by nature."
45. Cf. Tocqueville, *Democracy in America*, 734–735, Note Y: "Men think that the greatness of the idea of unity lies in means. God sees it in the end. . . . To encourage endless variety of actions but to bring them about so that in a thousand different ways all tend toward the fulfillment of one great design—that is a God-given [divine] idea."
46. *Politics* III, 1281b38–41. The doctor judges the "maker" (*poietēs*) of health. Cf. Plato, *Protagoras* 340d–e: Socrates, in correcting a poet, refers to himself as a doctor.
47. Compare *Politics* III, 1278a36–37 to 1285a10.
48. Elsewhere, Aristotle refers to Sparta or the Peloponnesus, thus distinguishing his use of "the Laconic regime."
49. *Politics* III, 1279a37–1279b1. Consider also *Nicomachean Ethics* III, 1115a4–6: Courage is the first virtue discussed.
50. *Nicomachean Ethics* V, 1134b17–1135a5. The conventional element in political justice exceeds the natural in dignity, except in the case of the best regime. Cf. Tocqueville, *Democracy in America*, 2.3.18; supra ch. 2, note 50.
51. Compare Plato, *Protagoras*, 342b–343b.
52. This might be said to be the posture of virtually all of modern philosophy, from Machiavelli's rape of fortuna, Bacon's "torture of nature" for "the relief of man's estate," Descartes's *Cogito ergo sum*, and Hobbes's state of nature in which life is "solitary, poor, nasty, brutish, and short" to Nietzsche's ultimate conquest of nature with the "eternal return."
53. Compare Locke, *Two Treatises of Government*, 2:104–112, 116–120. The peaceful origin of all ancestral regimes must be supposed to have been consent to a monarch. Present consent is tacit consent to the ancestral regime for the sake of acquiring the ancestral estate.
54. *Nicomachean Ethics* VII, 1145a18–22. Plato, *Republic* III, 391c–d.
55. Aristotle later speaks of a part, of excessively great age, that has happened to surpass all.
56. *Politics* I, 1256b31–34. The apparently unjustified criticism of Solon is justified in that Solon did say that a man could never cease his toils with the assurance of having enough because of the caprice of the gods. Fragment 13.
57. A king is apparently necessary only in war. Cf. Tocqueville, *Democracy in America* 1.1.8,126. The American president has "almost royal prerogatives," which he has no occasion to use because of the circumstance that the Union has no neighbors to fight.

58. *Politics* III, 1285b17–19. The king worth speaking about is a leader in polemics beyond the boundaries.
59. Supra, 3.3, "We have yet . . . according to nature."
60. Supra, 1.1, "Since the starting . . . of the examinations."
61. *Nicomachean Ethics* VI, 1141b23–28.
62. Ibid. I, 1102a5–26. The true political scientist or statesman must know the virtues, which requires the kind of knowledge of soul that a doctor has of body. Greater precision is *perhaps* unnecessary.
63. Cf. Plato, *Republic* V, 473d.
64. Cf. Hobbes, *Leviathan*, intro., 1: "Nature (the Art whereby God hath made and governes the World) is by the Art of man, . . . so in this also imitated, that it can make an Artificial Animal. . . . For by Art is created that great Leviathan called a 'Commonwealth.'"
65. Hippodamus, for example, whose name is roughly "Horsiness of the *dēmos*," seemed not to have understood the difference between politics and art. *Politics* II, 1268b22 ff.
66. In addition to Hobbes and Hippodamus, recall the oligarchy in which political scientists might have large estimates. *Politics* III, 1278a21–24, supra, 1.5, "In all the other . . . educated in private."
67. Recall the "one *mina*" to which the oligarchic *logos* did not give due weight. *Politics* III, 1280a27–31.
68. *Politics* IV, 1290a24–29; supra, 1.2, "In the first . . . far from politic."
69. *Nicomachean Ethics* III, 1113a15. The deliberation of the serious man must be supplemented by the wish or intention (*boulesis*) for what is truly good. What is truly good seems to have no measure and standard other than that the serious man does wish or intend it.
70. *Politics* IV, 1296a3–6, and Book V generally. The philosopher, as the erotic man par excellence, is treated as one kind of tyrant.
71. Hobbes, *Leviathan*, intro., 2. Consider the importance of the passions in the whole of his political teaching.
72. *Politics* III, 1281a42–1282b3. Supra, 2.6, "The first is . . . order in it."
73. Hobbes *Leviathan*, 15:72–73. Hobbes's argument against Machiavelli is that, in general, tyranny is an unreasonable risk.
74. Some of Aristotle's heroic kings omitted their sacrifices. *Politics* III, 1285b16–17.
75. Supra, intro., "When do we . . . kinds of parts?"; 2.6, "Aristotle eventually will . . . other two realms."
76. Supra, 1.5, "Why this apparent . . . rhetoric, his poetry"; 3.1, "The democrat, we . . . and the demotic."
77. Plato, *Republic* VI, 505a–509b.
78. Ibid., VIII, 546a–569c.
79. Consider Aristotle's criticism of Socrates' teaching of the Phrygian mode in the *Republic* and of teaching of flute playing. *Politics* VIII, 1341a21–39, 1342a32–1342b3; III, 1276b6–9; IV, 1290a20–29. More important, consider the impression created by the *Ethics* as a whole.
80. Plato, *Republic* VIII, 546a–d.
81. Plato, *Epistle* VIII, 335aff.
82. Supra, 3.3, "The second form . . . according to nature,"
83. Aristotle, *On the Heavens* I, 268b11–271a35, 279b4–283b22; III, 300a20–302a9; *Physics*, II, 197b33–198a13, 199b15–33.

84. The tyrants, Periander and Thrasyboulos, neither spoke nor clarified their intentions. Supra, 3.2, "The tyrants understand . . . of political men."
85. Supra, 2.6, "Perhaps what Aristotle . . . has been established."
86. Supra, 1.2, "A citizen in a . . . a citizen are."
87. At *Politics* III, 1283a42–1284a3 it is suggested that those who make wealth authoritative do constitute a regime.
88. Supra, 1.2, "Others, however, do . . . or prior regimes."
89. Contrast Aristotle's apparent defense of democracy with his immoderate attack on immoderate democracy at *Politics* IV, 1292a4–38.
90. Supra, 1.3, "The distinction that . . . and impolitic philosophers."
91. Supra, 1.2, "Regardless of applicability . . . is another matter."
92. Supra, 1.2, "Others, however, do . . . any more reasons."
93. At *Politics* II, 1268b4–22, Aristotle criticizes Hippodamus's proposal of permitting qualified judgments.
94. Supra, intro., "Each of these . . . his friends imprudently"; 1.4, "The relations between . . . be taught him."
95. Supra, 3.2, "The tyrants understand . . . is to philosophize"; 3.2, "Yet if we . . . equal and men."
96. *Politics* III, 1277a19–20, 1277a24–25, 1278a36–37, 1285a10, 1285a37–38.
97. *Nicomachean Ethics* III, 1113a2–12. We deliberate about what means are within our power, presumably for the sake of some desired end, yet the desire is also said to be a consequence of deliberation.
98. Aristotle, *Metaphysics* XII, 1076a5. Aristotle's explanation of the god ends with a quote from Homer.
99. *Politics* III, 1285a3–14, the first form of kingship. Cf. Hobbes, *Leviathan*, 13:63;15:79–80; Locke, *Two Treatises of Government*, 2:3.
100. Supra, 1.2, "In characterizing the . . . of political justice." *Politics* III, 1286a6–7.
101. Supra, 3.1, "The mathematician's study . . . failed to do so."
102. *Politics* III, 1278b37–1279a16. Consider also the beginning of Book IV: the political scientist or statesman has the kind of knowledge a gymnastic trainer would need, as if he exercised souls (1288b10–30).
103. Aristotle, *De anima* I, 403a16–18, 403b17–19.
104. *Politics* III, 1281a16–38. Supra, 2.5, "We note a . . . creator or ruler."
105. Cf. *Politics* III, 1279a8–10 (the first political *archē*); 1282b23–30 (those who claim to have greater worth on the basis of "superficial differences").
106. Consider Hippodamus, a lover of honor, who wanted those who found things beneficial to the city to be rewarded, and whose love of honor also led him to wear cheap clothes, but with many ornaments (*Politics* II, 1267b22–28).
107. *Politics* V, 1301a39–1301b1. In "so-called aristocracy," claims to honors are made (1287a18–20).
108. Hobbes, *Leviathan*, 15:73.
109. Aristotle, *Metaphysics* XII, 1075a11–16. The good is either in the order of the whole or in what is separate, as the army's goodness is in its order and the general.
110. Klein, *Greek Mathematical Thought*, 64. He refers not to Aristotle's *Politics* but to *On the Heavens* III, 301a5f; *Metaphysics* XII, 1075a11–23.
111. Hobbes, *Leviathan*, 46:371 and generally.
112. Hobbes, *Leviathan*, 21:109; Locke, *Two Treatises of Government*, 2:22, 128–130.
113. Jean-Jacques Rousseau, *Social Contract*, 3:15.

114. Hobbes, *Leviathan*, 17:85; Locke, *Two Treatises of Government*, 2:123–124. Consider the Declaration of Independence: "All men are endowed by their creator with certain inalienable Rights, that among these are Life, Liberty, and the *pursuit* of Happiness. That to secure these rights, Governments are instituted among men" (emphasis added).

115. Hobbes, *Leviathan*, 20:104: "The Rights and Consequences of both Paternall and Despoticall Dominon, are the very same with those of a Sovereign by Institution; and for the same reasons: which reasons are set down in the precedent chapter." In that chapter (19), arguments for the superiority of monarchy are given. Locke, *Two Treatises of Government*, 2:14, "Of Prerogative": "A good prince, who is mindful of the trust put into his hands and careful of his people cannot have too much prerogative, that is, power to do good. . . ."

116. Cf. Plato, *Republic* VII, 523a–525c.

117. *Nicomachean Ethics* VI, 1141a9–20.

118. Aristotle, *Metaphysics* XII, 1074b15–1075a11.

119. *Democracy in America*, 2.4.8, 704. The "almighty and eternal being" is perhaps not the Christian God of whom Tocqueville speaks initially.

120. Plato, *Statesman*, 297b–c, 303a–b. *Politics* IV, 1289a39–1289b5. *Nicomachean Ethics*, 1160a35–36.

121. Xenophon, *Memorabilia*, 1:2.

122. Plato, *Apology*, 19a–c.

123. *Politics* IV, 1289b1–5: Democracy is at least "measured."

124. Cf. *Politics* III, 1279a8–13.

125. *Politics* III, 1286a14–15. "It appears that the best regime is not according to the written things."

126. Machiavelli, letter of December 10, 1513.

127. *Politics* III, 1279a17–19, supra, 2.1, "What he means . . . the political community"; 1279b11–19, supra, 2.2, "Aristotle begins what . . . demonstrate their reasonableness."

128. *Politics* III, 1282b14–18, supra, 3.1, "Hence Aristotle's assertion . . . philosopher's serious attention."

129. Cf. Marsilius, *The Defender of Peace*, 1.11.3.

130. *Nicomachean Ethics* V, 1137b10–1138a3.

131. *Politics* IV, 1292b11–21: The law of the regime and the customary way (*ethos*) of those who lead do not always correspond.

132. The following summary and quotes are taken from *Democracy in America*, 1.2.8, 262–276.

133. Ibid., 1.2.5, 150.

134. Supra, 3.5, "In suggesting as . . . interests of others."

135. Supra, 2.4, "Virtue or justice . . . perfection a possibility."

136. Homer, *Iliad*, 2:372 and context.

137. Ibid., 10:224 and context.

138. Supra, 1.4, "Praise of citizens . . . moral virtue seriously." Consider Book VI of the *Ethics*: There is no apparent doubt of the sufficiency of prudence and moral virtue for performing virtuous actions, but there is no adequate explanation of what the first principles of moral virtue are (1143a33–1143b14).

139. Supra, 3.3, "The king in . . . the 'divine' things."

140. *Nicomachean Ethics* X, 1179a35–62.

141. There is no evidence that the text is corrupt at this point, incredulity of the commentators notwithstanding.

142. *Democracy in America*, 1.1.5, 70; 1.1.6, 100; 1.1.8, 142–143, 150, 168–169.

143. Supra, 1.2, "Aristotle may have . . . the democrat found"; 1.5, "The third regime . . . resemble man's cities." Cf. *Politics* V, 1309b35–1310a38 for the means of preserving democracies.

144. *Politics* III, 1286b16–20. Consider the similarity of a certain kind of tyranny to a certain kind of democracy: V, 1313b32–39.

145. Chief Justice Roger Taney, *Luther v. Borden*, 7 Howard 1, 40 (1849). Cf. Marsilius, *The Defender of Peace*, 1.10.1, 1.11.1.

146. Supra, 1.4, "The moral virtue . . . said to correspond."

147. Klein, *Greek Mathematical Thought*, 108–109.

148. *Nicomachean Ethics* III, 1109b30–35.

149. Ibid., 1111b26–29.

150. Ibid., 1114a31–1114b12.

151. Ibid., 1114b16–19.

152. *Politics* IV, 1292a13. The reference to *Iliad*, 2:204, leads us to the distinction between Odysseus's speeches to the lords and his blows struck against the many with the scepter Zeus had given Agamemnon.

153. Hobbes, *Leviathan*, 46:373.

APPENDIX 1

1. Aristotle, *Politics*. Thomas Taylor, trans., 1811.

2. Aristotle, *Politics*. H. Rackham, trans., 1932.

3. Aristote, *Politique*. Jean Aubonnet, trans., 1971.

4. Aristotle, *Politics*. Ernest Barker, trans., 1958.

5. Aristotle, *Politics*. W. L. Newman, ed., 1887.

6. Aristotle, *Politics*. F. Susemihl and R. D. Hicks, eds., 1894.

7. Aristotelis, *Politica*. W. D. Ross, ed., 1957.

8. Newman, II, xxi–xi; Susemihl, 11–19; Jaeger, *Aristotle*, ch. 10; Barker, "Life of Aristotle and the Composition and Structure of the *Politics*," *Classical Review* 45, Nov. 1931.

9. Consider the opinion of Thomas Taylor in the introduction to his translation of the *Metaphysics*: "Those more ancient than Aristotle, thinking that it was not fit to expose their wisdom to the multitude, instead of clear and explicit diction, adopted fables and enigmas, metaphors and similitudes, and under these, as veils, concealed it from the profane and vulgar eye. But the Stagirite praises and employs obscurity, and perhaps accuses and avoids philosophical fables and enigmas, because some interpretation may be given of them by any one, though their real meaning is obvious but to a few. Perhaps, too, he was of the opinion that such obscurity of diction is better calculated to exercise the mind of the reader, to excite sagacity, and to produce accurate attention. . . . That this obscurity, however, in the writings of Aristotle does not arise from imbecility, will be obvious to those who are but moderately skilled in rhetoric: for such is the wonderful comprehension, such the pregnant brevity of his diction, that entire sentences are frequently comprised in a few words; and he condenses in a line what Cicero would dilate into a page. His books on *Meteors*, his *Topics*, and his *Politics* likewise evince that he was capable of writing with perspicuity as well as precision. . . ."

APPENDIX 2

1. Brackets in the translation are Delba Winthrop's, not the editor's.

2. Reading *ton de politikon anagkaion einai phronimon* at 1277a15.

3. Euripides, *Aeolus* fr. 16 (Nauck).

4. Homer, *Iliad*, 9:648 and 16:59.
5. Reading *mallon* at 1283a4.
6. Reading *aretēs megethos* at 1283a7.
7. Homer, *Iliad*, 2:391. The last line is not in the original.
8. Alcaeus, fr. 37A (Bergk).
9. The text is corrupt.
10. Reading *basileias* at 1287a4. The alternative is *politeias*, regime.
11. Homer, *Iliad*, 10:224.
12. Ibid., 2:372.

BIBLIOGRAPHY

TEXTS OF ARISTOTLE'S *POLITICS*

Aubonnet, Jean, trans. Paris: Société d'édition "Les Belles Lettres," 1971.
Barker, Ernest, trans. Oxford, UK: Clarendon Press, 1946.
Newman, W. L., ed. Oxford, UK: Clarendon Press, 1887.
Rackham, H., ed. Cambridge, MA: Harvard University Press, 1932.
Ross, W. D, ed. Oxford, UK: Clarendon Press, 1957.
Susemihl, Franz, and R. D. Hicks, eds. London: MacMillan, 1894.
Taylor, Thomas, trans. London: R. Wilks, 1811.

OTHER WORKS OF ARISTOTLE

Metaphysics. Hippocrates G. Apostle, trans. Bloomington: Indiana University Press, 1966.
Nicomachean Ethics. L. Bywater, ed. Oxford, UK: Clarendon Press, 1894.
Nicomachean Ethics. H. Rackham, trans. Cambridge, MA: Harvard University Press, 1926.
On the Soul. W. D. Ross, ed. Oxford, UK: Clarendon Press, 1956.
Physics. Philip H. Wicksteed and Francis M. Cornford, trans. Cambridge, MA: Harvard University Press, 1929.

BOOKS

Diogenes Laertius. *Lives of Eminent Philosophers*. R. D. Hicks, trans. Cambridge, MA: Harvard University Press, 1925.
Euripides. Arthur S. Way, trans. Cambridge, MA: Harvard University Press, 1912.
Filmer, Robert. *Observations upon Aristotle's Politiques*. London: R. Royston, 1652.
Herodotus. *Histories*. A. D. Godley, trans. Cambridge, MA: Harvard University Press, 1920.
Hobbes, Thomas. *Leviathan*. Harmondsworth, UK: Penguin Books, 1968.
Homer, *Iliad*. A. T. Murray, trans. Cambridge, MA: Harvard University Press, 1924.
Jaeger, Werner. *Aristotle: Fundamentals of the History of His Development*. R. Robinson, trans. Oxford, UK: Clarendon Press, 1934.
Klein, Jacob. *Greek Mathematical Thought and the Origin of Algebra*. Eva Brann, trans. Cambridge, MA: MIT Press, 1968.
Locke, John. *Two Treatises of Government*. Cambridge: Cambridge University Press, 1960.
Marsilius. *The Defender of Peace*. Alan Gewirth, trans. New York: Columbia University Press, 1956.
Nauck, August. *Tragicorum Graecorum Fragmenta*. Leipzig: Teubner, 1889.

Nietzsche, Friedrich. *Beyond Good and Evil*. Walter Kaufman, trans. New York: Random House, 1966.

Plato. *Apology of Socrates*. Harold North Fowler, trans. Cambridge, MA: Harvard University Press, 1914.

———. *Epistles*. R. G. Bury, trans. Cambridge, MA: Harvard University Press, 1929.

———. *Gorgias*. W. R. M. Lamb, trans. Cambridge, MA: Harvard University Press, 1925.

———. *Laws*. R. G. Bury, trans. Cambridge, MA: Harvard University Press, 1926.

———. *Phaedo*. Harold North Fowler, trans. Cambridge, MA: Harvard University Press, 1914.

———. *Protagoras*. W. R. M. Lamb, trans. Cambridge, MA: Harvard University Press, 1924.

———. *The Republic of Plato*. Allan Bloom, trans. New York: Basic Books, 1968.

———. *Republic*. Ioannes Burnet, ed. Oxford, UK: Clarendon Press, 1902.

———. *Symposium*. W. R. M. Lamb, trans. Cambridge, MA: Harvard University Press, 1925.

———. *Timaeus*. R. G. Bury, trans. Cambridge, MA: Harvard University Press, 1929.

Strauss, Leo. *Natural Right and History*. Chicago: University of Chicago Press, 1953.

———. *The City and Man*. Chicago: Rand McNally, 1964.

Taylor, Thomas. *Theoretic Arithmetic*. London: A. J. Valpy, 1816.

Thucydides. *History of the Peloponnesian War*. Charles Forster Smith, trans. Cambridge, MA: Harvard University Press, 1919.

Tocqueville, Alexis de. *Democracy in America*. George Lawrence, trans. New York: Doubleday, 1969.

———. *Oeuvres complètes*. Vol. 1. J. P. Mayer, ed. Paris: Gallimard, 1951

ARTICLES

Barker, Ernest. "Life of Aristotle and the Composition and Structure of the *Politics*." *Classical Review* 45, Nov. 1931.

Stocks, J. L. "Composition of Aristotle's *Politics*." *Classical Quarterly* 21, July 1927.

Wolfson, Harry A. "Knowability and Describability of God in Plato and Aristotle." *Harvard Studies in Classical Philology* 56–57, 1947.